10/13/11

For Fran —

"The Girl Who Does It All"

Always follow your dreams —

I did

Donald Young

THE ONLY BOY WHO DANCED

A JOURNEY

FROM OKLAHOMA TO BROADWAY AND BEYOND

with

RONALD YOUNG

authorHOUSE®

ENDORSEMENTS

Angela Lansbury – Kennedy Center Honoree
"My friend Ron Young illustrates with wit and charm how Talent, Ambition and Practicality combined add up to a life well spent and beautifully realized!"

David Hartman – Original Host, ABC's "Good Morning America"
"Life is not a rehearsal. Do it NOW!" Ron Young's "Journey" inspires and empowers us to "live every moment...to GO FOR IT!"

Georgia Engel – Actress
"Have always known that Ron makes an art of friendship. He's made an art out of his life's journey, also. Inspiring!"

Lee Roselle – Former First Vice President of Marketing/ Communications, Merrill Lynch
"… This tall guy walks in with a resume that reads like Gene Kelly's. Being a show biz nut I'm eager to talk to him about his theatrical experience. By the time he left an hour later, he had organized my office, given me a few good ideas for the museum I was about to build and taught me a tap dance step I can still do today… He also left with the job, which he handled with agility right up until his retirement."

Chita Rivera – Kennedy Center Honoree
"What a remarkable career Ron has had, and how wonderful that his story has been told. A wonderful book."

Valerie Harper - Emmy Award Wining Actress
"A wonderful read, fun and inspiring. Ron reminds us there's not just one dream in life and always a new fulfilling path to take."

Judith Drake – Actress
"Required reading for every worker-bee actor!"

Charles Busch – Actor and Writer
"Ron Young's Journey "The Only Boy Who Danced" beautifully mixes irresistible show business anecdotes from a long musical comedy career with a true no nonsense approach to managing retirement with intelligence, grace and usefulness. His Oklahoma background and solid values have allowed him to smoothly navigate the rough waters of the professional theatre and have given him the toughness of character to know when to move on and reinvent himself."

ENDORSEMENTS

Suzie Jary, LCSW, CP, PAT, Client Services Consultant Career Transition For Dancers
"This is an excellent, encouraging, can-do, guide and real life story for any individual concerned about their future."

Sandy Duncan – Actress
"By the end of this personal and inspiring book, I wanted to know this man. Then I remembered I do! This is by my friend, Ron, who makes everyone's life he touches richer, as certainly his book will make yours."

Julie Morgenstern – Writer and Public Speaker
"If you are looking for an example of an authentic, adventurous and well-organized life...along with all of the rewards that go with it, look no further. My dear friend and colleague Ron has been taking life by the horns since he was a small boy, and we can all be inspired by his philosophy and approach."

Tommy Tune – Nine Time Tony Award Winner
"Totally Inspirational!"

Jack Lee – Broadway Music Director
"How definitive can one exciting theatrical and a beautifully normal existence be?"

Michael Lirtzman - Former Music Chair, LaGuardia High School of The Arts, NYC
"A must read for anyone with performance (or other career) aspirations. It is positively uplifting because Ron Young's natural optimism is present in every line, propelling the read forward. This fascinating and rewarding journey is infused with a unique brew of joyful enthusiasm and common sense."

Paul Critchlow - Vice Chairman, Public Markets, Merrill Lynch Bank America
"Ron Young refuses to sugar-coat the painful conflicts of faith, sexuality and a compulsive need for approval that drove him forward against all odds. His quest for love and attention morphs into a genuine passion to entertain. Still, a childlike sense of awe and wonder permeates every page, and the reader can't help but smile as 'the only boy who danced' transforms himself into a multi-talented trouper sharing world stages with international stars."

AuthorHouse™
1663 Liberty Drive
Bloomington, IN 47403
www.authorhouse.com
Phone: 1-800-839-8640

First published by AuthorHouse 7/21/2011

ISBN: 978-1-4634-1763-5 (e)
ISBN: 978-1-4634-1764-2 (hc)
ISBN: 978-1-4634-1765-9 (sc)

Library of Congress Control Number: 2001012345

Printed in the United States of America

This book is printed on acid-free paper.

This book is dedicated to everyone who longs to
follow their dream... and does.

SYNOPSIS

Sometimes Broadway dreams do come true.

Fresh from the obscurity of living in the small farming community of Grove, Oklahoma, Ronald Young, at 22, is catapulted onto New York City's "Great White Way"... BROADWAY.

After arriving in Manhattan on a Friday, he auditions for his first Broadway show on Monday. Bingo! After three call back auditions he snags his first dancing role in the soon to be mega hit "HELLO, DOLLY!" directed and choreographed by Gower Champion and starring Carol Channing.

Armed with three music degrees and lots of enthusiasm he embarks on his career on Broadway. His resumé includes working with some of the legends of the theater: Ethel Merman, Shirley Booth, Angela Lansbury, Tommy Tune, Bernadette Peters, Joel Gray, Chita Rivera, Sandy Duncan, Georgia Engel and many others. He appeared in a host of shows: "MAME," "GEORGE M!" "THE BOY FRIEND," "MY ONE AND ONLY," "A CHORUS LINE" and the films "HAIR" and "ANNIE."

"THE ONLY BOY WHO DANCED" is a series of compelling, riveting stories about Ronald Young's personal quest to make it on Broadway. If you or a friend have hidden aspirations to make it on the New York theatrical scene, you will enjoy his tips and suggestions on how to break through this tough barrier.

ACKNOWLEDGEMENTS

What's the phrase? "It takes a village..." In this case it's true. "The Only Boy Who Danced" would not have seen the light of day without the help and encouragement of my friends. First, Naomi Buck gave me the original title, "Retired ... with my Ducks in a Row." Then Julie Morgenstern put me in the writer mode.

Along the way there was input from Jinny Ewald, Charlie Evans, Angus McLean, Hillary Pereira, Connie Kitchens, Jim Shewalter, Lori Kennedy, Suzie Jary, Bill Berloni, Diana Brill, Nicole Barth, John DiLeo, Joe Landau, Juanita Owens, Gracey Tune, Jimmy Vaughn, Anna Ivara, Pamela Shaw and Victor Syrmis. Michael Lirtzman was very helpful with ideas on the structure of my story. Julia Landau was invaluable for her studious editing and proofing of my manuscript. Bill Ecenbarger then gave me his professional eye for added refinement.

Suzanne Boles and Leyna Gabrieli helped me locate photographs. Chandra Inturi was instrumental in getting all the selected photos scanned.

Now the stars really shined on me. One of my golfing buddies was the very technically adroit and visually ingenious Rob Rees. He laid out the book in InDesign and also created the eye catching book cover. Kudos, my friend!

Both Paul Critchlow and Michael Lirtzman picked up on a line from the first chapter, "The Only Boy Who Danced," and suggested it as a title that would motivate a theater audience.

A special "thank you" goes to all those who gave me endorsements for my book: Angela Lansbury, David Hartman, Georgia Engel, Lee Roselle, Charles Busch, Suzie Jary, Valerie Harper, Judith Drake, Sandy Drake, Julie Morgenstern, Tommy Tune, Michael Lirtzman, Paul Critchlow, Chita Rivera and Jack Lee.

And finally, Paul Wisenthal walked me through the publishing process and gave me a business plan.

You can tell this was a group effort and for all those who prodded, coaxed and buoyed this fledgling writer I am most grateful.

WHAT COULD THIS LITTLE BOY GROW UP TO BE?

A JOCKEY?

A SAILOR?

A SCHOLAR?

WHAT OTHER POSSIBILITIES WOULD
APPEAR IN HIS LIFE?

CONTENTS

PREFACE

Here I sit on the deck of my home on the shores of Grand Lake O' the Cherokees on Monkey Island, Oklahoma, having a cup of coffee while the birds serenade me... . How did I get here?

My journey has been interesting and amazing, with unexpected turns, painful disappointments and a bag full of surprises. The telling of my story up to and arriving at this point in my life is simply that ... a narrative of my life's journey. This is not a "how to" book! That would be presumptive of me. My book will have served its purpose if any of my decisions inspire you or lead you to a new way of thinking about your life and pathways.

My choices have always been a combination of following my passions and being practical. This made for a balance of treating myself well as well as planning for the future. It hasn't always gone smoothly. There have been times when my direction was unclear, and other times when the unexpected took me in an entirely different and unplanned direction.

Growing up in Grove, Oklahoma, a small rural farm community much like the Texas town in Peter Bogdonovitch's "Last Picture Show," did not give me an inkling of where my life would go, but it certainly was an adventure. After attending the University of Tulsa and receiving three degrees in music, Broadway and New York City beckoned. This led to a thirty-three year career in musical theatre. At a crossroads, Career Transition For Dancers helped me find work in the Marketing Communications department of a large financial institution, Merrill Lynch, for almost twelve years. Along the way I discovered the world of Professional Organizing, and currently go around the country helping people get control of the clutter in their homes and offices.

Why write a book? My friend, Naomi Buck, suggested that I give a seminar entitled "How to Retire with Your Ducks in a Row." She said she had been telling her friends in Naples, Florida, about how a friend of hers in New York had retired in pretty good shape from his beginnings as a tap dancer.

1

When I mentioned this to Julie Morgenstern, my Professional Organizing guru, she said, "No, not a seminar ... you have to write a book!"

I replied, "Julie, it's just my story, no one else would do it that way."

She responded, "I don't care, it is an inspiration. I don't know of anyone who has managed to do what you have done with your life." Thus began my fourth career.

After writing the first chapter, I asked some friends for feedback. Two very good writers, Paul Critchlow and Michael Lirtzman, picked up on the same line, "It was difficult being the only boy who danced in a small town in Oklahoma," and thought that "The Only Boy Who Danced" would be a strong motivational title.

Sounded good to me.

So, let's get started ... a FIVE, SIX, SEVEN, EIGHT!

EARLY YEARS

This would be my first time to ever work in an office environment. "A-FIVE SIX SEVEN EIGHT" had now morphed into "Nine to Five." Lee Roselle, the Vice President in charge of creating The World of Merrill Lynch, had hired me as a consultant to assist him. This high-tech museum would have a 75 by 20 foot timeline on one wall that combined Merrill Lynch history, world history, United States history, financial industry history and pop culture history. There would also be an interactive center, a hi-def movie theater and other items on display. This was going to be a unique exhibit in the world of financial institutions and was highly anticipated. It was crunch time toward completion of the museum. That's why Lee now needed an assistant.

Once again, you never know when all your skills are going to come into play. At my last interview Lee showed me a flip chart of the exhibits in the museum. As he explained what he had in mind for each section, the theater director in me came out:

"Will the speaker in that exhibit have direct sound, so that it will only be heard by the guests looking at that display?"

"Have you considered the traffic flow of the viewers?"

"Where will the directions be for the interactive?"

With each question he would look at me as if to say, "You get it, don't you?"

This seemed to seal the deal for my getting the job. You must realize that he took a huge chance on me. Here was a man in his mid-fifties, who had never worked in the business world, with minimal computer skills. When the job was offered there was still the salary to be determined. Every book on the subject of negotiations had the caveat that the applicant didn't name the first salary number, management did. My agent Bret Adams had handled this area for me for years. I was the proverbial fish out of water. Lee would say, "What salary do you want for this job?" My reply? "How much do you feel it is worth? This is all new to me." He would not respond except to ask me the initial question again. Before this final interview several friends were asked for help in this particular area so there was a number in mind that was hopefully not too high to nix my landing the job. Finally, my figure had to come out, since Lee was so much better at the negotiating process. To my surprise he came back with an offer that was $10,000 higher than mine. "OK. That should work" was my grateful response.

~~~~~~~~~~~~~~~~~~~~~~~~~~~~~~~~~~

In the spring dance recital with Suzanne Crawford.
Photo by Orrick Sparlin..

It was difficult being the only boy who danced in a small town in Oklahoma.. Several years into my career as a dancer/singer on Broadway I asked my father if he had any idea why the entertainment field had become my chosen profession. He recalled an incident when I was five years old watching a musical variety show on television. It seems I stood transfixed in front of the TV for the whole hour's program jumping up and down saying, "That's what I want to be. That's what I want to be." There is no recollection of that event in the deepest recesses of my mind, but evidently it essentially shaped my life.

So starting at the age of five there were tap, acrobatic and jazz dance classes. Now put this in perspective: a young boy (the only boy) in a small rural town in Oklahoma who wanted to take dancing lessons. My mother drove me once, sometimes twice, a week 25 miles from Grove to Miami, Oklahoma, to take classes with Virginia Lee Wilson. She shared the driving duty with Helen Crawford, my first grade dancing partner's mother. They were both dedicated to making sure that Suzanne, her sister, Linda, and I always got to those dance classes. They also made all our costumes for the dance recitals every June at the Coleman Theater.

What kept me at it when there would be comments about that "sissy" who danced? It's hard to break this down completely. First of all, I loved to dance! Later on, after a few years of psychotherapy, the discovery was made that I started performing to get attention. You might say, "Duh, isn't that why all performers get up on stage?" Yes, but there was an added incentive for me. You see, at that early age attention from anyone, anywhere was equated with earning the love of my parents. Where this concept came from beats me.

My mother and father were loving parents, but from a distance. It was always evident that they loved me and were very proud of me, but it was just taken for granted that we loved each other. There were not a lot of hugs nor much saying, "I love you." It's enlightening now hearing friends on the phone with a loved one, ending the conversation with "I love you." We never did that in my family. Being an only child led to my being spoiled, but not feeling deeply loved. Therefore, the attention gained by performing never quite filled that empty little pit inside me. So my thought was, "I must not be doing enough. Do more! Do More!" An endless cycle spiraled into motion.

There's that "Do you love me now?" look on my face. Photo by Ed Gibson.

There is a photograph of me, playing the accordion at about the age of eleven, with this searching look on my face. I'm sure that I was focused on my parents in the audience and the look on my face was saying, "Do you love me now?"

It took many years to get beyond this and become an entertainer in the true sense of the word. I had to learn to create a space on stage where it was important for those in the audience to have the experience of a laugh, a tear, a memory – not me. But in the beginning this served me well, by giving me an inordinate drive. This will to succeed in anything and everything could also be attributed to the drinking water in Oklahoma. But in my case there was that little added incentive: attention equals love.

Then there was the influence that the Methodist church had on me, both positively and negatively. My parents started taking me to Sunday school and church practically as soon as I could walk, but by the age of seven or eight, if they didn't want to go, Sunday morning would find me at the church anyway. Imagine, what would possess a child of that age to make his parents take him to church, drop him off and pick him up if they didn't want to go that particular Sunday? Well, there was this lure of a "perfect attendance" pin that got a bar added on for each year that you didn't miss a Sunday. Even there the need to be the best, get attention and be that "nice little boy" was front and center. However, that finally came to a screeching halt when a choice had to be made between Sunday school and dance class.

This decision took place some time around the sixth grade. My dance teacher learned of a weekend of dance classes to be held in Oklahoma City, led by Louis DePron, a well-known Hollywood choreographer. Saturday was the class for all students and Sunday was the advanced/professional class. I wanted desperately to go to that Saturday class and talked Suzanne, still my dancing partner, into begging her mother to go, as well. So we all drove down for the Saturday class: Suzanne, Linda, Helen, my mother and I. We had planned to stay over Saturday night, go to church somewhere in Oklahoma City and come back on Sunday afternoon. The perfect attendance record could be kept intact by going to a church other than our own and bringing back a note that we had attended.

The tap class on Saturday was very exciting: I just loved every minute of it. When it was over, as "Dudley-Do-Right" personified, Mr. DePron had to be thanked.

After my gushing "Thank you," he surprised me. "You did a good job in class today and picked up the combinations very quickly. Why don't you come back tomorrow? You will be one of the youngest in the advanced class, but I think you can do it."

Thrilled, but torn: a dilemma. Dance class would preempt Sunday school and my perfect attendance record would be broken. What to do? Looking back it seems like the decision should have been a no-brainer, but I agonized over it and didn't decide until after a sleepless night of worry and prayer. What do you think? God spoke. The dance class won out, and it turned out to be amazing. Mr. DePron taught a number called "Drumming on a Chair" with a wooden chair and drumsticks. I was able to keep up with everyone in the class and learned the whole routine in a single session. Back in Grove and floating on air, that routine was used in many per-formances. However, the following Sunday reality hit. There would be no more bars on my "perfect attendance" pin, and Suzanne would continue with her record. Dang, sometimes you just can't have it all.

One other sign of spunk showed up in the third grade when one of my Sun-day school teachers made a point of telling me that it was a sin to dance. This really bothered me. After praying about it and pouring through the bible, Psalm 150 turned up with a passage that read, "Praise him with the timbrel and dance." Practically running to church the next Sunday, I chal-lenged the teacher with that passage saying, "See, I can dance!" The look on her face was priceless. That was one of the few times I bucked authority. Dancing continued to be front and center in my life.

At about the age of four I noticed that other kids were getting spankings and I wasn't. "Hey, Momma, why don't I get spankings like the other kids do?" (Looking back it seems like such a dumb question, but it did involve being touched.)

"You've had your share already, honey," she responded.

A relative once told me that in my "just beginning to walk" stage, it was constantly: "Ronnie, don't touch that. Ronnie, sit down. Ronnie, behave," and having my hands slapped and bottom spanked for not following the directives immediately. Years later, when recalling this on a psychiatrist's couch, I wondered how any level of creativity was achieved, when those initial reaching out and searching impulses were thwarted. Evidently I was always this paragon of "goody-two-shoes." At my 50th high school reunion, one of my classmates told me that her mother used to scold her by saying, "Why can't you be good like Ronnie?" Oi vey!

During elementary school my cousin came to live with my grandparents. Johnny was a year ahead of me at school but it was like having a brother. It was always Johnny and Ronnie. That period provided the experience of having an almost-brother. Johnny was the one who asked me, "you don't really believe in Santa Claus, do you?" as I looked out the car window one night trying to see the track of his sleigh. Isn't it funny how you never for-get the person who burst that bubble?

7

My father worked as a Waterproofing Engineer (tuck pointer on brick and stone buildings) and would schedule work in Iowa or Minnesota in the summer and fall and then back in Oklahoma in the winter. That meant that I started the fall term of school "up north" and then transferred back to Grove in November. It wasn't until the sixth grade that a whole year of schooling was completed in Grove. During this migration period of my life there were two telling events:

In the second grade in Waterloo, Iowa, one day my after school recital of the daily activities was prefaced by happily telling my parents that my teacher had told me I didn't have to say "yes ma'am" and "no ma'am" because none of the other children did. My father's reaction was to invite the teacher to dinner to set her straight

"Ma'am, if you don't mind my son will continue to say 'yes ma'am' and 'no ma'am' at school, just like he does at home, regardless of what the other children say."

Manners were made part of my DNA at that early age, manners which remind me that I was not "entitled," manners which emphasized the worth of other people. As a result, to this day I am impelled to stand up when a lady sits down at the table, open doors, take my hat off in an elevator, walk on the outside of a sidewalk, precede a lady down stairs or an escalator and follow her up. These are things I am inwardly driven to do. All of my female friends can thank my father for that.

The seminal event happened in the third grade in Cedar Falls, Iowa. It was November and we were preparing to come back to Oklahoma. My teacher and the principal called my parents in for a conference and told them that had I remained in the school system in Cedar Falls, I would have been promoted to the fourth grade after the fall term. The principal wrote a letter to that effect for my parents to take upon my leaving the school.

The day my mother took me to reenter school in Grove we went to see Mr. Huggins, the grade school Principal, and she handed him the letter. This had never been done in the Grove school system. Can you imagine his quandary? His reasoning and how he reached his decision remained a mystery, but he did enter me in the fourth grade. This decision altered my life forever and put me on the path to my current destination.

Looking back after the painful adolescent experiences of being a year younger than my peers, my advice to parents is to never push their child ahead, even if their grades and test scores indicate an advanced child. Just think of the embarrassment of having your mother drive you and your date to the junior prom, then picking you up and driving your date home. Fairly mortifying. That being said, I love my life and the people in it so much now, it is hard to imagine this life taking a different trajectory. There was, however, another minor downside: the third grade was when penmanship was taught. Missing most of that year left me with a rather cryptic handwriting. In fact, it's lousy.

Living part-time on a farm with my grandparents had its fringe benefits. My Grandpa Butch was known as a real old fashioned horse-trader. One day after school there was a little palomino mare in the barn. He greeted me with, "Ronnie, I think it's time you had a horse." What? It was never high on my wish list, but he must have gotten a real good deal at the weekly sale at the auction barn and used me as an excuse for getting it.

"Thanks, Grandpa. She sure is pretty" was about all I could get out. I named her Kay. Every morning she had to be fed and her stall mucked out. She was a little frightening to me and I think she knew it. She would push me around in the stall, but she was fun to ride.

During the time of parking our trailer house outside of Grandpa and Grandma's, there were two different dogs in my life. First, a wonderful little black mutt with a white slash on her chest named Bibs, who was my love. She was able to come inside sometimes during the winter and we could snuggle. Later Laddie, a black and white collie mix, ruled the farm. We had great times running through the woods. We had 88 acres to explore and we knew almost every foot of it.

Our itinerant lifestyle continued all during my grade school years. Part of my fifth grade was spent in Guthrie, Oklahoma because Dad was working on the Masonic Temple there. That spring there was an all-city track meet for the kids of the town. Dad worked with me after school on three events: the fifty-yard dash, the high jump and the broad jump. At nine years of

9

age my division was "11 and under." My first place finishes in the dash and the high jump, and a second in the broad jump, weren't bad against those bigger boys. That was also the end of my track career. There were only so many hours in the day and something had to give, but the event did garner a few more kudos for me. It was in Guthrie that my mother was called, "the mother of that boy who dances." She loved it.

The same time conflict happened in junior high and high school. Music and band took place during the same hours in the school day as the sports programs. My junior high basketball experience was cut short because of band practice. My junior high football tryout lasted one day. That was my choice. Getting hit over and over was not my idea of a good time. From my now "senior vantage point," that was a wise decision. My life has been one with no broken bones and a minimum of arthritis, unlike that of many re-tired football players.

Christmas caroling for the neighbors with Mom and Dad.

The accordion was mentioned earlier. That came into my life through an unusual circumstance. We traveled so much that Dad purchased a 28-foot trailer house. When we were up north we would live in a trailer park. In Oklahoma we parked it outside of my grandparents' house on their farm, a little outside of Grove. My parents wanted me to study a musical instrument, preferably pi-ano, but a piano wouldn't fit in our trailer. The answer to that problem? An accordion. Luckily there was an accordion teacher in Miami, Oklahoma, Mr. Payton. So along with dance classes, accordion lessons became part of my weekly routine. Very quickly this skill, along with singing, was added to my performing act. A one-man show was born. Get that attention! It was interesting that later, when starting to play the piano for the first time, my right hand went in place, and then I leaned my head down with the left side of my face on the keyboard, to attain the same view as when playing the accordion. It gave a whole new meaning to "playing by ear."

During the Christmas season the family would go caroling to some of our friends and neighbors. Dad would sing lead, Mother harmonized the alto part and Yours Truly would be the tenor on the accordion. The rehearsals were a happy family activity and our surprised audiences clearly loved the little performance.

The outlets for performance were varied, from Rotary clubs and garden clubs to county fairs and 4-H Club events. One of the more unusual of these venues was the state mental institution in Vinita, Oklahoma. Once every spring, for about four years, I would perform on a program for the patients. It was unusually touching to talk with some of them. One incident in particular stands out.

A patient approached me after my performance to give me a hug. "I have a little boy just like you at home. I sure wish I could see him". She didn't want to let me go. It was one of the reasons that kept me coming back every year. There was always a feeling of having done something good after those performances. Somewhere deep inside the inkling of what it took to touch people as an entertainer was beginning to grow. It was just going to take many years of exhausting my need for attention in order for it to blossom.

The 4-H Club was an important organization for the farm youth of the country. Even living in town from the sixth grade on, there were enough areas in the program to be interesting for me. The main area was the "Share the Fun" contest. Yes, you read correctly. The talent contest was called "Share the Fun." As a freshman in high school I put together a three-minute routine with the help of my music teacher, Elsie Smith, and my dance teacher, Virginia Lee Wilson.

My 4-H Club "Share the Fun" number at the National Convention. Check out the argyle socks. (Photo by Orrick Sparlin)

"Let's Go On With the Show" was a song and dance routine, with tributes to Bill "Bo Jangles" Robinson and Pat Rooney's soft shoe, complete with straw hat and cane. It ended with a one-handed handspring, a double pirouette and a "Ta Da" finish.

I won the Delaware County contest, the Tulsa District contest and went to the state contest at the 4-H Club Roundup in Stillwater, Oklahoma. They didn't choose a winner at the state level. Instead all the acts were put on film. That fall sixteen acts from all over the country were asked to perform at the national 4-H Club Convention held in Chicago. Yep, Chicago was a go that year!

This was a big deal. My mother, my music teacher (Elsie Smith) who accompanied me on the piano for the act and I drove to Oklahoma City and took an overnight train to Chicago with the entire Oklahoma delegation. It was a wonderful experience. My own act was received well, and, paired with Joan Hunsberger in a completely new comedy/dance routine, we pulled off a double. The big night arrived and the show went off without a hitch. You can imagine my level of euphoria. There was a lot of press coverage. For a while the "attention" level was off the charts with telegrams, newspaper articles and lots of photographs and interviews.

Another area of the 4-H Club of interest to me was the "Timely Topic" contest. It consisted of giving a two-minute speech on something of current interest that tied in with the 4-H Club. As a junior in High School my progress stalled as the district winner. My senior year found me as the state champion. Recently my friend Lee Roselle transferred an old movie of that speech to a DVD for me. It's a little difficult to watch, but it is sincere. Others who have seen the DVD have said they could see the beginnings of a politician in that earnest young man. Luckily that didn't happen.

Every spring each 4-H Club member was encouraged to submit a record book of their projects in the past year for county, district and state contests. Ah, here we go again, another chance to get noticed! These big, thick binders with the extensive reports, essays and photographs would be due in March. My activities ran the gamut from Assistant Church Organist at the Methodist Church, to home beautification projects and mowing lawns around Grove, to compiling a 12-page booklet, "Fun the 4-H Way," on planning a party (complete with party games) to all the numerous appearances and speeches made throughout my entire time at school.

Each year around January, my mother would begin, "Ronnie, honey, have you started on your record book yet? Remember it has to be in by March." "Not yet, Momma, but I will" was my dutiful reply, putting it off as long as possible.

It would usually be submitted in several different categories. The required reports were so daunting to complete, I would procrastinate in this area and wait until the last minute to finish, just getting it in on the due date. In some ways it was a little rebellion on my part. It is interesting that this resistance continued into my adult life with paper work, until the discoveries of the whys and wherefores were made, once again in therapy. It was basically saying to my mother, "I'm tired of the endless cycle of achievement to get attention. I just want unconditional love!" Didn't happen. Remember, this is all from an adolescent point of view. My parents did the best parenting job that they could. Years later that passage in the Old Testament, Exodus 34:7, rang a bell for me. "Visiting the iniquity of the fathers upon the children, and upon the children's children unto the third and fourth generation," now had an enlightened meaning for me. My parents could only give to me emotionally what they were capable of with their own unresolved hang-ups and issues. It had little to do with my emotional needs. They did the very best that they could, and though they are both gone, I love them dearly for that.

Mom and Dad on their wedding day.

Walking down the street in Calgary, Canada.

Standing in front of our trailer in Guthrie, Oklahoma.

My record book won the state contest in Recreation my junior year. In my senior year it won state in Community Relations and placed in the national contest. That same year I was in the top ten boys in the candidate group for the Oklahoma 4-H Hall of Fame, where one boy and one girl were selected each year. That award was very high on my "want list," but my insides told me that the honor would have to go to someone who had grown up on a farm. That was indeed a correct assumption. Reading through that record book now is exhausting! How there was ever time to eat and sleep is beyond me. The activities were unceasing. However, that impressive work ethic which started at a very early age has paid off in spades throughout my life.

Two of my classmates, Angie Perry and Tommy Swisher, danced in a wonderful American Indian dance troop, the Turkey Ford Dancers. The group had been invited to New York City to appear on the televised "Ted Mack Amateur Hour." My Mother contacted the leader of the group, Romere Darling Martin, to check on the audition process for the show. We had been friends with Romere from appearing on several programs with the troop. She graciously called her contact at Ted Mack's to tell them about me, and came back to us with the information that they wanted me on the show. There was even a date set for the airing. It seemed too good to be true.

We naively drove to New York City for the live show, with Mother writing notes along the way and mailing them to all of our friends to let them know the news. There was even an article in the local paper about my upcoming appearance. It was my first time to see that breathtaking view of the Manhattan skyline when you drive down that big curve in New Jersey going into the Lincoln Tunnel. This view would be indelibly etched in my mind for a lifetime. We settled in our hotel and called to find out the details for the show. There had been a miscommunication. What? We were told that this week's show was already booked, but that I could come by the studio to audition. It was a little unnerving, doing my number on a TV studio stage with no music, and the whole crew just going about their business. It couldn't have been very stellar. The end result was no appearance on the "Ted Mack Amateur Hour." Mother had to write and call everyone that she had contacted to tell them the news. To say that this was a major disappointment for me would be understating it. Devastated more aptly described my state.

OK, flip the coin over: New York City came into my life for the first time and my life-long love affair with that amazing metropolis was begun. On a sight seeing trip to the Statue of Liberty, it was the amazing experience of climbing to the crown and looking out at the Manhattan skyline. There is also a photograph of my

With Dad and Jack Dempsey, at his restaurant in New York City. Photographeer unknown.

father and me with Jack Dempsey, the former heavyweight-boxing champion of the world and our "new best friend," at his restaurant. Never down and out for too long.

Back in Oklahoma the high school band beckoned me. In the fifth grade we could choose an instrument to learn. For some reason the day of instrument selection, the baritone saxophone became mine. So I would lug that big case on the school bus out to my grandparents' home to practice. If you have ever heard anyone learning to play a reed instrument, you know it is not a pretty sound. The back porch was my rehearsal room. I would toot a note on the sax and then the cow would moo. It made for an interesting bucolic duet.

You'll notice that the "high school band" and the "fifth grade" were mentioned in the same line? A small school needs everyone who can walk and play halfway decently in the High School marching band. Starting in the sixth grade, that big old sax and I trudged along. I even had to lean back a little to keep it from dragging on the ground. Parades were very long for me. At one of the half-time performances at the high school football game the band made a formation that had me kneeling very close to the sideline. On one knee, with the sax on the ground I could just barely reach the mouthpiece to blow the horn. While dealing with this, my father materialized. He had made his way down from the stands and now stood right in front of me on the sidelines with his cheeks puffed out like he too was blowing a horn of some kind. He kept doing this the whole time the band was in that position. I was laughing so hard; there was no way any sound could come out of that sax.

We had moved into Grove city proper that year, purchasing a small one-bedroom house on Hazel Street. The sofa was my bed for the first few years, until we were able to build an extension onto the house to enlarge the living room and give me a small bedroom. Living in town was a big step. It meant no more school buses, as school was within walking distance.

That same year there was a memorable Christmas band concert with the high school band. For some reason the regular bass drum player was not available. Mr. Roe, the band director, asked me to substitute for the absent drummer for that concert. He must have thought that because of my tap dancing, a good sense of rhythm might be my specialty. Came the night of the concert and our big number, "Winter Wonderland," was to end the program. At the end of the song there is a two bar solo with a bass drum roll that started the finale. Picture if you can a little boy who was not tall enough to see over the bass drum making this loud rumbling sound. No one in the audience could see who was responsible for that noise. I really enjoyed that little deception.

Suzanne and I together again as the Drum Major and Drum Majorette of the Grove High School Band.

In my freshman year the baritone sax gave way to the tenor saxophone. A couple of years later my parents surprised me at Christmas with a brand new Selmer tenor sax. I loved that horn and continued playing it all through college. Also, that year there was a tryout for drum major of the band. The tryouts came down to Suzanne, my dancing partner, and me as the last two standing. She had been a baton twirler the preceding year. Mr. Roe resolved the issue by making me the Drum Major and Suzanne the Drum Majorette. We had off-white complementary uniforms and the big shako hats. The team was together again.

Halftime shows at the Friday night football games were always fun, but parades were a bit of a challenge. In Oklahoma there were always many horses in the parades. We always kept one eye on the street to avoid the gifts the preceding horses had deposited there for us. Occasional last minute changes in direction were necessary to avoid disaster. There was also an opportunity for me to learn to play the snare drum. The classes would consist of rolls, rim shots and flim flam paradiddles. (Don't ask me what a paradiddle is now. That name has just always stuck with me.) It came fairly easily to me and I was able to sub as the back-up snare drummer when needed.

It seems that several events happened that freshman year. Voice lessons started and vocal contests just had to be entered. My teacher was Dorothy Wilson, the school superintendant's wife. Mrs. Wilson had certain interesting attributes, like the look on her face was always as if she were detecting an unpleasant odor. Then she always seemed to sort of flutter about. Interesting combination, like she was trying to avoid whatever it was that she was smelling. She also volunteered as the choir director at the Methodist church. It was there that a tradition was started. For Easter that year I sang "The Holy City" for the main church service. This continued all through high school and college, with my returning to Grove every Easter to reprise that warhorse.

A couple of medical issues surfaced. One was impacted wisdom teeth. These had to be surgically removed with an overnight stay in the hospital. X-rays showed that all four teeth were turned on the side and growing into my back molars. For my first few days back in school my swollen face had me competing with the largest available grapefruit for "Most Bloated."

The second problem was a little more serious: epileptic seizures. My first one occurred at ten years old during the night while I slept. Because we had relatives in Rochester, Minnesota, I was taken there to the Mayo Clinic for treatment. This was my first airplane ride. Wow! After being checked and all the tests evaluated, it was determined that the seizure was caused by too fast hormonal growth at the beginning of adolescence. A medication was prescribed along with twelve hours of sleep a night. Only one other episode occurred about a year later. At my last checkup at the age of 15, I was pronounced cured. In fact, my whole history was written up in a medical journal, citing the treatment and the cure.

The Grove Sun, the weekly town newspaper, called the high school for someone to be the school reporter to write a weekly column for the paper. Guess who lobbied for the job! That's right. For two years, every week, my column would let the community know what was going on at the school. Of course with a byline guaranteed, my name appeared in the paper every week. Front and center, charge!

KVOO, a Tulsa TV station, had a live teenage dance party every Saturday afternoon, "Top Ten Dance Party." In my junior year Bennie Graham and I auditioned and were taken as one of the 10 couples to compete. A couple had to win the contest three weeks in a row to receive a small trophy. Oh, how we practiced! One of the telecasts even took place outdoors at the Tulsa State Fair, with Della Reese as the guest artist, singing her No. 1 hit, "Don't You Know." Did we manage to win three weeks in a row and garner that trophy? Never a doubt, and gallantly I insisted that Bennie keep the prize.

Standing on my head on the saucer made in shop class. See, it can be done. (Photo by Gibson Studios)

Bennie and her father had introduced me to water skiing during my junior high school years, which in the 50's meant the seventh through the ninth grades. My enthusiasm had a "duck to water" quality about it. So much so that my father bought a little 16-foot boat with a 35 horsepower outboard motor that was just powerful enough to pull one skier. My family had many days on Grand Lake of boating, skiing and stopping on a deserted shore for a picnic. Those were blissful times. Obsession is a strong word, but water skiing became very important in my life. Water ski books and magazines became my textbooks for learning new tricks. Dad was always very patient driving the boat for this process. There were times, however, when the spoiled brat in me surfaced.

Unable to master some new trick on the skis and falling multiple times, the accusations would come out: "Dad, why were you driving so fast? Why didn't you turn sooner?" I would blame his driving for my inability to accomplish the new skill. Recalling this is saddening, because he gave up countless hours of his time for me to indulge in this passion of mine.

In one of my water ski magazines there was a picture of someone standing on their head on a 36 inch saucer, being pulled behind a boat. It looked like it was just a flat circular piece of wood. Since there was no store in our area where I could buy a saucer, my eighth grade shop class provided me the place to make one and coat it with a waterproof seal. Then it was into the water. First you had to learn to just get up on the saucer while holding a rope and being pulled by the boat. Turning around in a 360 degree spin was next. Then the head stand was mastered, by kneeling on the back side of it with my feet dragging in the water and my hands on the back edge of the saucer, holding on to a two-handled ski rope, one handle on either side of my legs. Then with my head down on the middle of the saucer my legs just went up into the air in a headstand. Sounds simple, doesn't it? I just loved showing off. You can guess why.

Mastering the single slalom ski was exhilarating, with the added speed and deep turns. For long distance skiing I could rest my arms by holding the rope handles between my legs or clasping them behind my back with one hand. You might be thinking, "Why would anyone want to ski for 30 or 40 minutes without stopping?" Well, there was just this incredible feeling of gliding across the water with the wind roaring in my

Learning to rest my arms while water skiing by holding the rope-handle between my legs. Oh, and did you notice the two batons? (Photo by Gibson Studios)

ears and all of my muscles working in tandem to accomplish the feat.

The "piéce de resistance," going backwards on one ski, holding the rope with my foot and twirling two batons. Gee couldn't I have balanced a tray of water-filled glasses on my butt as well? (Photo by Gibson Studios)

Next, came the trick skis. These were shorter than regular skis with no rudders. You could ski sideways, the "side slip," or turn completely around and ski backwards. Of course in one of my magazines there was a picture of a skier going backwards on one ski, holding the rope with one foot with that leg extended straight back in an arabesque. OK, how do I do that? First Dad made me a special towrope with a piece of garden hose to be softer on my foot than the bar on the regular ski rope. Then skiing backwards on one ski had to be conquered. You accomplish that by skiing backwards on two skis, dropping one and continuing with both feet on the other. Finally, the ultimate trick was learned and there I was skiing down the lake backwards, on one ski, holding the rope with my left foot, with my left leg extended straight out to the boat. But wait, that wasn't enough! Remember my being a drum major? What does a drum major do besides lead the marching band? He twirls batons. Could twirling batons possibly be added to the water ski trick? But if I dropped one, it would sink. Solution? Floats! Picture this: you have a water skier doing his backwards thing, holding the rope with one foot, on one ski, but with the addition of twirling two batons at the same time. Do you think any boats followed me down the lake? You betcha!

Eventually, someone built a ski jump, located on the Honey Creek branch of Grand Lake. This is a floating wooden ramp, anchored in a stable position. The ramp rose to a height of four feet above water level at the jump-off point. No one on the lake knew how to go over a ski jump. Ah, another chance for a first! All the books were read on the "how to" of ski jumping. Then Dad read about the driving techniques – how far to be from the jump and when to start turning the boat away when the skier "pops off" the end of the ramp to keep the rope taut. OK, this seemed fairly straightforward.

The big day comes for my first attempt. We have found a day with not much wind, so that the lake surface was smooth. Mother wouldn't come with us, being more than a little nervous. A little apprehensive, we head over to the jump. Once there we water it down, so the skis will slip over the wood. Then it's into the water. We make a couple of passes to check speed and proper distance of the boat from the jump. Then I head for the outside edge of the jump, because the minute you hit the jump the momentum will drag you back toward the boat. My knees were flexed with my upper body in position, but nothing can prepare you for the first feel of going from water resistance to the feel of slippery wood.

The first attempt was not successful. The good news is that the fall occurred on the other side of the jump. Analyzing the jump, it was just a matter of adjusting my balance on the transition. The next try, it was up and over the jump landing on my feet! Now there was a feeling of accomplishment that was really shared with my Dad. Over that summer my skill level increased until I could start outside the right wake of the boat, ski across to the left, building up speed, hit the bottom right of the jump and "pop off" the upper left corner. This gave me much more airtime on the jump.

Golf was my dad's first passion, and then my mother became quite skilled at the game as well. We spent a lot of time together on the golf course. My dad had managed Mohawk Golf Course in Tulsa, Oklahoma in his early twenties. He continued there after my parents married, but when his responsibility became a family of three, he wasn't making enough money to support us. He left golf to work in an oil refinery in Duncan, Oklahoma. He had taught my mother to play while they were still in Tulsa. She was a natural athlete and developed a beautiful, graceful golf swing. She was also the competitor in our family. dad was a good teacher and I was an enthusiastic player, but she was the one with the winner's instinct on the course.

My first introduction to golf was at the age of two, with a cut-down set of clubs that dad made for me. He also made some little putting holes in our back yard in Duncan. So golf has always been a part of my life. A love of the game and a lot about the swing technique was learned from my dad, but being an average "bogie" golfer was to be my zenith in the sport. In the beginning there was a little promise of something better. At the age of seven on a driving range in Rochester, Minnesota, there was a "closest to the pin contest." It was about 120-yard shot and my best shot was about 12' from the pin. Got a mention in the newspaper article about the contest. Oh boy, another area to garner kudos! Didn't happen. My one junior golf tournament in Miami, Oklahoma, preserved a telling incident for me. I was leading in my match going into the back nine, then choked and started to fall behind. My mother, who had been following me around for the match, left and went back to the clubhouse. She couldn't stand to watch this collapse. Yep, the match was lost. Evidently her competitive DNA strand didn't transfer to me. I did continue to play golf, but no more tournaments for me until a couple of charity events as an adult. Mother went on to win several club championships and dad became a successful teacher. Now, even playing golf socially only a few times a year, the fluid swing that dad taught me is still in place. It looks so right that when a bad shot caroms off my club, one of my partners has been known to comment, "How did that happen? you looked so good!" Ah, form is everything.

What other ways could attention be garnered? Well, the band had a fundraising contest every year. Band members sold magazine subscriptions and the one who sold the most won a small trophy. Who won that contest several year running? You guessed it. Moi. It would be a little boring to detail all of the organizations, local and state, in which I held elective office during my school years. That bountiful list would run on a little long. Years later it was discovered that my dad and I had shared a unique double. We were both Valedictorian and President of our Senior Class in High School. Now remember, "more is better." My senior year alone, I was president of five different organizations and 2nd vice-president of the state 4-H Club!

Talk about attention. Dad loved getting a new car almost every two years. During my senior year he surprised Mother and me with a two-toned green Ford convertible! Can you imagine, being able to drive a convertible in a small Midwest town in the fifties? On one of our first trips to Miami for dance class it was, "Mom, can we put the top down?" It was a spring night and still a little on the cool side, but she did. There we were, tooling down a little Oklahoma highway, coats buttoned, windows rolled up and the heater turned on, but with the top down and music blasting on the radio.

I'll bet many a first time convertible owner has done the same thing.

Oklahoma has sometimes been referred to as the "buckle of the bible belt." The summer before my senior year I attended five different church camps. It is difficult to explain the lure of religion on this impressionable young mind. The need to be the good boy was so front and center in my life that this seemed to be the ultimate showcase for me. At the final camp of the summer there was a closing event on the last night. During the service there was a direct appeal for those who felt the calling to give their life to Christ. Sitting in the back of the open-air auditorium in prayer, not knowing what to do, my stomach was giving me fits and hurting a lot.

My prayer began, "God, I don't know what to do. Do you want my life? If you do, make my stomach stop hurting." Surprisingly, it did. Uh-oh. On shaky legs I walked down to the altar and completed the confirmation. Don't ask me to clarify this. It is as inexplicable now as it was then.

What to do next? Did this mean I had to stop performing to concentrate on being a minister? What?? My parents had to be told. Dad was away working. Mother was, as always, very supportive. There were tears and hugs (yes, hugs), and discussion about the direction of my life. It wasn't decided at that moment, but over the course of the year two possibilities emerged: a minister of music and a Christian entertainer. When Dad was told, he too was supportive, but a little mystified.

My idyllic life had taken a downward path at the age of thirteen. Mother was diagnosed with breast cancer and had to have her left breast removed. The preceding year she had had a lump removed that was benign, But just a year later she required a complete mastectomy. During her recovery period she needed assistance changing the dressing on the still-fresh wound. The scar that was left from the radical surgery was like a big plus sign on the left side of her torso. The bottom of the incision had to be drained every day for the first few weeks. Dad was away working during this time, so there was no one to help her but me. It was a traumatic task for this adolescent boy to go through.

My Mother was a remarkable woman in many ways. After she had recovered, her left arm remained swollen because of the lymph nodes that were compromised during the procedure. Even with her arm in that shape she came back to win another golf club championship at the Miami Country Club. That was quite a feat, but she topped that. I helped her conquer the slalom ski. To be sitting in the boat watching her ski on one ski, after what she had gone through, was just amazing. She had upped the definition of "indefatigable" for me.

Another telling moment about my mother occurred when I was acting as the Master of Ceremonies for the state "Share the Fun" contest the year after my trip to the national convention. At one point during the show a moment was set aside to acknowledge my parents:

"There are two people in the audience I would like to thank who have been so supportive and without whom I wouldn't be here today - my parents. I would like them to stand up and take a bow."

Before the 2,000 or so members of the audience they stood, each in their own way taking the applause. Dad shyly smiled, ducked his head a couple of times and kept his hands clasped in front of him. Mother was a different story. She stood there with both hands raised, turning around and waving to the audience. I now know she earned every second of that bow. At my 50th class reunion several friends made comments to me about my mother being so beautiful and being such a class act. That was nice to hear after all these years.

All of the pursuits previously cited in those early years developed three important principles in my life: follow your passions, explore all possibilities and develop a killer work ethic. My initial reasoning for doggedly pursuing these principles may have been suspect, but each one proved to be vitally important as my life progressed and served me well throughout all of my careers. My parents gave me unbridled support in all my pursuits. This was also paramount in my attaining those elements in my life. I can't remember being truly depressed when a major disappointment occurred in my life. I would be down but not inert. It seems like my recuperative powers always kicked in. There was always another avenue or venue to pursue. This has a bit of a "Pollyanna" quality to it, as has been frequently pointed out by my friends. However, the truth is that positive energy does win out over negativity. This is not to be confused with unrealistic expectations or self-entitlement. Those two ego-centered life pursuits will bite you in the ass every time! For me it was often just a matter of rolling with the punches. As you get up from the "roll," you are usually facing in a new direction and it just takes a little courage to take that first step. Then it becomes less fearful to take the second. I'm not saying that it is an easy process, but it can be a fulfilling one.

On to college!

LESSONS LEARNED

- Follow Your Passions

- Explore All Possibilities

- Develop a Killer Work Ethic

- Roll With the Punches

COLLEGE

It was going to be a first in my family for me to go to college. Neither my father nor my mother had been able to pursue a higher education. We began to look at possibilities during my senior year in high school. It wasn't quite the same as today when students and parents begin to look for schools at a much earlier age. To show the extent of our search, the University of Miami, in Miami, Florida, and the University of Houston were on my list. Why? Miami offered scholarships for water skiing and Houston for accordion expertise. What? Go figure. These were not realistic considerations, but because of my passions, were researched nonetheless. I was offered a full scholarship at Northeastern Oklahoma Junior College in Miami. With only two years of schooling, it didn't seem right for me. There was also a smaller scholarship to attend Oklahoma State University. Not right, either.

My father knew Glenn Dobbs, the Athletic Director at the University of Tulsa. After meeting with him and auditioning for the band director, Dwight Dailey, a full tuition, room and board with books scholarship was offered to be one of two drum majors for the marching band, play tenor saxophone in the concert band and work as the Assistant Trainer for the freshman football team. The Assistant Trainer duties consisted mainly of cleaning up the locker rooms after the practice sessions. Hey, whatever it takes to reach your goals, even if it means doing menial labor for a time. Even then there was never any task for me that fell into the category of "that's not in my job description." My living quarters consisted of a cubicle on the wide-open top floor of the athletic dorm. That lasted for the first semester of my freshman year.

It had been difficult deciding the direction of my college education, due to of my many and diverse interests. Also, there was my life dedication to the church to be considered. I decided on a double major in the music department, vocal and instrumental, working toward two degrees: a Bachelor of Music Education in Voice and a Bachelor of Music in Church Music. The instrumental part of the double only lasted one semester. For me the tenor saxophone was not a good choice for a major instrument. Every instru-

27

mental major had to take a minor instrument class. In the string instrument class that first semester, the double bass and I made for an interesting combo. We were both tall.

Along with continuing to play the tenor sax in the concert band, that big old baritone sax came back into my life during my junior year. There was a classical saxophone quartet in the music school and I was enlisted in the baritone sax position. We played a few recitals and made an interesting little splash in the music school. Our main claim to fame centered on our stellar first alto sax player, Burl Reed, who later became the principle bassoonist with the Chicago Symphony under Maestro Georg Solti.

The summer before my entry into college was spent looking ahead to see what edge could possibly be obtained before school started. The jump into the drum major position would be from a very small high school to a medium sized university. First, I contacted the head baton twirler at the university for twirling lessons to improve that skill. This paid off in an unexpected way. During the half-time performances the drum majors led the band and the twirlers twirled. The pep rallies were a different matter, anything to create a buzz and high energy for upcoming games. Sometime in my sophomore year a pair of fire batons were purchased and the prerequisite tricks were learned. Remember my modus operandi, "Get that attention!"

That same summer there was a national band camp at Gunnison, Colorado. Attending that camp gave me first-hand experience in the expertise expected at the college level. Memory tells me I held my own in the competitions, but was not singled out as the top drum major. That was one of my several disappointments in striving to be the best, but the entire week was an eye-opening learning experience. That summer was evidence that my developing sense of exploring all possibilities and preparing in all areas was beginning to take shape.

Tulsa was only an hour and half from Grove, but it was still the first time for me to live away from home. It was a little bit more difficult for my mother than it was for me. She had been so wrapped up helping me with all my performances and achievements, there was more than a bit of the "empty nest" syndrome that crept into her life. This was before cell phones, but I did try to keep in touch.

Back to the band. The other drum major's name was Donnie and for three years there was an intense rivalry between Donnie and Ronnie to be top dog. This really became evident at the half-time performances with each of us trying to out "high step" the other. A telling incident occurred after band practice one day. It was a particularly hot afternoon and we had gone through our routine several times in the stadium. Mr. Dailey ended the session with the announcement that he would buy a Coke for the winner of a 100-yard dash. What a prize! Everyone who was thirsty lined up on the

Ronnie and Donnie, Drum Majors of the University of Tulsa Marching Band, with the band mascot. (Photo by Bob McCormack, University of Tulsa McFarlin Library Special Collection.)

goal line. We were off! Donnie and I had lined up together and it was evident after the first 50 yards that we were the fastest. I edged him out at the far goal line and was sore for several days, pushing some of those muscles not used since that grade school track meet.

"Rush Week" for the fraternities happened the week before classes commenced. It was a little overwhelming with all the parties and the upper classmen seeming to be so worldly and wise. As active as my participation had been in every level of my small high school, this was an entirely different experience. Many things were considered in perspective pledges, including high school grades, activities, social facility and potential comradery. There were other fraternities interested in my pledging, but Sigma Chi held the most promise for me. I moved into the fraternity house for the spring semester of my freshman year during the pledge period and after being initiated stayed for the remainder of my college life. The room-and-meals part of my scholarship that had me living in the athletic dorm and cleaning the locker rooms was given up. Thus my janitorial expertise was only honed for one semester. Couldn't have been a very high caliber. But this meant incurring a cost to live in the fraternity for room and board. My parents supported me in this and paid for it. The real upside of this move was meeting my roommate for the next three and a half years, Don Doss, who became a lifelong dear friend. We didn't have much in common when we met, although he had lived in that same athletic dorm on a football scholarship his first semester. He was a football player, I was a performer. He was from Texas, I was from Oklahoma. He was an engineering major, I was a music major. He was Baptist, I was Methodist. He was vertically challenged, I was tall. My story was always that I had to take the top bunk in our fraternity room because he couldn't reach it.

There was one incident that sums up an unfortunately strident "holier than thou" attitude that was all pervasive in my life at that time. The pledges of Sigma Chi had a beer bust that first spring which Donnie attended, but not me. Having signed a total abstinence pledge at the church, I didn't drink, but stayed in the house studying. Later in the evening when Donnie came back to the room it was pretty evident that he had had a few too many brews. Suddenly he jumped up and headed for the communal head. I followed him and as he was down on his knees in front of the porcelain bowl I pushed open the door to the stall and said, "Doss, was it really worth it?" Oh the arrogance of that statement haunts me to this day. It's a wonder that he continued to be my friend. There have been profuse apologies over the years for that incident and now we can laugh about it, but that attitude of mine remained a burr under my saddle for years and years.

The Modern Choir was one of the focal points of the music school. The director, Arthur Hestwood, affectionately known as Hesty, had formerly sung with "Fred Waring and the Pennsylvanians," a popular nationally-known singing group, and had quite a reputation for choral conducting. The preliminary auditions had been held the preceding spring and the final selections took place at the beginning of the fall semester. The big deal about being in the choir was the choir trip. Every January between semesters there was a road trip to New York City. Several concerts would be booked on the way there and on the return trip, with three or four days to enjoy the wonders of that phenomenal city. I was selected and remained a member for all four years of college.

When we were rehearsing the numbers for our concert that first year, my first solo, "Long Ago and Far Away," created a problem. The word "away" was beyond my ability to pronounce in an understandable manner. With my Oklahoma accent the word sounded like "awahyee." There were several private coaching sessions until the diphthong was removed, practically with forceps, and the lyric was intelligible. We all worked extremely hard and the concerts were always well-received. The trip to New York that first year was memorable for seeing my first Broadway show, "Gypsy," starring Ethel Merman. Can you imagine that being your introduction to Broadway? From that point on I was really hooked. Somehow, sometime, I had to get to New York and perform on Broadway. On every trip for those four years I would see a show every night and every available matinee, even if it meant getting a standing room ticket.

Another important direction was initiated at the beginning of my freshman year. My cousin, Shala, who had attended TU, suggested Beaumont Bruestle as an instructor for freshman English. His class had an opening that first semester. All right, enroll. He also happened to be the head of the Theater Department. One day he asked me to stay after class:

"Ronald, I would like for you to audition for the spring musical. Are you interested?"

"Yes sir, when are the auditions?"

It was an original musical about Catherine the Great of Russia, "The Name is Jones," written by Beau with music by his long-time collaborator, Charles Swier. My role was Ottokar, a Russian sailor, who had a barcarole to sing on the deck of a ship in the second act. That cameo performance became a bit of legend in the theater department and is actually documented on an audio recording. Standing on the prow of the ship, looking out into the wings where other cast members were murmuring low, I uttered, "Oh bless us all, those gypsies are at it again. Just listen to 'em," and then sang the song. First there was the sight and sound of a Russian sailor with this broad Oklahoma accent, and then there was my naiveté about the theater definition of "gypsies." It was much later that someone clued me in about that particular moment in TU theater history giving everyone, but me, a big laugh.

That started a connection with the theater department that lasted throughout my college career, including a scholarship from the Broadway Theater League of Tulsa during my graduate year. The downside for every spring musical was that Beau always wrote a new show, and we never had the experience of working on any of the great musical theater repertory. The upside for every spring musical was that Beau always wrote a new show, which meant there was the excitement of creating something new. So we had this double-edged sword. It was what it was. Those musicals, coupled with the plays in which I was cast, were the crux of my college theatrical training.

My ballet training with John Hurdle was beginning to show results. (Photos by John Hurdle)

John Hurdle became my first real mentor. We came in contact in that spring semester of my freshman year when he choreographed "The Name is Jones." He taught speech classes and choreographed all the shows for the theater department. Formerly he was with the Richmond Ballet and then spent time in New York working as a dancer. He had also toured with Mary Martin in the national company of "Annie Get Your Gun." During my graduate year he even gave me ballet classes during my lunch breaks. Tap had been so exciting for me it had been very difficult to get me to study ballet in high school. One could say I was "balletically" deficient. He worked very hard to bring me up to "passable" in that area. He also became a great friend to our family, painting a portrait of me for my dad.

His greatest gift to me was his encouragement and advice in pursuing a career in musical theater. During my senior year choir trip to New York he even arranged a private audition for me with Mary Martin! She graciously invited me to sing for her in her Sutton Place apartment. After the audition she told me that if I was going to be in New York that coming fall there would be a spot for me in her new show, "Jenny." This was another tough decision. Plans were already afoot for me to continue my studies the following year to earn that second Bachelor's Degree in Church Music and a Master's Degree in Voice. I wrote the appropriate letter turning down the offer and thanking her profusely. It was a wise decision. That fall "Jenny" was a bomb on Broadway. It was one of Miss Martin's few misses, if not her only one. My thought process for this decision was that there would always be auditions for shows in New York, even if I didn't have an "in" with the star, but if I left school after graduation the chances of my coming back for additional studies were slim. Here again a combination of pursuing all possibilities, following my passion and being pragmatic fueled my decision-making process. This time the killer work ethic won out, allowing me to obtain the additional degrees. John's last gift to me in college was a scrapbook of all my college memorabilia. It proved to be invaluable in reconstructing those years.

The University Methodist Church choir became my church away from home. For one cantata Mrs. Fowler, the choir director, needed someone to play a recorder, a small wooden wind instrument with a medieval sound similar to a flute and the fingering similar to a saxophone. I jumped at the chance, learned it quickly and played it several times for services. Remember, drinking the water in Oklahoma makes for over achievers.

My sophomore year the beautiful Sharp Chapel opened on campus and I regularly sang there as well. In my fifth year on campus one of my graduate scholarships was to assist the chaplain and direct the volunteer choir. The church remained an important part of my life throughout my school years. Knowing that one of my degrees was going to be a Bachelor's in Church Music, some religion and philosophy courses began to appear on my schedule. This was eye opening for me. Suddenly many of the precepts that had been accepted on blind faith were being seen in a new light. Questions were raised and beliefs were challenged. It was the beginning of my search to find out what was relevant for me in the church doctrine that had been spoon-fed to me during my first 18 years.

One of the curriculum requirements was a gym course. The natural for me was golf, but only two semesters were allowed in the same sport. In my sophomore year gymnastics sounded interesting, considering my acrobatic background. A lot of the football players also took the class, thinking it would be an easy "A" for them. Surprise! One task in the class was daunting for everyone. Thick ropes were hung from the ceiling and we had to sit on the floor with our legs in a "V" and climb the rope with the legs straight out, using only our hands and arms. The "jocks" didn't fare so well. One by one they would reach their heavily biceped arms up the rope and try to pull themselves toward the ceiling. Slowly, after two or three pulls, their legs would drop from the ninety-degree position and be dangling weights. They would then have to give up with about a third of the climb accomplished, grab the rope with their legs and work their way back to the floor. Only two of us in the class could make it all the way to the top. The secret was in taking small sections of the rope with each grasp, keeping your elbows close to your sides and engaging your lats, abs and pecs (remember the legs were still squarely out in front). It was a real achievement and gave me a little status boost in the class. How could this tall, skinny kid accomplish this fairly difficult maneuver?

Here's how. The summer between my freshman and sophomore years Dad decided that I should work with him on a tuck-pointing job. This would entail mixing cement, carrying the buckets to scaffold, climbing the ropes to get to the scaffold (aha, climbing ropes!), working on that scaffold four or five stories from the ground, knocking out the old mortar between the bricks, applying new cement, and surviving. We were working in a small town in Arkansas, staying at a motel during the week and then coming home for the weekends to be with Mother. It was exhausting. Eat, work and sleep. I would come back to the motel and just fall on the bed. At the end of the summer Dad finally told me, " Son, I wanted you to work with me this summer doing manual labor to realize that this is not the kind of job you would want to take in the future." He made his point. It worked. It also got me an "A" in gymnastics.

As a voice major there were voice lessons to be taken. Hesty was my first teacher. It soon became evident that the better voice students studied with another teacher, Louis Cunningham. It was a difficult switch for me. Working several days a week in the choir with Hesty, how could this transition be accomplished smoothly? Confrontations, large and small, have always been avoided at all costs. That is an area that is difficult for me even now.

The day arrived and it was time for my lesson. "Hesty, I feel that I need to change and study with Mr. Cunningham."

"Well, I'd like to have you stay, but if you feel that is what you need, go ahead," he replied.

There. It was done. The actual confrontation was usually never as bad as it played out in my imagination. The one residual fallout was that his wife was very cool to me for quite some time. I survived it.

So the change was made and Mr. Cunningham remained my teacher throughout my tenure in the music school. These studies led to a joint senior voice recital with Peggy Horn and two solo recitals during my graduate year. Thinking about the "away" episode, imagine what work was required for me to sing in French, German and Italian, as well as Oklahoma English! Ah, the challenge. Research was done to find very special material for these recitals. "On Wenlock Edge" by Ralph Vaughan Williams, complete with string quartet and piano, was selected for the senior recital. This was a beautiful setting of A.E. Housman's "A Shropshire Lad." There was the added challenge of conducting the string quartet in rehearsals. It was a thrilling experience. For a special effect in one of my graduate recitals I brought in a harpsichord for the Bach cantata section. In addition, a little-known version of Gioacchino Rossini's "La Danza" surprised the audience and was a hit. The two most unusual finds were Maurice Ravel's "Cinq Melodies Populaires Grecques" and "Les Illuminations" by Benjamin Britten. Both were haunting creations that enabled me to cast a brief musical spell on the audience.

Early on in my first music history and music theory classes it became evident that there was an enormous lack in my background in many areas of musical knowledge and experience that put me way behind the other students. The music library became my hangout of choice, spending hours listening to records of famous symphonies, piano concertos and operas. Going to my first Tulsa Philharmonic concert allowed me to hear a French horn in all its glory for the first time. Wow! So what could be done to gain knowledge and close the gap with my fellow music students? Bring on the killer work ethic! In addition to hours in the music library, more hours were spent in the practice rooms and the regular library. At that point my own version of time management was born. Practically every minute of my day was scheduled. That kept up until I felt that I could compete on a fairly equal footing. By then the habit was ingrained and was just continued, enabling me to excel. Here was one of those times to assess the situation, look at my options, select a path and work my butt off.

Plans can be made, but snags usually develop. There were two hospitalizations during my college years: one for severe strep throat and one to have my tonsils removed. During the strep throat episode my grandmother on my dad's side, who had been a practical nurse, would come and sit with me during the nights in the hospital. She was a wonderful, petite woman who was very comforting.

"Now Ronnie, I'm right here if you need anything. Here, gargle this hydrogen peroxide. It'll make you feel better and get rid of that infection. You just get some rest now." She had developed the habit of doing different forms of needlework and knitting while on the night shifts. I still have two beautiful afghan blankets that she made for Mother and me. At 18 the tonsil episode necessitated a longer recovery process. Ice cream and Jell-O became my sustenance for a few days.

During the fall semester of my sophomore year Mother's cancer returned with a vengeance. She had been told that if she remained cancer-free for five years she would have it beat. This was the fifth year and it came back in her lungs. During one of her series of radiation treatments in the fall she came to Tulsa and stayed in a hotel downtown right next to the medical center. I would go to see her every day, squeezing the short trip into my already bulging calendar. One day it was just impossible to work in a visit. The next day when I got there she said, "Oh, I thought you had forgotten me." That statement was seared in my memory and stayed with me for years.

"If I had just gone every day she would have been able to beat the cancer and wouldn't have died." The guilt was palpable. She did die the next spring. Dad and I were in the hospital room when the nurse pushed the last breath out of her liquid-filled lungs. To lose a parent any time is devastating. To loose one before you become an adult is almost too much to bear. Rehearsals for the spring musical and my first leading role had already begun. A few days of rehearsals were missed and then it was "on with the show," because that was what Mother would have wanted.

It turned out that I had to be the strong one in the family, at eighteen. Family members and friends would come by to offer condolences to Dad and me, but I would end up comforting them. "As much as we loved and needed her, God must have needed her more" was my practiced response. At one point when Dad and I were alone we both broke down and let all the hurt come out. But, as everyone who has lost someone knows, that pain doesn't abate for a long time. Mother had touched so many people's lives. At her funeral the floral tributes filled the chancel area and the side aisles to the very back of the church. The sanctuary overflowed with family and friends. Then the service was over, she was interred, and all of the mourners were gone. What a void. Dad and I still had each other, but I would be going back to school and would be busy. What was he going to do? That first Mother's Day was the first of the holidays we had to experience without her. It occurred right away and gave us a bleak inkling of what the rest of the year would hold.

We made the mistake of giving away a lot of Mother's clothing and personal effects too soon. There had been a family tradition that we would go shopping with Mother to help her select her clothes. We had a hand in picking out most of her wardrobe. There was an emotional attachment there that we ignored when parceling out her possessions. We tried to end the grieving process too soon and go on with life. We just didn't give it enough time.

Dad was really at a loss. During that first year he sold our little house in Grove, purchased a lot on the lake and built us a new home. It gave him focus and purpose. My cousin, Mary Ann, had drawn up the plans and Dad acted as his own contractor, doing some of the work himself. The beautiful stone floor in the great room and kitchen area was his pride and joy. He had mixed a mortar with a little silica in which to set the subtly hued Arkansas stone. He hand ground the entire floor and then applied a waterproof sealant. The effect was stunning, with all of the natural beauty of the stones being set off with just a hint of sparkle in the mortar. Anyone who ever paid a visit to our home never failed to comment on that floor.

During that time he went back to Guthrie to finish a waterproofing job. The local dry cleaning establishment was run by LaVon Gibson, whom he had known from frequenting the dry cleaners during his previous work stints in Guthrie. He began to date this very attractive divorcee, who I first met when Dad invited her up to our newly finished home on the lake. There was an immediate connection. She was warm, friendly and beautiful. On one of her later visits she brought her daughter, Linda, who was just two year younger than I. At one point they both took me aside.

LaVon seemed to summon up her courage, "Ronnie, what do you think?" she asked as she extended her left hand to show me her new engagement ring. Dad had not confided in me, so it was a surprise, though not a total one.

I immediately hugged them both and said, "Welcome to the family." We were all just beaming.

Dad and Lavon, my new Mom.
(Photo by Gibson Studio)

LaVon also had a son, Chuck, who was just a few years older. The wedding took place in May, just about a year after Mother had died, with just the family in attendance. For those who think that was too soon for my Dad to remarry, you just didn't know him. He had loved my Mother and she would continue to have a deeply special place in his heart. But, he was the type of man who simply couldn't be alone. He turned out to be the luckiest of men to have found two such wonderful women to complete him in his lifetime. Suddenly, this only child had a sister, brother and sister-in-law, with Chuck already married to Charlene. This built-in family eventually grew to include nieces who married, and then great-nephews and nieces. After all, dancers and new "steps" are a match made in heaven. My experience of combining with a "step" family was one of commitment and love. I have been one of the lucky ones to experience that lifetime of love and support from a "step" family. In fact, from this point forward they will be referred to simply as my family.

My college life continued at a very fast pace, with additional activities being picked up along the way. One of the local funeral homes asked me to be on call to sing at funerals when the families did not have a soloist for the service. Rushing to the funeral home and standing behind a screen to sing the requested hymns was a way to pick up extra spending money and improve my musical sight-reading.

The "Tulsa Spotlighters" was a combination of a dinner theater and a local nightclub. It was a nonprofit organization that provided fine arts scholarships and contributions to local charities. The guiding light was Georgia Noel. Playing only on Saturday nights, it featured a production of "The Drunkard," a popular melodrama that encouraged audience participation. After the play there was an "Olio" portion, featuring individual variety performers, that Georgia emceed. It was a great venue for trying out new material. This became a Saturday night fixture for me, and my performance skills went to a higher level from this experience. Georgia wrote me a note after my final performance, before going off to summer stock and New York, that I still cherish. She signed it, "your ever lovin', foster fat mother, Georgia."

There is documentation that has me belonging to seven honorary fraternities during my tenure at TU and, of course, holding office in most of them. Grades were always important to me. Every semester for four years it was all "A's" except for one "B." That would always just kill me. Give me that 4.0! My grades did earn me a partial tuition Faculty Honor Scholarship for my senior year. Finally, in my graduate studies both semesters were 4.0. By that time some of the music faculty had been conned by my persistence and perseverance. There was no way my composition class should have resulted in an "A," unless it was an acknowledgement of diligence. In reviewing some of those pieces now, the workmanship shows through, if not the creativity. Walking across the platform after receiving my master's degree a salient thought did cross my mind "You dummy! You don't deserve this.

All you did was work for grades!" It was at this point that the real student in me began learning for the sake of knowledge.

Following my tradition of running for every office possible, Junior Class President became the next feather in my cap. There was also the presidency of the Wesley Foundation, the Methodist youth group on campus and the Modern Choir. By that junior year a student was also eligible to be considered for membership in Who's Who in American Colleges and Universities, based on a combination of grades and activities. The achievement of being selected that year started a run of three years of my being on the Who's Who roster, extending through my graduate studies. That was considered very unique and seldom accomplished. During my graduate year I was the only student to have been named for three successive years. Oh boy, another first with another picture in the paper!

The annual Varsity Nite Show occurred every spring. This all-school talent show was a magnet for me. There was a panel of judges to select the best acts and the audience voted on the Varsity Nite King and Queen. Winning had not been on the plate for me the first two years, so in my junior year all stops were pulled out. Overkill is an understatement here. In addition to directing and choreographing the Sigma Chi group in "A Girl Named Fred," from "Once Upon a Mattress," I entered the solo competition and was nominated for Varsity Nite King. My solo act consisted of dancing, tumbling, playing the accordion, twirling batons and singing a bit of an aria from Pagliacci. All of this while dressed as a clown. How could that combination not win? Look at all the talent it took to pull this off! Well, a popular Kingston Trio type group won. The best fraternity act was also lost to the Kappa Alphas. Even being selected Varsity Nite King that night and being given a large trophy didn't mask my disappointment. There is a photograph of all the winners in a faded newspaper clipping of the event, showing me holding that big trophy with a fake smile plastered on my face. This is evidence that even then a "poker face" was not in my repertoire.

Graduating from college was a milestone. One of the traditions was to ring the bell at Kendal Hall. There is a photo of me in cap and gown and my father, looking dapper in his suit and tie with spectator shoes, pulling the rope together. There is a look of great pride and accomplishment on both of our faces. I still have that pair of Dad's shoes and squeeze into them on occasion.

The spring before graduation in 1962 I auditioned for a spot in the chorus of the Kansas Starlight Theatre summer musical season. This was a large 7,000 seat outdoor theater in Swope Park in Kansas City, Missouri. Going through both the singing and dancing auditions, I was hired to be in the singing chorus at $75 per week. This was a big step, enabling me to join the Actor's Equity Union. One of the Tulsa newspaper articles about my selection described me as: "in many respects, the most active male student at TU." That just about says it all, doesn't it? Mission accomplished.

Dad helping me "ring the bell" at Kendall Hall, a tradition for all the graduates at the University of Tulsa.

That summer was an exciting introduction to professional theater. We rehearsed one show during the day and performed another at night, having a run of six shows for the summer season. They would be broken up with two touring shows to give us a little extra rehearsal time. My first show was "The Music Man" and my first line to be spoken on a professional stage was "What da ya talk, what da ya talk, what da ya talk," during the opening train sequence. The memory of that opening is still so vivid, standing in the wings under a burgeoning starlit sky, listening to the overture. "This is what I want to do, this is what I want to do." Oh, remember that total abstinence pledge from my freshman year? Bye, bye. At the opening night party Harding Dorn, the choreographer, bought me my first drink: a screwdriver. Yes, you read correctly. At the age of 21, liquor touched my lips for the first time.

That summer was exciting and very hectic, but it was the life for me. Another vivid memory was working with Chita Rivera in "Bye Bye Birdie." At the closing night party I got up the nerve to ask her to dance a jitterbug. We were so into it that the rest of the dancers stopped dancing and formed a circle around us to let us take off. Oh boy! The billing for the show had Brenda Lee starring over Chita. This was unusual since Chita had originated her role to acclaim in New York. Aha! This is the world of summer stock. Brenda Lee had a hit record out and the object was to sell as many tickets as possible. The toughest part was when the season ended. Many of my newfound friends were going to New York to seek their fame and fortune and I was going back to school. Oh, the envy!

Returning to TU for work on a master's degree, my residence became a garage apartment shared with Doy Cole, another Sigma Chi, at his parents' house. We remained so busy that year that we barely spent any time together. There is one incident that comes to mind: a chocolate cookie test. We were trying to determine which was the better cookie, Oreo or Hydrox. We got a box of each, a quart of milk and commenced this very scientific process: bite the cookie, chug the milk. After going through at least a half a box of each one the decision of the judges was unanimous: HYDROX!. Sorry, Oreo.

Looking back after that first summer of stock, there was a downside. Being a member of Actor's Equity gave me a certain status. Oh really? That put me a peg above the "mere students." Oh, not again! Up on a pedestal. The proof was in my performance of Little Bat, the simpleton brother in the opera "Susannah" that spring. This could have been a great learning experience because Norman Triegle from the New York City Opera was the guest artist in the production. Years later John Hurdle told me that I had shamelessly overacted during one of Susannah's major arias to pull stage focus. This time "get that attention" was a bummer. It was an accomplishment to be a member of Equity while still in college, but there was so much more knowledge to acquire about being a performer. A big dose of humility would have been nice. But remember, my operating system was still one of "more, more, more!"

Leading the band and conducting the various choirs gave me a background for the conducting class required for the Master's Degree. It was exciting to conduct the university orchestra in a rehearsal of a Mozart symphony. For the final, "L'Histoire du Soldat" by Igor Stravinsky was assigned. After hours of preparation I conducted the complex rhythmic score to a recording for Mr. McKee, the conducting instructor. It was a success. In addition to conducting the various church choirs there were countless renditions led of "The Sweetheart of Sigma Chi" over the years at the fraternity.

There were two roads to a master's degree: a dissertation and an oral examination, or give two vocal recitals and an oral examination. Either way there was no escaping that dreaded oral exam. After the work it took to learn all the material for the two recitals, that time was immediately devoted to cramming for the exam. I received notification that it would be on May 3, 1963. The board was stacked in my favor, with half of the six having been beneficiaries of my zealousness and the other three highly aware of it. Still, it was a nerve-wracking experience. What would they ask? To prepare for this is like reading the encyclopedia. The ominous day arrived. I can remember giving an appropriate answer for stating the difference between a French chanson and a German lied of a certain period, but that is the only question that comes to mind. The main memory is one of sitting in the center of that semi-circle with everyone looking at me expectantly. Survival and victory!

My next summer season at Kansas City after my graduate studies provided more learning opportunities, connections to the world of theater and performing spots. That season we mounted seven musicals. One of the shows was "Carnival." At his first rehearsals with all the chorus members, Harding asked, "Does anyone

Twirling fire batons and walking on my hands across the stage at the Kansas City Starlight Theater in "Carnival."

have any skills that could be used in our staging other than just plain old singing and dancing?"

That was like a red cape in front of a bull for me. "I could twirl two fire batons or walk on my hands across the stage if you needed it." Of course he did. Here are the photos to prove it.

In "Gypsy" there was a chance for some bovine antics as "Caroline," the cow. For whatever it's worth, my position was the front end, not the rear.

The most important event occurred in the last show of the season. It was meeting Georgio Tozzi, who played the lead in "South Pacific." His advice to contact his vocal coach, Max Walmer, led to my finding a voice teacher in New York.

Nothing has been mentioned thus far of my social life. It was there in high school, but not with too much enthusiasm. Dating was what all my peers did, so I did too. Part of the problem was being a year younger, but the main part was that I just felt "different" and didn't know why. This was nothing that prayer and being "good" couldn't fix. Life continued.

With Jackie Alloway at one of the Sigma Chi fraternity parties. (Photo by Winesburg-Davis.)

College fraternity parties required dates and the façade continued. In my sophomore year Jackie Alloway entered the music school. She was stunningly beautiful and talented. When she joined the choir we spent more time together. We then began to perform as a duo, becoming the Tulsa version of Janette McDonald and Nelson Eddy, singing at a variety of events, including the Spotlighters Club. Dating became inevitable. In fraternity parlance we were soon "dropped" and then "pinned." In the spring of my senior year we took the next step and became engaged. A snag occurred. I was going to Kansas City for the summer and she would be staying in Tulsa. I don't recall when we became unengaged, but that summer we went our separate ways. She played Adelaide in "Guys and Dolls" for the Tulsa Little Theatre and there met her future husband. The good side of the breakup is that we remain dearest friends to this day.

Looking back there was a disappointment that we were not to be together, but also there was a little sense of relief on my part. I cared for Jackie a great deal, but there was still that sense of being different. It would take me years to come to grips with being gay. First there was the bible-belt church dogma that made me a sinner. Then there were several years in New York with the wrong therapist working to make me "normal," or straight, if you will. There would be years of living with the feeling of being not only different, but somehow wrong and sinful as well. Acceptance of myself was the most difficult thing to ever achieve in my life. Only after the realization that being gay was not a "wrong" choice that I had made, nor was it caused by outside effects, could a feeling of identity finally flood my life. This total acceptance did not happen until sometime in my fifties. Now that's way too long to live with guilt. The need to prove that I was still an OK human being, that I was worthy of my own body temperature, probably sparked the urgency of my need to accomplish, to succeed, throughout all those on-coming, on-rushing years. Who knows?

Another dilema was upon me. New York was calling me strongly that fall after the second summer of stock. What to do about my commitment to the church? As stated earlier it had been narrowed down to two choices for me: minister of music and Christian entertainer. Was it possible to be a Christian entertainer in New York? This was the path I had to follow. Ever since seeing "Gypsy," it had been my dream and focus to be in a Broadway show.

At the end of the season in Kansas City it was back home for a few days. Then my final performance in Oklahoma was singing at my sister's wedding in Guthrie. She married a great young man, Bob Corlett. Now there were five of us in my family, all within four years of each other's age: Linda and Bob, Chuck and Charlene and I. Eventually my family would grow to four married nieces and include ten grand-nieces and nephews.

Then it was off to New York with $500 in my pocket, no job and only a temporary place to stay with one of my summer stock friends.

What would happen to this old Okie in the big city?

LESSONS LEARNED

- **Excel in Time Management**
- **Do Whatever it Takes, Even Menial Labor, to Reach Your Goals**

HELLO, DOLLY!

A dream comes true. New York City! I arrived on a Friday in September of 1963, having arranged to stay in an inexpensive hotel on the Upper West Side with Jimmy Powers, a friend from summer stock in Kansas City.

"Hey, you got here just in time. There's an audition for the role of Barnaby in 'Hello, Dolly' on Saturday. It is a cattle call for Equity and non-Equity performers. This is a big new Broadway show, directed and choreographed by Gower Champion. Let's go."

Gower Champion, wow! In town one day and it's off to my first audition. We trouped down to stand in line with all the others on Saturday, hoping there was an outside chance that we would be cast in the role. I was "typed out" immediately: too tall. However, it did give me my first chance to feel the sensation of standing on a Broadway stage. Memorable. On the following Monday the audition for Equity singers would be held, with dancers being seen on Tuesday. Why not go to both auditions? Only later was I told that in those days this was very rarely done, if ever. You know, sometimes ignorance is bliss.

Monday morning dawned. My choice of what to wear is still very vivid: black slacks, black blazer, black vest and white shirt with a scotch plaid red tie. It was a step up to be able to attend the Equity call, rather than the open call. We arrived and were given numbers. Mine was up in the hundreds somewhere. My time finally came to step on stage and hand my music to the accompanist to sing sixteen bars. My choice of song that day was "If Ever I Would Leave You" from "Camelot," because the last sixteen bars had a high "G" that fit my voice very well. After my audition, Gower asked me to come back the following Monday for the singers' final. Oh boy! Years later upon meeting Robert Goulet, I thanked him for helping me get my first Broadway show. See, he had originally sung that song in "Camelot," and it had made this Canadian actor a big star in the United States.

The next day was the Equity dancers' call. Here, the green Oklahoma kid stood out a little bit in a strange way. At most dancers' auditions the

47

dancers wore dance pants or tights with T-shirts or tank tops. I wore the same ensemble from Monday without the blazer, just exchanging the black slacks for black dance pants. Whoever in their right mind would wear a shirt and tie to a dance audition? Once again we were given numbers.

When my number was called, Gower looked at me and said, "Did I ask you to come back to the dancers' call today?"

"Oh no, Mr. Champion, I just came on my own." The choice of attire worked. He remembered me.

Then it was on to the dancing. Ballet was first. Oh no, that wasn't my strong suit. Gower's assistant demonstrated the combination. Whew! This was going to be doable, maybe not the best, but passable. It was glissade assemblé to the right, repeat to the left, second, fourth and double pirouette to the right. Then repeat the entire combination to the left. Sure enough my best was good enough and I made the cut. Then it was on to the tap combination, which was fairly simple for me. At the end of the audition Gower asked me to return for the dancers' final the following Tuesday.

At the final singer's audition the following Monday I was allowed to sing my entire song and was immediately asked to come back the next day for the final dance call. At that audition another dancer was having trouble learning one of the combinations, so off in the wings of the stage I worked with him. It really didn't occur to me that he was competing with me for a limited number of positions in the show. He just needed help. When the last selection finally came, it was literally like a scene from a later Broadway show, "A Chorus Line." All the dancers who had made it past the all-day culling process were standing in a line on stage.

"Ron, will you come downstage to the front line?" He pulled other dancers down front as well. Then there was an interminable wait until Gower said, "I would like those in the front to be my dancers. Rehearsals begin in two weeks." Wow! I wanted to run down to Times Square, screaming, "I just got my first Broadway show!"

You can imagine the thrill of being one of those chosen to be in the show. My first audition and here was a plum job as a dancer/singer in "Hello,

Dolly!" starring Carol Channing, directed by Gower Champion, with music and lyrics by Jerry Herman and produced by David Merrick! It's a little embarrassing to say that it almost felt inevitable. Being so prepared with those years of study and performing behind me, it would have been more surprising to me to not have been hired. However, my timing was impeccable, arriving in New York just before that first audition. After the rehearsal in New York, there would be out-of-town tryouts at the Fisher Theater in Detroit and the National Theatre in Washington, D.C. before opening on Broadway.

Those two weeks before rehearsals started were filled with apartment hunting and other auditions. Jimmy and I found a two-bedroom apartment at 310 W. 85th St. to share with Justin Morley and Steve Rydell. The rent would be about $75 each a month, affordable. We jumped at it and moved in, each of us buying a single bed and finding other bits of furniture on the street. We quickly learned which days furniture was left on the streets on the ritzier East Side, and would then go hunting for useful items that we could carry back through Central Park. The apartment was sparse at first, but eventually became quite livable.

On one of my days off, during that initial rehearsal period in New York, I contacted Max Walmer, Georgio Tozzi's vocal coach, to help me in my search for a voice teacher. He asked me over to sing for him. After what felt like another audition, he said he wanted to make a call. It was to Beverley Johnson, who happened to be Georgio Tozzi's teacher, and lived upstairs in the same building. She also taught at Julliard Music School and had a waiting list of student's wanting to study with her. It was because of this waiting list that Mr. Tozzi had not suggested that I contact her initially. At Max's suggestion arrangements were made for me to sing for her. Somehow the waiting list didn't seem to matter and she took me on as a voice student. That changed my life. She not only became my voice teacher, giving me a strong, durable vocal technique, but became a life-long friend as well. It turned out that she lived and taught on W. 86th St., just a block and a half from my new apartment. Could things work out any better?

The New York World's Fair in Flushing Meadow, Queens was going to be held in 1964 with several live musical shows that would play for the entire run of the fair. After auditioning for the General Electric Show a contract was offered. When they gave me the schedule, it conflicted with the show times of "Dolly!" Doubling, doing both shows simultaneously, was not a possibility. Yes, there was still that push to do everything, the endless cycle forever spinning: "Do more! Do more!"

Finally the rehearsals started on October 2, 1963. The salary stated in my contract was $150 per week for the tryouts outside New York City and $117.50 for performing 8 shows a week when we opened on Broadway. Rehearsals were held at the old Mark Hellinger Theatre on W. 51st St. The first two weeks of those rehearsals were devoted almost exclusively to staging the title song, "Hello, Dolly!" and "The Waiters' Gallop." Gower would only allow the performers in the numbers and the necessary production staff to be present in the theater. The atmosphere was very intense. If he had asked me to jump off of a bridge at some point in the number, I probably would have. Once those two numbers were completely staged they remained intact. Despite all of the revisions in Detroit and Washington, not a step in those two numbers was altered. Gower's vision had been so clear from the beginning that there was no need for improvement.

It's hard to describe the feeling of going to rehearse a Broadway show every day. Having dreamt of this for so long, it just seemed impossible that it was actually happening. One day when we were working on "Dancing" in the hat shop scene, Marge Champion, Gower's wife and dancing partner in the movies, came in to assist him. Now remember, all the MGM musicals with Fred Astaire, Gene Kelly and Marge and Gower had been my not-so-secret vice back in Oklahoma. So when Marge did a little waltz across the stage and back with me, I thought I had died and gone to heaven. Those hands that had danced with Marge Champion weren't washed for three days! Years later when Marge heard this story, her smile seemed to convey to me, "Well that was a little strange." Maybe not, but memory does skew events.

When the dancers would have vocal rehearsals to learn the music, the standard method was for the rehearsal pianist to plunk out the notes on the piano until everyone learned the song. Having acquired sight-reading skills in college I would just sing the music as written. This received several quizzical looks from the music director, Shep Coleman, until he realized that even a dancer could sight read music, if trained. That was not common among dancers in the sixties. It seems that I was one of the forerunners of the multitalented performers of today, being equally trained as a dancer and as a singer.

Then it was off to Detroit. Actually, it was an overnight train trip. After long and arduous technical rehearsals we performed the show for an audience for the first time at the Fisher Theater. It was thrilling for me, but evidently the critics found fault with the show. Changes were made, songs were taken out, new songs were written. I was not aware of all the various people called in to "doctor" the show and write new music. The backstage antics here and in D.C. could probably provide fodder enough for another show. However, we improved. It was in the basement of the Fisher Theater that fateful day in November of 1963 that the wardrobe mistress told me President Kennedy had been shot and killed. The earth shook. My feet became lead. Something youthful in me fell silent along with him. Everyone has seminal events in their lives where they can remember exactly where they were and what they were feeling. This was one of those for me. We canceled the show that night, and spent healing time comforting each other.

With Carol Channing backstage in our "Sunday Clothes" from "Hello, Dolly!"

In Washington we played the historic National Theatre. Washington was filled with sights to see and I wanted to experience them all. One particular day rehearsals didn't start for me until the afternoon, so the Washington Monument seemed like the thing to see that morning. Yes, I climbed to the very top and then hurried back for the rehearsal. We were staging "Before the Parade Passes By," and my character was one of four firemen. The steps were fairly athletic and being on in the beginning of the number, these steps had to be repeated many times as new characters were brought on and new steps created, until the number was staged to its completion. Halfway through the rehearsal my legs began to scream at me, "You fool, why did you climb to the top of the

Washington Monument this morning?" The rehearsal came to an end with my limping off, only to remember that there was a show to do that night. Ah, youth! Of course I made it through the show, even with those jumps in plié in the "Waiters' Gallop."

Opening night was memorable. Mary Martin was a guest of Marge and Gower and at the party that night and took a spin around the floor with Gower. It was a magical moment, watching the two of them! I didn't have the nerve to go up to Miss Martin to reintroduce myself as the Oklahoma boy who had sung for her in her apartment two years ago.

After improvements were implemented during the run at the National, it was back to New York for the opening on January 16, 1964 at the St. James Theater on W. 44th St. My folks came up from Oklahoma for the event. A lot of my new friends got tickets in the second balcony. Then it was show time! That performance is seared in my memory. There were two separate standing ovations during the show for "Hello, Dolly!" and "The Waiters' Gallop." Being on stage in both of those numbers was electrifying. The opening night party was at Sardi's and Dad and LaVon were able to accompany me. This was a thrill for them as well, meeting all the stars that were there. The reviews were fairly ecstatic and we seemed set for a long

run. My first Broadway show and it was a hit! My timing for coming to New York had been extremely fortunate.

Dorothy Kilgallen, a well-known theater writer at the time, mentioned me in her column after the opening of "Dolly."

Soon after the opening, an item appeared in the New York Journal-American about me. Dorothy Kilgallen, a well-known columnist who penned a Broadway column for the paper, wrote, "…Watch the agents scramble for Ron Young, a dancer in David Merrick's new musical, 'Hello, Dolly!' He's a Tyrone Power look-alike." Can you imagine? Of course we scoured New York until we could find multiple copies of the paper. Dad and LaVon even told me that later, when an old Tyrone Power movie would play on TV, they would hold up my latest headshot to see if there actually were some resemblance. That was pretty heady stuff for this old Okie. It was later learned that the item had been "planted" by Lester Shurr, Gower's agent. It seems that he was interested in signing me and wanted to build up some interest. I did sign with him but nothing ever materialized in the form of additional work. Not surprisingly that association ended after about two years.

We settled in for that anticipated long run. Performing only eight shows a week felt a little bit like loafing, after filling every moment of every day in my college schedule. The weekly voice lessons were added. Then dance classes in ballet, tap and jazz commenced. My tap teacher was Paul Draper, one of the greats in the world of tap dancing. Under his tutelage, there was a marked improvement in my tap.

My ballet teacher, Harry Asmus, was very acerbic. One day in class he gave a combination that required a double pirouette (two turns on one foot). My balance just happened to be spot-on that day and instead of two turns I did six! Feeling very full of myself at the end, I was shot down with, "You were late on the step after the turns." Can't recall ever doing six pirouettes again in my life, but at least that one moment lives in my memory.

In addition to a voice teacher one had to find a vocal coach to work on material for auditions. Beyond this, three remedial speech classes a week gave me hope of overcoming my Okie sound. It had reached a "crisis point" in our apartment. I would say something and my roomies would laugh at me. "But y'all don't understand. I won the state 4-H Club Timely Topic Contest and spoke before 6,000 people with the governor," I drawled. Well they laughed even more at the sound of that. Those remedial speech classes became of paramount importance in eventually being hired for speaking roles, as well as avoiding being a laughing stock.

Acting classes were a necessity. I audited a few teachers and decided on Walt Whitcover at the Herbert Bergoff Studio. This was eye-opening as well. The acting process was never intuitive with me. There was this long-standing practice of being presentational in my performances, rather than experiential. That initial need to get attention led me into a method of literally showing off for the audience. How could you not like me? Look at all this talent! Remember the overkill in my Varsity Night performance in college? Well, over the years it eventually became evident to me that by being "in the moment" on stage and playing the character from my unique point of view, both the audience and I had the best experience. However, for those first few years of dancing in the chorus, the presentational method prevailed. That was OK. The experiential way was being learned. At times it was a little like having teeth pulled without novocain, but the journey was started. Uta Hagen also taught at the Bergoff studio, since she was married to Herbert. This famous actress was known as a no-nonsense teacher. After interviewing with her, another teacher switch was made. Hers were very technical classes with exercises designed to help the actor learn how to "endow objects." The props that were worked with on stage became not only a book, but "the" book, for instance. She also had her students execute an imaginary telephone conversation, learning how to make the audience believe there was an actual person on the other end of the line. She was a dynamic personality and the classes were exciting to attend.

Someone told me that there were church agents in New York who booked singers for church services. Can you imagine? After finding one and auditioning, my new agent would send me out on Sunday mornings to different churches as a paid professional to substitute for the regular tenor soloist, of course paying him a ten per cent commission. My commitment to the church continued. Every week I sent a tenth of my earnings back to the Grove Methodist Church as my tithe. Once again it seemed to be the right thing for the wrong reason. It was important for me to hear that the preacher had mentioned me in his sermon as that "nice young man" who continues to support his church, even though he is far away in New York. Will this need for attention ever end? It'll take a long, long time to work this one out.

There was still a consideration of pursuing my higher education and working on a doctor's degree in music. Now here comes a humiliating confession: my reason for wanting a doctor's degree did not come from the purest of motives. Walking down Broadway and looking at all the theaters, I would fantasize what a marquee would look like if it read, "Starring Dr.

My first composite. I will never live it down. (Photo by Ken Duncan)

Ronald Young." Is that not embarrassing? Needless to say, the doctor's degree was never added to my résumé.

Every actor and performer in New York had to have a head shot, a photograph to leave at auditions and with agents. A friend recommended Ken
Duncan for my first photos. He later became one of the most sought-after
photographers by Broadway performers. His shots were clean, crisp and
alive. He even put together my first composite that included dance pics. It's

a little ironic that in the eighties he would also take my last dance shots.

The Tony awards were held in the spring of 1964 with "Hello, Dolly!" being nominated for 11 awards. We won all 11, with Carol even winning Best Actress over Barbra Streisand in "Funny Girl." That record number of awards stood until 2005 when "The Producers" won twelve. That was a nice 41 year record. The cast was invited to go to the awards dinner, which was not televised at that time. In addition to just being there, the big thrill was seeing Elizabeth Taylor and Richard Burton. They looked so spectacular! They even used "doubles" that night to lead the paparazzi astray when they needed a break.

In August of 1964 one of the dancers in "Dolly," Jari Lynn, told me that her girlfriend needed to move from New York and had to give up her apartment on W. 13th St. in Greenwich Village. She needed someone to take over the lease. It was a five-flight walk-up (think "Barefoot in the Park") and the rent was $92.56 a month. It was four small rooms with less than 500 square feet of total space. After an initial worry that the rent might not be affordable on my $117.50 per week salary, I took the chance and jumped at the prospect of having my own place. My thought was that this would be for just a few years until the move to a penthouse. Guess what? It is still my home, as of this writing. The rent has increased incrementally, and no elevator has ever materialized. Having been a healthy dancer without knee problems could be attributed to all those years of climbing 75 steps several times a day. However, it does weed out one's friends. They tend to come by, buzz me on the intercom and say, "Come on down." The fairly inexpensive rent also made it possible for me to maintain a residence in New York when traveling out of town with a show.

In those days the performers in all the Broadway shows were like family. Once a week we would go bowling after the show was over. Each show had a team and the competition was fervent, if not highly skilled. Also, when a big movie was released, there would be a special midnight showing for all those performing on Broadway. We loved those times, and memories of them make us rich forever.

One matinee day during the second year of the run I came into the theater whining, "Oh, I'm so tired. This has been such a hectic week. Do I have to do the show today?"

Gene Wilson, the wardrobe master for the show, who had been in the business a long time, stopped me in my tracks. "So why don't you just quit? There are ten more at the stage door just like you!"

Boy, did that turn me around! It was like a bucket of cold water in the face. My own career world may have centered around my continued existence, but the world of the Broadway Musical most certainly did not. Never again would I complain about the privilege of performing in a show, on any stage, anywhere!

The evening that Gene Kelly saw the show was memorable for me. When the performance was over he came backstage and after seeing Carol asked to see the male chorus. We were all stuck in a small dressing room in the basement of the theater. He came in to see us and said something to each individual of the ensemble.

When he came up to shake my hand, I blurted out, "Oh Mr. Kelly, I've loved everything you've ever done!"

"You're not that old." He chided me.

Well, that provided fodder for the gypsies in the room to rag me for several weeks. I didn't care. It was about meeting Gene Kelly, one of my idols.

The Tony Awards came around again. We were not eligible, having opened on Broadway the previous year. However, this year the show was going to be televised locally and each musical currently running on Broadway was asked to select a member of the ensemble to assist in handing the awards to the presenters. The "Dolly" company management selected me to represent our show. We were all seated in a row of chairs on stage and at the appropriate moment, stood up and gave the Tony to the presenter to give to the winner. My friends who were watching the show from home accused me of bribing someone on the production staff. It seems that my chair was directly behind the presenter's position and in line with the camera, so that my beaming face was visible throughout the whole telecast. I swear I didn't pick that seat, the director assigned me that spot. That's my story and I'm stickin' to it!

During the second year of the run, the International Company of "Dolly" was cast with Mary Martin as the star. It was going to tour around the world, including Viet Nam. One of my TU theater classmates, Judy Drake, was now living in New York and was right for the role of Ernestina Money. Lucia Victor, our stage manager, was holding the preliminary auditions for Gower and agreed to let her audition. While Judy was not a trained singer, she could belt out the necessary "Sweet Rosie O'Grady." After the reading, Lucia was going to pass on her. I literally begged her to let Gower see her. She reluctantly agreed. Well he loved Judy, and she got the role. This virtually started her career in theater in New York.

Carol Channing was replaced by another one of my screen idols, Ginger Rogers. That meant that by now I had met or worked with Marge and Gower Champion, Gene Kelly and Ginger Rogers. Only Fred Astaire remained as the last icon to meet on my MGM Musical Star list. That would happen later. For the changing of the stars, the photographs of Carol on the theater marquee were taken down and Ginger's were put up. The famous shot of Carol on the ramp with all the waiters presenting her with open arms was among those stacked in the basement.

Frank Dudley, the assistant stage manager, knew of my covetous interest in the picture. "Do you really want it?" he asked.

"Do I??" It was a done deal.

My treasured "Hello, Dolly!" poster. That's me, third from the end on the right side. (Photo by Eileen Darby)

One afternoon I came to the theater, wrapped the six-and-a-half foot long photo in brown paper and made off with it out the side door. After a friend helped me make a frame, it was hung on a wall in my apartment and stayed there for over 40 years.

The "Dolly" company was a very special group of people. Several have remained friends to this day. That is unusual. In most shows, you strike up a friendship with some of the cast during the run and go your separate ways when the show closes. To keep in touch with one or two, is unique. To have about a dozen remain as friends after the run of the show is quite rare. Two of those have since passed away but several members of that cast have remained my good friends.

Walt Whitcover, my first acting teacher, contacted me. "Ron, I have a new project. I'm in the Director's Unit at the Actor's Studio, under Lee Strasberg. I've decided to tackle Verdi's 'La Traviata.' Would you be interested in singing Alfredo?"

He was going to do one act of the opera at a time, in Italian and as musically correct as possible, with a modern sensibility. I jumped at the chance and started working on the score with Beverley and rehearsing with Walt. Performing that first act wasn't to be. A conflict of performing schedules would keep me from the initial performance, but eventually all four acts were performed over a period of two years. What was that conflict that would take me out of town?

Along came "MAME."

LESSONS LEARNED

- **Utilize Your Own Uniqueness to Stand Out**

- **Work at Maintaining Friendships that Matter**

- **Never Complain When You Have the Privilege of Living Your Dream**

.

MAME

According to the Broadway scuttlebutt, "MAME" was going to be the next blockbuster. Everyone was excited about it and wondered who would be cast in the show. Angela Lansbury was announced as Mame with Bea Arthur as Vera, her sidekick. Gene Sacs was going to direct and Oona White (who would go on to become the only choreographer to be given an academy award for a specific film, "Oliver") was set for the dances and musical staging. Jerry Herman, fresh from his "Hello, Dolly!" triumph, was composing the music and lyrics for the show.

One night Jerry showed up at the St. James Theater and sought me out. "Ron, I'm doing a new show, 'Mame,' with Angela Lansbury and would like you to audition for it. Are you interested?"
"Sure, I'm interested. Would it be for the chorus, or a role in the show?" I enthused.
"It would be as a dancer/singer with the possibility of a small role or an understudy," he explained.
"Just tell me when and where, and thanks, Jerry." Wow!

He must have cleared it with someone in the Merrick office, because it was unusual for a composer to try to take a cast member out of his currently running show to be in his next untested production. At the dance audition for "MAME" I showed up as a proven Broadway dancer. It had a very different feel to it. Gone was my naïve expectation of the inevitability of being hired. In its place was the knowledge of just how many talented dancers there were competing for a limited number of jobs. There was the inside track that the composer would be a vote for me, but I still had to prove myself to the rest of the creative team: Gene Saks, the director; Oona White, the choreographer; Don Pippin, the conductor; and the producing team. The ballet part of the dance auditions was more difficult than that first "Dolly" combination. Here's where the preparedness part of my mantra paid off. Remember all those dance classes during the day while performing "Dolly" at night? My dance technique was much improved. My voice had begun to blossom as well under Beverley's tutelage. That combination

61

got me hired as a dancer/singer, playing the cameo role of Ralph Divine, the avant-garde beatnik who ran the nudist school in Greenwich Village (hardly type-casting), where Mame sent young Patrick. There was the possibility of understudying older Patrick, but that hadn't been decided.

So, after two and a half years in "Hello, Dolly!" it was time for a change. Excitement, coupled with apprehension, were the overriding feelings of the moment. It was always a risky business to leave a hit show. That is why some performers in shows like "My Fair Lady," "Cats," "A Chorus Line," and "Phantom of the Opera" stayed for years in the same job: security. That safeguard against unemployment is very hard to come by in show business. So when the possibility arises for long-term employment some performers latch on to it. They take the safety of the long run over the uncertainty of chancing a new show. That individual decision must take into account financial responsibility, providing for a family, one's drive to be a success and a myriad of other factors. So, scary as it was, I took the leap. There was also sadness at leaving my "Dolly" family. However, assessing all the pros and cons, it just felt right to take advantage of this opportunity. This assessment literally consisted of listing all of the pros and all of the cons on opposite sides of a piece of paper a la Benjamin Franklin. I find that if you just keep running over all that information in your mind, the same reasons keep popping up, over and over. If you write everything down, no matter how small the consideration, there it is in black and white. It soon becomes evident which column is the path to take.

Rehearsals were exciting and arduous. At one point in the "Mame" number Oona had all six male dancers do double tours to the knee in unison. For the laymen reading this, that means launching yourself into air from a standing position, making two complete revolutions with your body, landing on one foot and dropping to your other knee. That unison capability was usually only found among soloists in ballet companies. We gave it a game effort, but the unison was elusive and the step was eventually changed.

When the completed number was first performed in rehearsal for the rest of the cast for the first time, Bea Arthur was unreserved in her critique: "Let me tell you something. After we opened in New York I was going to buy new sterling silver with a place setting for eight. Now I'm going to make it for sixteen!"

We were off to Philadelphia and the Schubert Theater for the first of our two out-of-town-tryout cities. The first run-through of music with the orchestra was off the charts. When the time came for Angela's eleven-o-clock star turn, "If He Walked Into My Life," we thought we had heard it all. Then the conductor brought his baton down and started the number. It was a single clarinet

With Angela Lansbury and Bella Shalom in the rousing "MAME" number. (Photo by Bill Ray from Life/Getty Images)

playing this hauntingly melodic introduction. It ended. There was silence. Then Angela simply broke down in tears and threw her arms around Jerry. She just knew that performing this number would be the cherry on the icing for her impending jump to real stardom as a leading lady. It was a magical moment.

The purpose of out-of-town tryouts was to find out what worked with an audience and what didn't. One of the numbers that took a lot of effort before achieving the final version was "Open a New Window." In this number Mame showed Younger Patrick all the vistas that were possible for him to explore in life. At one point there were several of us as firemen sliding down a fire pole. Cut. Then there were 2 couples doing a parody of a modern dance in orange and yellow tights. One couple was cut, Diana Brill and myself. She was upset, but I was thrilled not to have to go on stage in yellow tights with those skinny legs. A tango in a speakeasy with all the male dancers in black patent leather wigs was kept. It was a fun part of the number that featured Angela dancing with Frankie Michaels, young Patrick. The "Mame" number was built in a very slow crescendo to a rousing finale that ended the first act. Jerry had done it again with this show-stopping anthem. The audiences loved it.

In the second act there was a big jitterbug number, "That's How Young I

Partnering Angela wtih Hank Brunges in "That's How Young I Feel." (Photo by Friedman-Abeles, ©Billy Rose Theatre Division, The New York Public Library for the Performing Arts)

Feel." I was Angela's partner during the part of the number where we did the hip to hip and swing over the back lift. Angela was not a trained dancer, but she was a natural. The way she controlled her body and danced from her core made the lifts very easy for me to handle, as did the knowledge that it was actually Angela Lansbury I was lifting.

Then it was on to the Schubert The-ater in Boston with more changes and improvements. I marveled at the way Angela took last minute line changes that were being thrown at her nightly and integrate them into her performance. It was watching a real pro in action. She had followed her passion for acting, by taking many roles that were fulfilling and many that were just jobs, learning and improving her craft with each one. That was another lesson for me to soak up: always keep your long-term goal in mind and do whatever it takes to achieve it.

Back in New York we opened at the Winter Garden Theatre on May 24, 1966. (By the way, I have no idea why "theater" is used sometimes with the British spelling "theatre.")It was another magical night. My folks had flown up from Oklahoma once again for the opening and were allowed to accompany me to the opening night party at the Rainbow Room, high atop Rockefeller Center. When Angela made her grand entrance into the party it just so happened that her only open avenue led her past my little party. She hugged me and greeted my folks. Being on "cloud nine" was an understatement.

The reviews were great and we settled in for another long run. I had been hoping to be cast as the understudy to older Patrick, but that didn't hap-pen. A little vindication did occur the night that Judy Garland was in the audience. After the show she came backstage to see Angela.

As she passed me in the hallway she said, "Say, Patrick, you were just wonderful in the show tonight."

"Thank you, Miss Garland," I managed to get out, without reverting to my gushing response to Gene Kelly or pointing out her error. I was tall with dark hair like Jerry Lanning, the actor who played the role. So the mistake was understandable. I could have played that part!

Two other dancers in the company, Diana Brill and Bella Shalom, and I would meet at the half-hour call on stage to do a warm-up ballet barre. The dancing in the show was fairly strenuous, including a double attitude turn sequence in the "Mame" number, and required a good warm-up for the body to perform well and not suffer any injuries. The meeting of the three of us started haphazardly, but quickly grew into a routine. Diana and Bella remain friends to this day. Another lifelong friendship developed with Dolores Childers, Angela's dresser. Even though she lives in California and it is a bi-coastal friendship, we stay in contact.

We were invited to parties galore. One in particular stands out. Luigi Gasparinetti, a dancer in the show, and his partner, Howard Gillman, had a very large East Side penthouse with a terrace, overlooking the city. One night we were picked up at the stage door after the show and whisked away in a double-decker bus, complete with trays of Champagne. The penthouse was like something out of the movies. One expected Fred Astaire and Ginger Rogers to come dancing out at any moment. Here again it was very heady stuff for this old boy from a small town in Oklahoma.

There was still this need to fill my days with productive activity. Fencing and gymnastics classes were added to my schedule. The remedial speech lessons had served the greater purpose. I could now speak without eliciting laughter. With those three hours off the weekly schedule, there was time available. Fencing

Gymnastic classes solidified my form on the parallel bars. Photographer unknown.

was not my thing. It required aggression to go after the opponent. The moves could be learned almost like dance steps, but when it came time for an actual bout with another student, my stomach did flip-flops. It made me nervous. Luckily, there were a couple of friends in the class and we could laugh about it afterwards. The gymnastics classes were a different matter. They were exciting. I was too tall to ever be a real gymnast, but working on floor exercise, still rings, parallel bars and trapeze was an exhilarating experience. Some of these skills would come into use in later productions.

In a modern dance concert with Hava Kohav. Photographer unknown.

Another opportunity presented itself. One of my acting partners, Hava Kohav from Walt's class, had a small modern dance company. One day after class she stopped me, "Ron, would you be interested in dancing with my company for our next concert?"

This was a surprise because I had no training in the field of modern dance. "Do you think I could pick up your technique and fit in with your other dancers?" was my reply.

"Why don't you come to a rehearsal where we do a technique warm-up to start and see how you feel about it," she encouraged.

Well, that started a two-year odyssey of working with Hava and dancing with her troupe. Never having danced barefoot led to some blisters on my feet, but nothing I couldn't survive. There was also the introduction to the Martha Graham torso contractions, which were central to modern technique. It was a broadening experience.

Always looking for additional income to supplement my Broadway salary, the Powers Modeling School offered me temporary employment, teaching speech and discothèque dancing. No, they were not taught in the same class, but isn't it a kick that my own speech had improved enough to teach a class in it? This was the closest I ever came to taking a job outside show business.

66

During the run of the show the dance captain would hold periodic "clean up" rehearsals to keep the show in tip-top shape. Our dance captain, Pat Cummings, had a bit of a "Little Caesar" complex when it came to running those rehearsals. One particular rehearsal stands out for me. He was asking each dancer to do the double attitude turn sequence in the "MAME" number in front of the whole company. Let me explain this dance step. It was a turn done to the right on the right foot with the left leg extended to the back and bent at the knee parallel to the floor for the entire sequence. You had to start by bending the right leg and hopping twice to make one turn. After two of those turns you raised both arms overhead and did a double turn on the right leg with the left leg still extended to the back in the attitude position. This entire sequence was done three times in a row, staying in the same spot on stage. It was a difficult combination. This rehearsal was being held for dancers who had been in the show over a year and performed those turns nightly on stage. For some reason, having to do this stuck in my craw. Rather than bucking his authority I managed to channel my hostile feelings into my body. When my time came those turns were whipped off with panache. There might have even been a little flourish at the end, because the rest of the cast applauded.

After a preliminary audition Sandy Meisner, one of the prominent acting teachers in the city, took me into his professional acting class, for the beginning of a two-year stint. This was another approach to learning how to utilize your whole self in a role on stage. We would be assigned one partner to work with over a period of time. The first year my partner was Victoria Wyndham, who would later become a famous soap opera actress. My scene partner for the second year was Larry Fuller, who evoled into a well known director/choreographer and remains a good friend to this day. You might be thinking, "Isn't this your third acting teacher?" Yes, that's right. Acting was much more difficult for me than singing or dancing. The basic concept that I, with all my unique attributes and flaws, was enough in a role just didn't quite compute for me. All my life there had been this overpowering feeling that the basic "me" was just not enough. More, more, more! To even consider that without embellishment, I would be at all interesting on stage took a monumental leap of faith for me. It was going to take time, different approaches and all the courage that could be mustered. Was there anything else that would help me?

Psychotherapy. My friend Bella was in therapy at the time and would discuss it with me. This seemed like an avenue that might open new doors for me in my discovery process. What a can of worms that turned out to be! My first therapist practiced Freudian psychology. So twice a week I would lie on a couch and be analyzed. This was the beginning of intermittent years of work with different therapists. It was enlightening. However, because of my deep desire to be "normal," a lot of time was wasted.

My last therapist, Richard Soll, who was not a practitioner of Freud, told me that he would not have taken me if my reason for seeking therapy had been based on my desire to be straight. I was in my fifties by then, but it was the work with Richard that ultimately led me to the total acceptance of myself. You are what you are. It took me years to achieve this state. So my advice is to look at your own life right now and lovingly accept everything. This doesn't mean to stop tying to be a more complete entity. It does mean that you didn't ask to be born, but now that you are alive, you have a right to exist, just to be. Proving yourself is unnecessary! What would my life had been like if that concept had been learned at an earlier age? But hey, better late than never, right?

Throughout the years there would be several therapists, work in group sessions and participation in various trainings. There was always something to be gained in this last type of exploration. First there was EST, developed by Werner Erhart. "What is, is," became understandable on a gut level for me. Say you are in a traffic jam and it is making you late for an important appointment. You have a couple of choices. You can get upset and anxious because you are late, or you can realize that your feelings and opinions about the reality of the traffic jam don't alter the situation. It will be over when it's over. That awareness resonated deeply with me and came in very handy in many other situations when reality was about to be ignored.

Next was Primal Therapy, espoused by Arthur Janov in his book, "The Primal Scream." This was done in a group setting to get one more in touch with one's deepest feelings. This did not work as well for me. Barbara Cook, the Broadway Star and inveterate cabaret singer, was in the same group. We were both afraid to really scream for fear it would damage our voices.

You win some, you lose some. In the Sedona Training the idea was to release and let go of anxiety and fear. This added to my burgeoning ability to accept the reality of what was. Ki training was my last foray into group enlightenment efforts. This was Eastern in origin and was a combination of physical and inner exercises with a period of chanting. Each time at the end of a class, I seemed more centered. They lost me by including prayer in the sessions. It was purported to be a non-religious technique but it didn't appear that way to me. All these trainings took place over a period of about 30 years, and each added elements to my life.

Singing in church on Sundays had settled down to one church for me, the Broadway Congregational at 55th St. and Broadway. (Today it no longer exists, having been replaced by a residential tower.) Wally Klaus was the musical director and organist. Part of the arts program of the church was to sponsor artists in showings or recitals.

After choir rehearsal one night, Wally asked me, "Would you like to do a voice recital as part of our arts program?"

Boy, that was out of the blue. Always being up for a challenge I replied, "I would love that. When did you have in mind? I have to see if there is enough time to put it together."

Oh boy, dancing in a Broadway show and doing a classical voice recital simultaneously - probably something that no one else had ever done! The date was set, February 12, 1967. Through Beverley, Sam Sanders was available as my accompanist. He would later become a very sought-after classical accompanist, also teaching future accompanists at Julliard.

The music was selected: a Handel section, a group of Schubert leid, four Faure songs and the centerpiece, "On Wenlock Edge." My string quartet for that piece was made up of Julliard students. Wally sat in on a couple of rehearsals and commented that as a conductor I was a bit of a taskmaster. The end result, however, was very good. They played beautifully. Of course one little sticking point had to arise. Ever since college, the flu, sore throat or laryngitis would track me down before every important singing event. True to form, some malady found me. One of the best of throat doctors at that time, Dr. Wilbur Gould, treated me. Then, unbeknownst to me, he attended my recital with medication in his pocket. If he detected trouble, he was prepared to administer it to me at intermission. Luckily, it wasn't needed. I was not 100%, but I could get through the program. This tired old boring routine seemed to say to my audience, "Hey, I'm doing my best under the circumstances, but if I were completely whole, just imagine how much better this would be. How could you not like me for trying?" It took another few years to get over that one.

It was on a Sunday afternoon in the church sanctuary. There was a nice turnout and the biggest surprise of all was that Angela attended. This was the first day of her one-week vacation and she held off her departure until after my recital. I will never forget that. Each section of the recital built to Wenlock Edge. That grouping of songs always had a special resonance with me. For an encore there were four Haiku, short Japanese writings that had an unusual twist at the end. It proved to be a perfect ending for the afternoon. Mission accomplished.

Later that year, Beverley wanted another opinion about my voice. She had to have known, but didn't want to have to tell me that as a tenor with no "high C" there would not be a career in classical music for me. She arranged for me to sing for Hans Heinz, one of her colleagues at Julliard. Sure enough that was his take as well. Once this was decided, my voice became more relaxed and eventually became more of a baritone-tenor with a sound that was very right for Broadway. Here again it was a matter of exploring all possibilities until the ultimate path was revealed.

It was around this time that serious questions surfaced about the church and my dedication to it. One Sunday after the service I posed a very direct question to the pastor: "In the service every Sunday there is a section where the congregation is encouraged to ask God for forgiveness of our sins. Ask forgiveness of what to whom? I feel like I try to live a decent life without hurting anyone. Why is there a need to confess?" It was really a question about the Judeo-Christian concept of a patriarchal deity.

He replied, "Now with your newfound insight, you should go back and read the bible."

After mulling over that inadequate answer, it seemed to be the straw that broke the camel's back in my spiritual search. It was during the ensuing period that my break with the church happened. Following a Christian path was not to be for me. Most of the teachings are good basic guidelines for living, and somewhere in the universe there has to be a life force bigger than we are. Beyond that, I simply allowed my already-waning powers of self-delusion to shut down. Belief in the deity of Christ as the Son of God and the concept of God the Father were just no longer available to me as literal truths. My spirituality became one of my own creation. God would live in my song, in my dance, in my heart. My cup runneth over. Being a minister of music was not in my future. One treasured quality in particular that has developed over the years is my ability to be a good, true friend. Giving and caring have become paramount in my life. Now, looking back on my life so far, it has been a pretty good run. Something must have gone right.

Being in a hit Broadway show gave one a little bit of visibility and there were opportunities to be asked to do additional gigs that didn't conflict with your performing schedule. Soon the Ed Sullivan TV Show came a knockin'. The gigs were usually as a back-up dancer with popular singing stars of the sixties, like Lana Cantrell and Johnny Mathis. Another time Angela was asked to do the Perry Como Christmas Show. I partnered her with two other dancers for her two numbers. Then for the finale we all sat down at a Christmas dinner table and Perry sang "Bless this House." Just pinch me, this must be a dream.

Walt called me to start working on "La Traviata." Rehearsals for Act 2 were built around my performance schedule. It was fascinating work. Walt's approach to fleshing out each character and giving the piece a modern take was exciting. Violetta was played by Leyna Gabriele. She had sung at City Opera and currently owned and ran an Italian restaurant on the East Side, where she would occasionally sing for the patrons. We would also rehearse some of the scenes at her

Fresh from waterskiing at the top of Act II in "La Traviata," Alfredo serenades Violetta, played by Leyna Gabriele. (All Three Traviata photos by George Joseph, ©Billy Rose Theatre Division, The New York Public Library for the Performing Arts)

71

swank apartment. She led a glamorous life in this Okie's eyes.

Act 2 opens with Violetta and Alfredo ensconced in their country hide-away. We found an idyllic spot by a lake to film the opening. Here's the surprise: we started the film with my water skiing. Yes, water skiing, and with Joseph, the caretaker, driving the boat. The camera panned to the empty seat next to Joseph in the boat and then to my face, while skiing. At that point we played scenes of Violetta and me in the garden and different places around the cottage. Suddenly there was the realization that without her in the boat, this wasn't much fun. So I signaled Joseph to turn the boat around and take me back. At that point the pianist started playing the Entr'acte for Act 2. We had practiced the next move until Joseph drove the boat the correct distance parallel to the shore. I skied to the outside of the boat and at the precise moment cut across the wake, let go of the rope, skied up to shallow water, stepped out of the skis and ran on shore. The film dimmed, the stage lights came up and I entered on stage, dripping wet, singing "Lunge da lei, per me non va diletto," into my first aria, "De' Miei

Breaking away from Germont, my father, played by Adair McGowan, when I find that Violetta has left me.

Bollenti Spiriti." I continued to dry off and then prepared breakfast for Violetta, all the while singing. The audiences were a bit stunned, but totally into it.

Another innovative sequence occurred later in that act. Violetta had left me a note that she was leaving me. My father, Germont, played by Adair McGowan, was there when I found the note. Distraught, I ran out of the house, tripped over some lawn furniture and skidded in a heap of dirt that had been specially placed for my face to land in. There was always a gasp from the audience. The trip and the fall had been rehearsed meticulously so that I would not be injured. Germont then ran after me, picked me up and carried me back into the house. He consoled me and bathed my face during his famous aria, "Di Provenza il mar, il suol." This again was an eye-opener for opera audiences. The usual staging is for Germont just to declaim the song as Alfredo sits there despondently. This act was presented in December of 1967 at the Actor's Studio.

"MAME" had been my life for almost two years, and there was an itch to take the next step in my career. Another Broadway show emerged on the horizon, "GEORGE M!" Aha, here was the chance to step out of the chorus and onto center stage.

"GEORGE M!" here I come!

LESSONS LEARNED

- **Take Educated Chances**
- **Stay the Course**
- **Accept Who You Are**

GEORGE M!

In assessing the pros and cons of leaving "MAME" after two years and making another leap of faith into "GEORGE M!," one reason stood out: being on a principal contract rather than a chorus contract. Here was my chance to take the next step in my performing career. Joel Grey would be playing George M. Cohan, Joe Layton would be directing and choreographing and there would be all of that glorious, flag-waving music. It was going to be a show that featured tap, so everyone cast would need to be proficient in that dance style. Jackie Alloway, my college sweetheart, had come to New York the preceding year and was auditioning for the show as well. Tapping was not her strong suit, so we hired a rehearsal studio for several coaching sessions. She learned the basics well enough and was hired to play Fay Templeton, a Broadway star at the turn of the century. Her moment on stage was truly memorable, standing at the top of a staircase in a long black strapless gown, singing the Cohan classic, "Mary." She brought a hush to the audience night after night.

The auditions were fairly intense. For the final audition I had prepared a song and dance number, complete with a little cane twirling. Don't ask me why for this next part: it consisted of wearing a white leather suit taken from an industrial show for a hat manufacturer. There was still the "anything to stand out" mode functioning. That last audition took all afternoon and, unlike the "Dolly" final call, we weren't told if we had the job at the end of the day. Now the crowded subway had to be faced. Feeling disgruntled and looking a little strange already in a white leather suit and sunglasses, I began to tap my cane while walking along on the subway platform to gain a little space. This odd sight gave the impression that I might have been visually impaired. The other commuters began to give me a wide berth and breathing was a little easier. Looking back I'm not proud of that politically incorrect moment, but it did show a bit of spontaneous creativity.

The next day the call came to come in and sign my contract. Excitement and sadness were both present. Angela was getting ready to take out the national tour of "MAME" and there had been an offer to go out with the tour. This had been another item on my pros and cons list. What fun it would have been to perform across the country with Angela, but keep that goal in mind! Another educated chance was taken.

"GEORGE M!" had a stellar cast of 25 very talented performers. We were all principals with a chance to stand out. That illusion ended after we began performances out of town. A representative from Actor's Equity came to assess the show and determined that there were only six principals in the show and that the remainder of the cast was to be signed to pink Chorus Contracts. Bummer. Well, there had to be other ways to stand out.

During the rehearsals in New York and the out-of-town tryout, once again at the Fisher Theater in Detroit, other opportunities did arise. In the third scene of the first act George's sister Josie sang "Oh, You Wonderful Boy" as part of a Cohan family audition. Bernadette Peters fetchingly portrayed this part in her last Broadway performance before her starring role in "Dames At Sea."

Joe Layton had a concept of utilizing as many of the cast's skills as possible in the show. "Alright, who in the cast can play an instrument? We need someone to play piano, drums and soprano sax to accompany Bernadette and the Cohan family in their audition numbers." My mind began to work. It turned out that Loni Ackerman could play piano and John Mineo could play drums. "Say Joe, I played tenor and baritone saxophones in college, I'll bet I could learn to play the soprano sax," I piped up.

Sonny Fox became my teacher and tutoring began. The learning curve was fairly fast, even though it was a strange looking saxophone, looking more like a gold clarinet. It was difficult to play in tune but Sonny told me I played it as in tune as any real pro.

At another rehearsal Joe starts, "We're going to be putting together the vaudeville section today. Anyone have any unusual skills?" Angela Martin turned out to be a ventriloquist.

He was going to select two cast members to perform with a couple of trained dogs. What could I do?

"Hey Joe, could you use a fire baton act?" I asked. He looked at me quizzically and said, "You're on!"

The costume designer, Freddy Wittop, dressed me as a fireman. Playing a fireman seemed to be a theme for my first three shows, even though my fireman was cut in "MAME."

In the second act there was a grouping of songs that included "Harrigan." "Joe, would you like to have someone play an accordion in that section?" This time the whole cast stared at me in disbelief.

Freddy Wittop, the costume designer for GEORGE M! *gave me a sketch of my fireman's costume for opening night.*

Joe staged the scene with my standing on a barrel in the barroom, singing "Harrigan" with an Irish accent, and playing the accordion. The first time I was ever out of the show in New York, Joel came on the backstage mike to announce how many other performers it would take to replace me.

The accordion scores again, backing up Joel Grey and Jerry Dodge in "Harrigan." (Photo by Dick Swift)

This show's out-of-town tryout had a much different feel than both "Dolly" and "MAME." Joe Layton was very gifted but had a caustic personality. He opened one rehearsal in Detroit by stating, "All right, you were hired for your supposed talent, let me see something." That attitude did not engender a lot of good feelings in a cast that was giving it their best shot. Somehow the show pulled together before returning to New York.

We opened in New York at the Palace Theater on February 10, 1968. LaVon couldn't come up for the opening, but Dad brought my 18-year-old cousin, Charlotte Rae. For opening night I hired a limousine to drive us around New

York and let them do a little sight seeing after the show and before the party. The reviews were good, if not over the top, and Joel was universally acclaimed for his portrayal. We settled in for a long run. The show was basically one big finale. It must have been a little exhausting for the audience to sit through. At that time it was unusual to have a chorus of performers who were all quite able of holding the stage on their own. So there was this massive jolt of energy that went through the house every night when the show began and the stage lights came up on a tableau of the entire cast looking out at the audience. From that point it was a mad dash to the finish line. Another union had to be joined, Local 802, the musician's union, for me to play the saxophone and accordion on stage. Throughout my theater career there was mandatory membership in seven different unions, just to have employment in the different aspects of the business. In addition to Actor's Equity, my parent union, there was membership in the Screen Actor's Guild, American Federation of Television and Radio Artists, American Guild of Musical Artists, American Guild of Variety Artists, Local 802 and the Society of Stage Directors and Choreographers. Union dues became a factor in my budget process.

After the opening it was back to learning the first act of "La Traviata." In May of 1968 we were able to present Act 1 and Act 2 together. After the short run of these two acts a lengthy article with photographs appeared in the December 7, 1968 issue of "Opera News," the monthly periodical for the opera world. The feature was entitled "Method Verdi" and created a little controversy in the opera world. Frank Corsaro had directed a new production at the New York State Opera that contained certain elements that seemed to come right from our first Act 1 showcase. Speight Jenkins, Jr., a respected music critic, wrote a comparative piece on September 19, 1968 for his Music and Arts column in the Sunday Post-Dispatch, noting the points of coincidence. This was after he had seen our Act 1 and Act 2 production. He noted that the similarities to the Corsaro staging were all in Act 1. Oh, Mr. Corsaro hadn't seen our Act 2 when he staged his production. So maybe he did borrow a little. Who hasn't?

For two instances of stage business my diversity of skills paid off again: water skiing for the film, and gymnastics and dance for the fall. You just never know. This was one of those times when past interests or passions were followed and then came into play later on down the line. This is an important point: if you have a desire to learn about something, follow it up. Even if it isn't currently useful in a concrete way, it will expand your horizons and makes you a fuller entity.

It was sometime during the run of the show that my throat problem was addressed by going to Dr. Abraham Weinberg, a noted hypnotherapist. During my six months of work with him, an interesting discovery was made. My throat problems probably stemmed from built-up stress in the area, which made me more susceptible to any passing malady. With self-hypnosis stress could be released from that area. My clockwork monthly visits to the throat doctor greatly decreased.

The conductor for "GEORGE M!" was Jay Blackton, one of the stalwart Broadway conductors. One night at the show he called me into his dressing room. "Ron, I'm going to be conducting a big benefit for the Lincoln Center Musical Theater department. Would you like to sing in my onstage singers? This group will sing backup for any of the performers who have arrangements that require augmenting."

"Jay, I would love to" was my pleased response.

Two segments of that night stand out. The audience discovered Beatrice Lillie, a legendary figure in the theater world, in our little singing group holding a note past the conductor's cutoff and then looking surprised, as only she could. Then, after she was introduced I escorted her downstage where she proceeded to perform her signature move, twirling a long strand of beads around her neck. I don't know when or where she started doing that, but it never failed to get a huge response.

The most exciting part of the evening was singing the original arrangements of two songs made famous by Judy Garland, including "Sing Hallelujah." The rehearsal with her was thrilling by itself. The performance night came and both the numbers were showstoppers. Then Harold Arlen came on stage to play the piano for Judy, as she closed the show singing his "Somewhere Over the Rainbow." It was achingly memorable. When she sang the last "Why, oh why can't I" and reached her arm out toward Mr. Arlen, tears were streaming down my cheeks. Embarrassed, I looked around to make sure no one noticed, only to see that everyone else on stage was in tear as well, including the orchestra. Talk about magical! On a sad note, that turned out to be her last performance in the states. She left for London shortly after, and it was there that she died.

The run of "George M!" had a different feel than my first two shows. There was some uneasiness that crept in from time to time. For me it stemmed from the basic deception from the very beginning that we were all going to have principal roles. After almost a year into the run, something caused me to spontaneously give my two-week notice to leave the show. The reason had to be miniscule, because it has been forgotten. This was a mistake. Another show was not waiting in the wings for me. After cooling down for a couple of days, I went to Jose Vega, the stage manager, and asked to rescind my notice. He said that wouldn't be possible. It seems like he had a certain glee in telling me. Yes, he was pulling me down a peg or two. It was probably deserved, and it did shift me into high gear to look for employment.

What was next on the horizon?

LESSONS LEARNED

- **Utilize Your Versatility**
- **Experience Highlight Moments as Fully as Possible**
- **Keep Focused on Your Goals**

BUILD A CAREER

This was my first time out of work after almost five years in New York City. There had been two one-week vacations, one in "Hello, Dolly" and one in "MAME." Other than that it had been steady employment for all that time in three shows. It is important to point out that all this time my skills were being improved and new ones added. This increased my future job possibilities by preparing me to audition as an actor, as well as a singer and a dancer.

My first gig after leaving "GEORGE M!" was immediately to go out on a cruise ship, hired as the "culture," performing one show going down to the Caribbean and one show on the way back. The shows consisted of a combination of Broadway show tunes and classical selections. It required me to bring music arrangements for the band, but there turned out to be very little actual rehearsal time scheduled with the ship's musicians. The two shows went fine. There was a first brush with seasickness on the downward voyage. The old proven formula worked for me, go sit on the deck and watch the horizon. The three island stops on this eight-day trip were St. Croix, Guadalupe and Granada. This was a vibrant experience, never having seen water this blue or sand this clean. It was great.

Upon my return in December, Walt Whitcover, the director of "La Traviata," invited me to his Christmas party. Who should be at the party but Tamara Long, from my tap dance classes in the fifth grade in Guthrie, Oklahoma! Show Business is a small world. She had just opened as Mona with Bernadette Peters in "Dames at Sea," off Broadway at the Bowery Lane Theater. It had received good reviews and was destined for a long run. The producer was looking for a male and a female stand-by for all six roles. I auditioned and was hired to stand by for all three men in the cast. It would be great to be working with Bernadette again, this time occasionally playing the role opposite her. It would also give me time to work on Acts III and IV of "La Traviata." They were having trouble finding a female stand-by, so I called Janie Sell, who was still in "GEORGE M!" Yes, she was interested in auditioning. When she was hired, it was a little like continuing a small version of my previous Broadway family.

The stand-bys were allowed to call in and not be present every night. This worked out extremely well until the night that we had scheduled the third act of "Traviata" for a time that was a little before the ending time for "Dames." It seemed to be a pretty safe bet: everyone in the cast had been healthy. It just so happened that night the actor who played Lucky, Joe Sicardi, did get sick. That meant going on for him and being late for the Actor's Studio show. I alerted Walt and then called a friend to meet me after "Dames" with my clothes for Act III of "Traviata." "Dames" came down and we hopped in a cab. On the way uptown I changed clothes and vocalized in the cab. The driver must have thought he had a nutcase as a fare. Walt had announced the reason for the slight delay to the audience. I ran in, took my place and it was "on with the show!"

Act III was a big party scene that Violetta threw and Alfredo was the party crasher, pursuing her after she had left him in Act II. We devised a fairly spectacular entrance for me, swinging in on a trapeze and doing a back release move into the center of the crowd.

In his comments about the performance, Lee Strasberg critiqued my performance, "If any tenor at the Metropolitan Opera House made that entrance he would receive an immediate standing ovation." Here again the gymnastics training added a color to my performance that would otherwise have been absent.

Violetta and Alfredo reconciled in Act IV.

Act IV was presented just about a month later on a much smaller scale, because it was focused on the reconciliation ofIVVioletta and Alfredo before her death. We had accomplished the nearly impossible task of modernizing the entire opera while keeping it in Italian, and as musically correct as possible. We even received a fan letter from someone who said it was so nice to hear an opera in English so that she could know what was taking place. There was no English on that stage at any time. I had proved to myself that even without the prerequisite "high C" I could sustain interest in an operatic tenor role.

"Dames at Sea" transferred to the Theatre De Lys in the Village. This was great because I could walk right down 7th Avenue to work. For one of the performances Janie Sell and I were both on as the stand-bys for Mona and the Ship's Captain. When we did the "Beguine" number in the second act, we stopped the show cold. It was very exciting and provided a lasting memory.

Now we come to one of the more obnoxious moments thus far in my career.: After having given my two-week notice, I was out of "Dames" and into rehearsals for my first leading role in "Irma La Douce" at the Meadowbrook Dinner Theatre in New Jersey. One day after my "Irma" rehearsal the producer from "Dames" called. "Ron, David just called that he is being delayed returning to New York today. The new stand-by is not up in the part yet and we were hoping that you could go on for David tonight. Is that possible?"

He was referring to David Christmas who played Dick in the show. Now, it was just a couple of hours before the curtain and I could easily have made it to the theater. What ever possessed me, I don't know. It could have been simple greed.

"I could do it, but I would like to have $200 for the performance." Remember this was an Off-Broadway show in the 1960's. A week's salary was less that two-hundred dollars.

There was a moment of silence, then "I'll have to check and get right back to you."

In a few minutes he called back: "We will not pay that amount. We will simply delay the curtain until David arrives, even if we have to hold it for two hours!"

Shocked, I was sure that word of this would get around show business circles and I would never be hired again. This was a moment in my career that was definitely a low point. It probably wasn't nearly as bad as I imagined, but for someone who likes to please and be liked by everyone it definitely struck a nerve. In looking back I know that it had to do with my craving for any acknowledgement that I was worth something. And, what better way to prove your worth than by being paid? Another big lesson learned.

My search for a theatrical agent had been ongoing. After an initial interview Bret Adams called me to sign with him. He turned out to be the right agent for me. Our professional partnership lasted for over 27 years. From that point on he negotiated all my contracts. Never again would I discuss terms with producers. His first contract to negotiate for me was the "Irma" contract. I hadn't called him about the "Dames" situation because that initial contract had been handled by me. It was such a relief to have him act as a buffer for me with the producers, that I never minded paying his ten percent commission.

'IRMA LA DOUCE' TRIO

Romantic lead Ronald Young (left) gazes fondly at star Monique Van Vooren, and comedian Will B. Able points out the virtues of "Irma La Douce," the musical production now at the Meadowbrook Dinner Theatre in Cedar Grove.

Publicity photo with Monique Van Vooren and Will B. Able for "Irma La Douce." (Photo by Len Leonards)

"Irma la Douce" was performed in a dinner theater, which is not unlike a summer stock venue where the producers will use any means to sell tickets. "Irma" was an all-male show, with the exception of the title role. In this production, Irma was played by a blond bombshell, Monique Van Vooren, who was an actress on the fringes of the Andy Warhol stable of personalities. She was quite voluptuous in the role, but evidently the producers needed more estrogen on the stage. Two female dancers were added to the cast and one of them, Louisa Flaningam, remains a close friend to this day. Monique wasn't too happy with their presence on stage. She wasn't above using little tricks on anyone to pull focus. One of her favorites with me was turning to one side or the other when we were singing a duet, so that my voice wouldn't be picked up on her body mike. Little things like that. Still, she was fun to work with for my first time in a leading role.

An incident happened that proved my work with the hypnotherapist had paid off. During the technical dress rehearsal the old tickle in my throat started up again. Oh no, same old, same old. So on a break I just stretched out under a costume rack in my dressing room and put myself through the self-hypnosis routine. At one point all the tensions from my throat area were sent down my shoulders and arms and out my fingertips on exhaled breaths. You might find that this next part stretches credulity, but it is true: after two or three exhales, the tip of the fourth finger on each hand began to cramp. I then brought myself out of the exercise, shook my hands and went on with the rehearsal. No more tickle. Call it what you will - mind over matter, not real, whatever. That technique worked for me, and still does.

This marked an end to consecutive employment for me. From then on there would be fallow spells between engagements when it would be necessary to live on unemployment or my savings. I had been very spoiled for over five years. Now it was reality. This helped teach me another lesson: delayed gratification. You don't always need to get what you want when you want it. Take into consideration your obligations, your assets and your proposed future earnings before making any large expenditure. From the very beginning of coming to New York a method of treating myself well and saving toward the future was developed. It wasn't without glitches, but the process was in place.

That summer Bret found a good summer stock role for me that was right up my alley: David in "Milk and Honey." The role had been originated by Tommy Rall in the Broadway production and required a strong dancer who could sing a

One of my favorite dance shots from a production of "Milk and Honey." Photographer unknown.

"high B flat" in one of his numbers. Molly Picon, the original star, was set for the production. My auditioning was continuing to improve and got me the role. Then the producers asked me if I would also be the driver for Molly and her husband, Jacob Kalish, affectionately known as Yonkel. This was going to be a tour in the northeastern part of the country and they needed to be driven from theater to theater. This had the unexpected benefit of getting to spend time with two of the stars of the Yiddish Theater with all of their history and theatrical anecdotes. They were both wonderful. The day we were to leave for rehearsals up on Cape Cod, I got the rental car and drove out to pick them up at their home in Westchester. Before we left they took me down to their basement, which was a treasure trove of all their theater memorabilia. They had to pry me away to get on the road to make it to our first engagement.

Suddenly a big dose of insecurity washed over me upon my arrival at rehearsals the next morning. The corps of dancers was made up of members of the Boston Ballet and a lot of the singers in the chorus were from the Boston Opera Company. For the first time in my career major doubts crept in that I could do this. Buckle down and bring on the kick-ass work ethic. It was a thrilling role to perform with a big athletic ballet and two songs. Yes, I did pull it off. Bret drove all the way to the Cape to see me and was quite proud.

That summer there were a couple of incidents that remain entrenched in my memory. The first one occurred during an after-the-show party on the beach for the cast. This show was extremely physical for me and my thirst was at a very high level by the end of the evening. Guess what? The only beverage on hand at the party was beer. Oh, no, I don't drink beer! Well, that night my life changed forever. Beer tasted so good that night it made me a beer lover ever since. See, you *can* teach an old dog new tricks.

Speaking of new tricks, I got accused of pulling one during the curtain calls at one of the theaters in the round. As each performer took their bow they would run down one of the four aisles, go to center stage and bow all around. My bow was a big stag leap that took me to center stage. This one particular night one toe got caught on the lip of the stage and sent me sprawling, rather that leaping, to center stage. Ever one with my wits about me for attention, I immediately pulled up on one knee, bowed and then wheeled around on the opposite knee to acknowledge the other side of the house, just as if it had been planned that way. Oh, the ham in me that never slept. The accusations from the other cast members came fast and furious that this had somehow been planned. The wardrobe supervisor knew better, because the knee on one leg of my pants was ripped. It was an eventful summer.

That fall a friend from the "Hello, Dolly" cast, Amelia Haas, called, "Ronnie, I'm down at the Bucks County Playhouse rehearsing the 'The Boys From Syracuse,' and the second male lead has dropped out. Would you be interested in the part?" Bret called and worked out the contract. The next day found me on my way to play Antipholus of Ephesus in the show. Boy, your life can turn around on a dime in show business. This turned out to be the first of three productions that the playhouse was presenting in their fall season. After "Boys From Syracuse" the producer asked me to stay and play Geoffrey, the second son in "Lion in Winter" and several small roles in the Scottish play, "Macbeth." This was a small repertory theater and the pay was low, but it provided much-needed experience. The actors were housed in the Lambertville Inn, just across the river. It was a charming inn but the walk across the bridge to and from the theater got to be a little more challenging as the weather got colder. It was also my first experience in the rather insular environment of a small repertory company. Lee R. Yopp was the producer and artistic director. This former football coach approached directing from an unusual point of view. But hey, learn to work with it. This was time well spent.

In the seventies Industrial Shows played a big role in employing musical performers. These were original shows with music created to sell a product. They would travel around the country and the pay was quite nice. My combination of skills made me a very viable candidate for getting work in this venue. In fact after doing several of these the nickname of "Ken Doll" was given to me. Hmm, was this an affectionate label, or a caustic comment? Never could figure that one out. Anyway, over the years my skill set came in handy for numerous shows for Oldsmobile, Cadillac, Ford, Chevrolet, Lincoln Mercury, GMC Trucks – can you believe it, the list goes on? – Admiral, America Leather Industries, American Millinery Institute,

An industrial show for the American Millenary Institute with Sheila Smith, Angela's standby in "Mame," and my infamous white leather suit. (Photo by Wagner International Photos)

Brown Foreman Distilleries, Stroh's Beer, Cessna, Fur Information and Fashion Council – and continues! – GM Terex, GE Silicone, RCA and RKO. Now you know why these "take the money and run" jobs were so life sustaining between shows.

What could make me stand out? With my "Ken Doll" image of the square pitchman in a suit and tie, it would have to be something a little off the wall. After searching through endless songs, there it was - "I'll Build a Stairway to Paradise." Very few people had ever heard the verse to the song, which ended with "When you practice here's the thing to do, simply say as you go," and then into the chorus. The verse would be sung very conventionally until that line. Then I would reach down, roll my pants up to reveal knee high American flag socks, and launch into a highly choreographed version of the chorus. The incongruity of this mixture never failed to get a riotous reaction, as in "I can't believe he just did that!" It usually sealed the deal for me, so it had to be used selectively. These jobs were not only lifesavers between shows, but usually provided interesting places to perform and were a ton of fun.

One of my secret ambitions was to sing on stage at Carnegie Hall. Did it happen? Well, yes. Was it a theatrical event? Well, no. My friend, Paul Richards, was the tenor soloist for a Sunday church service there every week. For two weeks he had a conflict and asked me to substitute for him as the soloist. Did I? Of course. Now I had sung on stage at Carnegie Hall.

By replacing Prisoner 105 in the Al Carmines Off-Broadway musical, "Promenade," I was reunited with Mary Jo Catlett and Alice Playten from the "Hello, Dolly!" cast. Furthermore, the musical director was Susan Romann, from my Kansas City "Starlight" stint. It really is true. Show business is such a small world.

The run with that show lasted only a month because "Hello, Dolly!" came back into my life. The Merrick office called to ask me to play Ambrose Kemper in the current production when Phyllis Diller took over the role of Dolly Levi. The role of Ambrose was small, but it was back on Broadway at the St. James Theatre again. Working with Phyllis was a trip. She would always give a curtain speech and the cast would have to stand on stage with her. This added time to the show and wasn't too popular with the crew

Ron —
You are so really wonderful! It's onward & upward for you —
Love
Phyllis Diller

Phyllis Diller's publicity shot for "Hello, Dolly!"
Photographer unknown

and some of the cast. During the show there was one point when I would go by her dressing room to pick her up for her next entrance. One night at that time her dresser was telling her what groups were in the audience that she might work into her curtain speech. She mentioned that there were 4-H Club members in the audience that night. Well, of course my time in the 4-H Club in Oklahoma had to be pointed out. Then surprise! She had been a member as well in Hawaii. So, together we recalled the 4-H club pledge and recited it.

Flash forward to the curtain speech. All was going along per usual until Phyllis says, "I hear we have some 4-H Club members in the audience." From high up in the second balcony we hear screams and applause. "Well, we have a 4-H Club member on stage tonight. Ron, come over here." I froze. Surely this couldn't be happening! She insisted until I came over to stage center with her.

"Ron, why don't you recite the 4-H Club pledge for the audience?"

What? You've got to be kidding! Backed into a corner, my adrenalin kicked in, as I said, "Alright all you 4-Hers in the audience stand up and say the pledge with me."

The cast on stage was pretty much in hysterics as we began, "I pledge my head to clearer thinking, my heart to greater loyalty, my hands to larger service and my health to better living for my club, my community and my country."

This was recited, complete with appropriate gestures. Something happened about halfway through, the laughter gave way to the deeper meaning of what was being said. The blending of the voices from the audience and mine onstage evidently touched a chord with some of the cast because the laughter changed to tears in some of their eyes. We finished, Phyllis told the audience "goodnight," the curtain came down and I collapsed in a heap on the stage. All the energy that that had been mustered to get me through had just completely drained me. "Phyllis, don't ever do that again!" I begged.

Phyllis stayed for three months and then Ethel Merman replaced her. This was big news on the Rialto. Ethel had been asked to do the show originally and had declined. Our first day to rehearse with our new Dolly was another dream come true for me, performing with Ethel Merman, the legendary star of "Gypsy." Remember, that was my very first Broadway show to see in New York while on that first college choir tour. We were into the opening scene, I said my cue line for Dolly and then a very Mermanesque thing happened. She snapped her head around and barked, "That's not in my script." It seems that we had altered the script for Phyllis and had forgotten to go back to the original that Ethyl had been given. The line was changed back and the rehearsal continued. Whew!

Jerry Herman was adding two songs for Ethel. One of them was "Love Look In My Window," which Angela had sung in the out of town tryout with "MAME" in Philadelphia and had been cut for the Broadway opening. The assistant stage manager let slip to me when the first rehearsal for those numbers was to be held in the theater. Somehow I was able to sneak up to the balcony and lie down between two rows to listen to the entire rehearsal, with Jerry singing the songs for her and then Ethel learning them. Wow!

Ethel was fascinating and a complete pro. During the feed shop scene the focus would alternate back and forth between Vandergelder downstairs and Dolly upstairs. When the lights were down on us, Ethel would go into a completely relaxed state. Then just before the lights were to come up, she would seem to awaken and the energy flowed through her right into her first line. It was amazing to watch.

My latest ballet teacher at this time was Nanette Charisse, the sister-in-law of Cyd Charisse, the MGM dance star. One day in class one of the other students, Sandy Duncan, asked me, "Say, are you going to audition for 'The Boy Friend'? You're very right for the lead in the show." She was already set for the role of Maisie.

"Sandy, Gus and I had a little falling out earlier on an agent-performer level, so he probably wouldn't even be interested in even seeing me audition," was my reply. Gus Schirmer was Sandy's agent, but would also be directing the show.

"Oh, go ahead. That wouldn't stop Gus from hiring you. I think you should try out anyway," and she was off to the barre.

Well, Bret set up the audition and surprise! Sandy was right. Gus hired me to play Tony Brockhurst opposite Judy Carne, a big TV star from "Laugh In." This was to be her first time on Broadway and my first leading role on the Big White Way. Thank you, Sandy!

There was a snag, however. Rehearsals started in a little over a week and my "out clause" in "Hello, Dolly" called for a month's notice to be given to leave the show. Bret called the producers and they were not to eager to give in to this request. We had a meeting in the Merrick Office with Lucia Victor, the original stage manager of "Hello Dolly!" who was now supervising the show and putting in all the replacement stars. Lucia had always been in my corner and she graciously let me out of my contract.

Rehearsal began and a British coach was immediately found for me to work on my upper-crust English accent. Laughter had to be stifled with this teacher. She was constantly working on my "oo" sound. "For the 'oo' vowel stretch your lips to the opposite wall." Then she would demonstrate, looking as if she had just been sucking on a lemon, "oooo." She must have been a pretty good coach. At the opening night party Judy Carne's parents were there on their first trip to the states. "Oh, and what part of England are you from?" queried her convinced mother. "Oklahoma!" was my reply in my finest British accent. She was momentarily stunned and then got the joke. Also, years later other young actors would tell me that they had studied my vocals on the original cast recording for their local productions of "The Boy Friend."

Back to the show. You can imagine my euphoric state during rehearsals. There were two duets with Judy, "Room in Bloomsbury" and "I Could be Happy With You," which had a rousing little tap solo in it. This part seemed tailor-made for the Dudley-do-Right part of me that was still present. There wasn't a lot of acting required, except for the British accent.

For this opening night one of my most practiced precepts came into play: "Life is not a rehearsal." In other words, live your life as completely as possible in every moment; you might not have another chance. Well, it was done up in spades for this opening night. Previously, at a costume sale for the New York Shakespeare Festival, a black Spanish suit, complete with short fitted jacket, pants with a high waist, kick pleats and silver buttons all down the outside of each leg had been found and purchased. This costume had been used in a production of "As You Like It," set in the south-

My caricature for the opening of "The Boy Friend" from the Sunday News in New York City. (Caricature by Sam Norkin)

west, starring Katherine Hepburn. What ever possessed me to buy it? Who knows? In any case, that was to be my opening night party outfit, with my hair slicked down, *a la* Rudolph Valentino. My rented limousine was a Rolls Royce with wood-paneled interior, and the chauffeur's name was "Prince Michael" of Austria. I swear that's the truth: who could make that up? Then a table for 20 had been reserved at Sardi's. My arrival elicited applause and more than a few curious stares. Phone calls were received at the table, including one from my folks back in Oklahoma, and we all had a grand time. Then it was on to the cast party at Tavern on the Green. To top it off I was introduced to Julie Andrews, the star of the original "Boy Friend." This opening night was made even more stellar by getting nice reviews from the press and a caricature by Norkin in The Daily News. It was disappointing that it wasn't a Hirshfeld in The New York Times, but what's a second banana leading man to do?

With Judy Carne in "I Could Be Happy With You", from "The Boy Friend." Photographer unknown.

Sandy got rave reviews and was literally catapulted on her road to stardom. Judy didn't fare as well, and the show was a bit of a hard sell for audiences. We only ran for about three months.

When the cast saw the writing on the wall, we all began to audition for other shows. There was also going to be a National Touring Company going out of "The Boy Friend." This turned out to be another difficult choice for me. They wanted me in the tour, but the second stand-by for the role of Bobby in the new Stephen Sondheim show, "Company," was also offered. What to do? It just seemed more right to be on stage than to be the second cover for a part. The tour won out. There was a bit of humor to the casting of the all-English girls' school. The star was Anna Maria Alberghetti, Maisie was played by Priscilla Lopez and Dulcie by Barbara Rubenstein. So much for the British roots! Let's hear it for early diversity!

The rehearsal time was short and Anna Maria, not being a trained dancer, was having a bit of a hassle learning her steps. She was able to learn the dance section for "I Could Be Happy With You" by the time we opened in our first city, but not "Bloomsbury." For the next two weeks we rehearsed before every show. When we included the dance section for our opening in Wilmington, Delaware, she received a glowing review that called her "a lovely dancer." She was proud of that. What she didn't know was that whenever we were in a ballroom dance position and my free hand was upstage, I would flip her skirt to make her turn look fuller. Then there were the glide steps. Whenever we were hand in hand going in my direction, I would gently pull her to make her take bigger steps. And vice versa, when going in her direction I would gently push her into a longer step. This partnering technique had been developed over the years to always show off my partner to the max. It came out of my initial idea to "always put myself between my partner and the floor." Whenever a dance partner would hear my theory about partnering, she never failed to look relieved. Also, seeing Rudolph Nureyev and Margot Fonteyn in "Swan Lake" at the Met was practically life-altering. As big as Nureyev's ego was, when he was partnering Fonteyn, she became the focus of his universe. Lesson learned. My job was always to show off my partner to her fullest potential and make her look good.

There was one incident on the tour that stuck with me. In Detroit there was not enough time to rehearse my tap number before the opening night performance, so I didn't realize that the stage was a little slicker that usual. Halfway into my number - splat - I was flat on my rear end! What a shock. Stage center and there I was down, but not for the count. Jump up and build to a big ending. Audiences love a performer who doesn't give up. So they gave me an even bigger hand than usual.

"The Boy Friend" proved to be an equally hard sell on the road. We only lasted two months. Maybe I should have taken the job with "Company," but then my life would have taken a completely different path. There would be two later companies of "The Boy Friend" to add to my résumé, one starring Rhonda Fleming as Mme. Dubonnet and the other with Gretchen Wyler in that role.

My vocal coach at that time, Ron Clairmont, helped me put together a dynamite combination of "When Johnny Comes Marching Home Again" and the folk song "Johnny I Hardly Knew You" for an audition piece. This very emotional number was one big crescendo from the pianissimo beginning to a triple forte ending. It never failed to get a positive response. This was used for my audition for Leonard Bernstein's "MASS" that would be the opening production at the new Kennedy Center in Washington, DC.

Bingo, got it!

Going into rehearsals, none of us knew the enormity of this work of Lenny's. There were vocal soloists, the Alvin Ailey Dance Company, a regular choir, a children's choir, an onstage band, the pit orchestra and the kitchen sink. Just kidding about the last one, but it almost could have been included, it seemed like everything else was. Rehearsals were exciting. Lenny's well-known and documented enthusiasm was always present. The composition was built around the Celebrant, who was played by an extraordinarily gifted young singer, Allen Titus. There were auditions for the cover for that role during rehearsals, because the cover would also be singing two performances during the run. My audition was good, but not good enough. That slot went to Walter Willison. Disappointment.

The time came in rehearsals to see the Alvin Ailey dancers for the first time. Suddenly a statuesque presence erupted onto the stage. It was Judith Jamison, Ailey's lead dancer. Never has there ever been a more mesmerizing performer. It was never less than thrilling every time she danced. We became friends during rehearsals and the run of the show, even meeting Miss Emma, her Great Dane. Fast forward to the opening night party. I escorted Judy to the party and that by itself became an event. The Ailey Company had toured all over the world, at times sponsored by the State Department. So many of the 2,200 people in the audience that opening night had seen Judy perform and wanted to meet her again. As we entered the party we became stuck in one spot as the well wishers lined up. Right away a little routine developed to check out the next person in the line. Generally their name would come up from snippets of their conversation, a nametag or anything. Then when they would reach Judy I was prepared with an introduction, "Judy, you remember General so-and-so when you danced in such-and-such?"

She would throw me a bemused look and say, "Why yes......"

After the party she asked, "Where have you been all me life?" That little technique worked like a charm that night.

After the solos were parceled out, mine was a small one. It was still very exciting to be part of the whole package. When rehearsals moved to the

Kennedy Center something strange happened. Walter Willison, the cover for the Celebrant, was asked to come in on a day off to work with Lenny on the Celebrant's material. He declined, for whatever reason. That was unimaginable to me, but he did. The result was that the director called me in to sing the material for Lenny. Again, I didn't quite measure up to his idea of the Celebrant, so singing the role on the Kennedy Center Opera House stage did not happen. Another disappointment. However, when it came time to make the recording of the piece, Walter was out, and I was moved into his slot as the First Rock Singer, singing "I Don't Know," the last track on Side One of the recording.

That recording was another memorable event. It was held in the Concert Hall of the Center. My part was broken up into two sections. The first was longer and the second only 32 bars. In between were six short sections by other soloists and the choir. When the time came for me to sing the last part, Lenny cued the orchestra strings into the pizzicato intro, then me to start singing. Normally he would have brought his baton up for my down-beat. Evidently, my eyes made such a connection with his across that vast space of the entire orchestra that he brought me in with a raised eyebrow. Those last 32 bars of sotto voce singing are my contribution to the world of music. And, it lives on in the recording. Hooray! On opening night Lenny gave me a treasure - a signed copy of my music, underlining, "I don't know" and writing "how to thank you, for so many things."

My opening night note from Leonard Bernstein, written on the piece of music that I sang in the "MASS."

The reverberation of working on the MASS stayed with me and gave me another short-term skill. The opening song sung by the Celebrant was "Simple Song" and he accompanied himself on guitar. So, let's get a guitar and learn that song. That task was accomplished, but the guitar and I never became good friends. Becoming an accomplished guitarist was not to be part of my future. That was my first and last attempt. My left hand just didn't wrap around the neck of the guitar easily. It was a gallant effort, but no dice.

"When Johnny Comes Marching Home" was used in a George McGovern Presidential rally in Connecticut. The best part of the rally was seeing Carmen de Lavallade, the famed modern dancer and actress, perform her "Creation." When we met after the performance effusive compliments flew both ways. Another memorable night.

Back in New York there were several industrials that were casting. "Stairway to Paradise" had been seen by almost everyone in the field, so a new piece of material had to be found. After searching and searching, a veritable unknown piece of music turned up: "There's Nothing like Dancing." It literally extolled the virtues of dancing to promote good health. A verse and two choruses should work for the routine. The staging started with my sitting on a chair and putting on tap shoes during the verse. Then the very simple tap steps grew progressively more difficult during the first chorus. By the second chorus I was on my back on the floor holding the chair upside down and tap dancing on the seat. Then "coffee grinders" led up to a few Gene Kelly traveling push-ups from his movie, "The Pirate." The routine culminated with a series of trenches into a front handspring and a double turn. At that point I clutched my heart as if having a heart attack and fell over dead. That was not the usual ending for an audition number and once again never failed to get me noticed. In fact, John Kenley had the number inserted for me in the production of "The Boy Friend" at the Kenley Players in Ohio, altering the "dead" ending so the show could continue.

Up to this point in my career one might think that there had been a little luck with timing, choices and circumstances in my life. Well, maybe, but someone once told me, "the harder you work, the luckier you get." Hard work has always been at the center of my performing venture. I never expected anything to be handed to me. Developing new skills and improving what was already in place would continue to be front and center in my life.

Would this continue to pay dividends?

LESSONS LEARNED

- **Continue to Improve Your Basic Skills**

- **Value Delayed Gratification**

BRANCHING OUT

The next several years saw a variety of performing opportunities, each one a unique adventure. There were two touring shows with Shirley Booth, one of the great actresses of the American Stage. The first one was "The Vinegar Tree," a drawing room comedy of little note except for Shirley's appealing role. The second was "Harvey," which found me playing the role of Dr. Lyman Sanderson, a young intern. By the time we opened that play after a short rehearsal period, the actor in me had not found the character I was playing. It was apparently nowhere in sight.

Opening night of the second week of our tour Shirley took me aside and said, "Ron Dear, why don't you play the part with a southern accent?"

What immediately came to mind were the hours and dollars spent trying to get rid of my Oklahoma accent. However, that night the stage manager came on the backstage mic to alert the cast of this "monumental" change in my characterization. Funny thing, later on in our run we returned to this theater for another week and the review was hilarious: "most improved in the cast was Ronald Young."

Working with Shirley Booth in two different touring companies was a gift. (Photo by Roddy McDowell)

In reality, Shirley had hit on something that made me a truer presence on stage in that role.

She was a wonder to behold. Night after night I would watch from the wings as she approached the end of a scene where she knew she would get a reaction. By that point in the show, she was incredibly fine-tuned to the audience. She knew if she would get a big enough reaction on her exit line to deliver it from center stage and have applause all the way to the wings. She also knew when to be at the door to have just enough laughter to make her exit.

Here was another time that I drove the star from theater to theater. Was it time to get my chauffeur's license? Once again the great stories came out, this time from Broadway and Hollywood. One of my big disappointments is having been too young to have seen her onstage in "Come Back, Little Sheba." Of course I've seen the movie, but by all accounts her performance on stage was up there with the immortals. Her big leap into the public's eye would come with her TV series, "Hazel."

Years later when in Boston with "My One And Only," I took my day off and drove out to her home on Cape Cod in Chatham, MA. By that time she had lost most of her vision but she was still at her charming best. After lunch she insisted on bringing out her photograph albums for me to go through. With the photos memorized and the images indelibly imprinted in her mind's eye, she would go from page to page showing me each picture and commenting on it. One stands out with Katherine Hepburn. "She has a scarf around her neck, doesn't she? She never liked for her neck to show. Wrinkles, you know." Vintage Shirley. That was the last time I was to see her, but I'm so glad I made the trip.

It was back to Broadway in 1972 with "Different Times." What's that, you say? Yes, it was a Broadway show with music and lyrics by Michael Brown, Book by Michael Brown, Directed by Michael Brown and Produced by Michael Brown. There was a rumor that he would have liked to play a role in the show as well, but was dissuaded. Wearing all those hats did limit perspective on the show. It would definitely have benefited from other opinions. Once again the show was cast with 15 extremely talented performers, all looking for their one spot to shine. For the third time the amazing Mary Jo Catlett, from my "Hello, Dolly" family was on stage with me. Michael had been known previously for his work in industrial shows. This was to be his shot at the big time on Broadway. The show had some wonderful moments and some good music, but several theater friends who saw "Different Times" said that it still had the look of an industrial. I had several roles with a big solo and a duet with Mary Bracken Phillips: "When They Start Again," toward the end of Act 2. During previews that number got a very good reaction every performance from the audience. The reviews came out, tepid as they were, with no mention of our number. Why was that? A little later word leaked out that the particular night the critics reviewed the show had coincided with the birthday of Douglas Watt from the Daily News. They all left the show early for his little celebration party. They never saw my two big numbers in the show! Somehow it just didn't seem fair after all the work, and considering how difficult it is to get those "one time" shots at a good impression. You win a few. You lose a few.

Speaking of losing a few. There was a short hospitalization caused by internal bleeding. After all the tests, the "assumptive prognosis" was a small duodenal ulcer. Those big words must have meant that the doctors didn't know for sure what it was. In any case, a bland ulcer diet was prescribed for the next few months. There was an interesting incident in the hospital. With my wide circle of friends there were a lot of visitors in my room. One day two girls whom I was currently dating showed up at the same time. (Yes, I was still trying to be straight. What can I say?) My way of dealing with the situation was a real copout: "Could you come back later? I'm really not feeling well. I think I need to sleep." What a crock! Hey, it got me through an embarrassing situation. Thankfully there was never another incident of any type of ulcer activity and my diet has never had to be curbed again. Hooray!

Musicals were my bread and butter. "Funny Face" with music by George & Ira Gershwin was being staged at the Studio Arena Theatre in Buffalo in 1973. This was being advertised as the "Lost Musical." It was last seen on stage 45 years before in London and had not been produced since then because the libretto and all the orchestrations had been lost. It had taken two years for Bill Cox to reassemble the show. Originally in 1929 it was an out-of-town flop, but then became a hit in New York. In the London production it was a vehicle for Fred Astaire and his sister, Adele. I was cast in the role of Peter Thurston, an

Was I dashing or what as Peter Thurston, the tap dancing, ballad-singing aviator in "Funny Face" at the Buffalo Studio Arena Theater? (Photo by Phototech Studios)

aviator, who just happened to be able to sing romantic ballads and tap dance like a fiend. Interesting combination. We had a limited run and then moved to the Ford's Theater in DC. This was a delightful show with great audience appeal. In fact, in 1978 when the Studio Arena Theatre opened their new theater, "Funny Face" was reprised for the inaugural event. It was recast, retaining only two of us from the original production. There was a very interesting dance number in the second act with the Fred Astaire role played by Denney Shearer, the comedian Jimmy Brennan and the romantic leading man, moi. Right before the number all three of our girls had left us. We began to pace the stage, only for the audience to discover we just happened to be wearing tap shoes. Well, "My One and Only," the wild number that ensued, never failed to bring the house down. It was just very unusual to find three such diverse characters tap dancing up a storm. That was great fun.

During the winter of 1974 the opportunity arose to perform in one of my favorite shows, "Jacques Brel is Alive and Well and Living in Paris," at the Alliance Theatre Company in Atlanta. This was a show with no dialogue, just music, but there was something about this material that was just fascinating. The music was haunting and the lyrics told a story. One song would stay in my performance and audition repertoire for quite a while, "Fanette." Overall, this was a very good experience.

There was a point during this period when some much-needed R&R time was spent in Oklahoma. After much work in therapy it seemed the right time to talk with Dad about my sexual identity. One night after LaVon had gone to bed early, I began to work the conversation around to the subject.

"Dad, we have never talked about this, but I'm having trouble finding my way sexually." This look came into his eyes like "Oh, no, we can't talk about this."

Instead he said, "Well, son, your Mother and I raised you according to the bible, the best way we could."

For some reason that just shut me down. It was another proof for me that they really did the best they could, but in certain areas they had their own demons that had not been addressed. After he went to bed I went out on the porch on that beautiful spring night with a full moon and cried. This was going to be my cross to bear. Deal with it.

Back in New York Don Smith, a well-known publicist, was putting on an event to announce a new biography of Judy Garland by Gerald Frank. He was asking artists to perform numbers from her movies, not necessarily ones she had sung. He approached Janie Sell, my cohort from "George M!" and "Dames at Sea," and me to do "It Only Happens When I Dance With You." Janie was fresh off of her Tony award for "Over Here" and was free. Wally Harper agreed to be our musical director. Interesting side note: He played for Paul Draper's tap classes when I studied with him back in the sixties, before going on to become Barbara Cook's long-time musical director. I agreed to choreograph the number, as well as perform in it. The event was to be in the Rainbow Room at Rockefeller Center. Janie wore her Tony dress, which flowed beautifully when she moved. I was in a white tails outfit. White tails? Stop! Don't say a thing! It worked, OK? We started the vocal on stage with the band, then segued down to the ballroom floor and guess what? We had on tap shoes! The number had been built to this big finish that just suddenly stopped. The night of the performance it all fell into place. We froze our position at the end of the number, there was a pause and then the audience erupted with a standing ovation. Pretty special.

My summer stock gig that year teamed me with Ann Miller, another tap dancing star from the world of Hollywood musicals. The role was Billy Crocker in "Anything Goes" with Ann's Reno Sweeney. Let me tell you, Ann was a bundle of energy. She was billed as having the fastest taps ever recorded, and she proved it every night. We had a couple of vocal numbers together, but no tapping. Dang it! My role was just singing and comedy.

Ann Miller as Reno Sweeney, with Coley Worth as "Moonface" Martin, and yours truly as Billy Crocker in "Friendship" from "Anything Goes." Photographer unknown.

On an evening off during our run at the Papermill Playhouse in New Jersey I was relaxing, watching the Johnny Carson Show on television. His guest was Truman Capote, who was answering Johnny's questions with his unique laconic drawl. Carson couldn't get a rise out of him, that is, until he brought up Sammy Davis, Jr. "You've got to admit the man has talent," Carson prodded. Capote paused and in that inimitable voice of his slowly lisped, "One must never confuse talent with energy." Whoa! I fell off the couch on that one.

My first number in "Anything Goes" was a Cole Porter standard with Ann: "You're the Top." She would already be on stage in a gleaming white gown, white fur piece, jet-black wig, bright red lipstick and three spotlights, energy blazing. Finding Capote's line apropos, I would stand in the wings quietly jumping up and down before my entrance for the number, repeating the line, "One must never confuse talent with energy." Then, as if shot out of a cannon, I would join Ann for the rest of the number. It worked. My energy matched hers. What a fun show!

Bob Hergett, a director and choreographer friend from previous industrials, was going to be staging a new piece for PBS, "Rachel, La Cubana." This was actually an opera by the contemporary composer, Hans Werner Henze. "When Johnny Comes Marching Home" was my audition again and they hired me to play seven different roles. Some of them were cameos and some had more meat to them. The range required singing, dancing, acting, mime and trapeze work. One of the singing roles, Alberto, was the love interest for Rachel, played by Lee Venora, formerly from the New York City Opera. Interesting connection, she had played Lili in "Carnival," my first summer of stock in Kansas City. One of the dance roles was that of Yarini, her pimp. This was replete with a purple and white striped satin zoot suit, fake nose and curled hair, definitely putting me in the mood to tango with Rachel. Do we have the beginnings of a character actor here? Let's hope so.

Every hit can't be a home run, or even a single. Here's one of my bunts, "Lucifer," billed as "A Great New Rock Musical!" My role was Jesus to Larry Marshall's Lucifer. My audition was OK, but the producers probably cast me in order to advertise that they had the "First Rock Soloist" from the Bernstein MASS in their show. The best part was the rider to my contract. It read, "In accordance with Equity ruling, Actor shall perform the

WORLD PREMIER
RONALD YOUNG in 'LA CUBANA'
by
HANS WERNER HENZE
WNET
Contact:
BRET ADAMS LTD.
36 E 61st Street
PL2-7864

APPEARS AS:
1. YARINI THE PIMP
2. YOUNG SAILOR
3. THE GANGSTER
4. TRAPEZE ARTIST
5. RACHEL'S COMPOSER
6. ALBERTO
7. THE BALLET MASTER

A composite of the seven characters I played in "Rachel, La Cubana," a world premiere opera by Hans Werner Henze for WNET television. (Photos by Carl Samrock, Copyright WNET 1974)

additional role of the Voice of God and for this shall receive $15.00 per week." Even though this was only in Paramus, New Jersey, it must be the big time. During the hectic rehearsals my communication with my agent was lax. Without an early warning Bret had booked a busload of friends out to see the show. Luckily he had drinks and snacks on the bus. That had to be the best part of the evening. On the other hand the cast had a pretty good time putting the show together. We had hopes that it was better than it actually was. Larry had appeared in the MASS with me, so reunited we had a great time in our numbers together.

It was a strange feeling to see my face that large on a set piece for "Girl Crazy" at the St. Louis Municipal Outdoor Theater.

It was that time again - summer stock. "Girl Crazy," another Gershwin musical was being staged at the St. Louis MUNI the summer of 1975. The MUNI is the largest of the outdoor musical theaters, seating almost 12,000 people. Everything there is done BIG, but more about that later. It was another good singing and dancing role for me. The two duets with Ann Reinking, one of the shining dance stars on Broadway, were the best part of the gig. With her long legs and mine we could really cover that grand stage. However, we had to do some adjusting in the vocal range area. I was a tenor and her voice was somewhere in the baritone range. "Honey, the only person who could sing a duet with you is Tallulah Bankhead" was my running joke. We worked it out. In one of our numbers, "Embraceable You," she was in a lavender chiffon flowing dress and I was in a gold lame suit. Gold lame? I didn't choose that outfit, I swear! You probably find that hard to swallow after the stories about my black Spanish number and the white leather suit, but the costume designer made me wear it! The number was beautifully staged by Edward Roll, the choreographer. For the ending we were on opposite sides of the stage and ran to meet stage center in a lift with my arms wrapped around her knees on my chest and she, straight above me with her arms raised. Slowly, I started to turn, letting her slide down until her legs were almost in a split with her feet skimming the floor. Then, I lowered to one knee and she lay straight out across my other knee, feet on the floor, arms extended. This was all done very smoothly until she just melted over my knee at the end. It stopped the show nightly for the week's run. Dolores Gray, the star, wasn't too happy with the audience reaction. After a couple of nights she began to stop the applause by yelling my name, "Johnny, Johnny," offstage before her next entrance. That was OK, we still stopped the show.

At one point in the show my character was running for local sheriff. Remember, everything was BIG at the MUNI. They made a 16-foot-tall billboard with my face on it as an election poster. During "Strike up the Band" the bottom half of my face parted and a local high school marching band was regurgitated on to the stage.

My billing was "Also Starring," which put me right behind Dolores and Ann with the third bow at the end of the show. That old itch to show off surfaced once again. One night about halfway through the week's run I decided to alter my bow without telling anyone. I came running out and threw in a front handspring before my bow. There was a big reaction from the audience. Then Annie came running in for her bow, gave me a wicked look and threw in a jump split. I think we kept those bits in for the remainder of the run.

At the end of the summer there was another trip to Oklahoma when Renee Baughman came back with me. Yes, I was still trying to prove to myself that I could be normal. Renee was a gorgeous dancer who would later play Kristine in the original Broadway production of "A CHORUS LINE." When we got to the house in Grove I moved Renee and myself into the second bedroom with two beds, without checking the arrangement with Dad and LaVon. After the first night LaVon spent the next day in bed with a migraine headache. That seemed a little strange until Dad pulled me aside to tell me that she was upset that we were staying in the same room. That stunned me. Of course it was wrong of me not to have checked with them first about the sleeping arrangements. It was their house. This also embarrassed Renee. For the rest of our stay I slept on the couch. LaVon got over her migraine and joined us for the remainder of our uncomfortable time there. This incident was to play out again later in my story.

Always looking to expand my job possibilities, choreography was being added to my arsenal of skills. With "Same Painted Pony," I was hired to choreograph and perform. The music for this show was written by Don Tucker, a brilliantly mad musician, and directed by Fred Chappell, who had directed me in the "Jacques Brel" show in Atlanta. This was a review with just musical numbers, some of which were astonishingly good. There were a couple of productions of the show, with improvements and new numbers added. At one point Don wrote a song for me, "I Did it For You, Daddy." This was a first and was loosely based on my stories about growing up in Oklahoma. It was a very emotional song about trying to please my father and not getting all the love I needed. In order to touch people in the audience it would be necessary to go deeply into my own experience. However, it would not be a good choice simply to indulge myself and wallow in the sentiments nightly onstage. I devised a one-time rehearsal technique and discussed it with both Don and Fred. This would be to sing the song straight through three times in a row without stopping and allow myself to go to the deepest emotion possible. They agreed to let me try this and see what would happen. At one point I was curled up in a fetal position under the piano, sobbing, but still singing. After that cathartic rendition, that deep spot never had to be visited again to touch the audience. In performing the number I could go right to the brink and then let each listener have his or her own emotional connection to the lyric. This was another step in learning how to create the space on stage for the audience members to have whatever feelings were appropriate for each of them, not to watch me indulge in my own emotions.

This was a hopeful production of bigger things to come. We wanted to bring it in to New York. That didn't happen. The producers did create a second company to play in Las Vegas and at one point had a party in New York for both casts. It was there I met PJ Benjamin, the actor who was playing my role in the Las Vegas company. I remember feeling a sort of rivalry with him at that time. After both shows closed we went our separate ways and both continued to have careers. Years later he would meet Louisa Flaningam, my friend from the "Irma" company, and they would get married. At their wedding he chose me for his best man, and they remain my close friends. So much for rivalry!

We now have the beginning of a budding choreographer and director, but this additional direction for my career would have to be put on hold. A new show had just appeared on the horizon: "A CHORUS LINE."

LESSONS LEARNED

- Be Open to All Opportunities
- Be Aware of the Consequences of Forcing "Your Way" in Every Situation

A CHORUS LINE

My first exposure to "A CHORUS LINE" was the off Broadway production at the New York Shakespeare Festival. This was before the show became the mega-hit on Broadway it was destined to be. Watching the show affected me so much that I could barely get out of my seat when it ended. That white line was my life. Those were my friends up there. Going backstage the words would scarcely come out to tell them what the show had meant to me. I needed to go home and think about that white line and my life. Of course there was the same reaction on seeing it when it opened on Broadway.

It was about a year later that auditions were announced and that two companies were being formed, the National Company for Los Angeles and the International Company to play in London. I auditioned several times, and let me tell you: Michael Bennett, the mastermind director/choreographer behind ACL, gave tough auditions. The role of Don was offered with an 18-month contract, including six months in London. That role was originally played by Ron Kulman, who had been with me in the chorus of "Funny Face" in Buffalo. I had been hoping for the role of Zach, the director, but that wasn't to be. The 18-month contract to play the character of Don was accepted, just to be a part of this historic show and to play in London.

Rehearsals were most unusual because Michael was rehearsing two companies at once. A space large enough to fit this many dancers was found: the basement of City Center. It was like an audition every day, proving that you were as good or better than your counterpart in the other company. There was another unusual aspect present. Having been given the choice, part of the New York Company had opted to go out with the National Company in order to play Los Angeles. There was always the chance of movie stardom. This meant that some of the new dancers would be going into the Broadway production and some to LA. So sometimes there would be three companies rehearsing. It was a little chaotic, but Michael was always totally in charge.

There was one tap number in the show that was built on very basic steps.

111

Ann Reinking had been hired for the role of Cassie and would be going into the Broadway production when Donna McKechnie left for LA. This all got very confusing, but Michael had it all worked out. Brilliant dancer that she was, tap was never Ann's strong point.

"Ron, come back here and help me learn this combination," she whispered as she grabbed me by the hand, taking me to the back row during the rehearsal. Of course she eventually learned it and looked like a competent tapper when performing it.

This brings me to an aside. Somewhere about this time a very useful concept was formulating in my mind.. In the rehearsal process some people learn the steps and the lines more quickly than others. Here's the point: when you are on stage, no one in the audience knows, or cares, who learned it first. Think about it. This is not a race! This bit of wisdom has been imparted on numerous occasions throughout my show biz career. At times I would see these amazed looks on faces as a light bulb dawned over their heads. But back to ACL.

When each company would do one of the production numbers, the opening or the finale, you could sense they were trying to best the other company. Michael planned this all out. He knew what he was doing. He wanted us to feel the competition and bring that urgency to our performance in the show. It worked. We were all possessed.

The International Company was scheduled to play the Royal Alexandra Theatre in Toronto before heading off for London. It was my first time traveling to Canada, and we were to be there for six weeks. Our stay started on a high note, literally, and just got better. The enormous CNN Tower was just being completed as the tallest building and freestanding structure in the world. To celebrate the opening the cast was taken up to the top on the outside viewing platform in our finale costumes. Helicopters then circled the tower with photographers snapping pictures and taking video footage. Later, those photos were splashed around the world to herald the opening of the tower.

Right before the opening Jeff Hyslop, who played Mike, was injured in rehearsal and would not be able to open in the show. Don Correia, who was

The cast of "A Chorus Line" photographed on top of the CNN Tower in Toronto to publicize its opening in 1976. (Photo by Mike Slaughter/Getstock.com)

in the LA company, was brought in to open and stay until Jeff could return. Since Jeff and I shared a dressing room, Don of course took over his place. Show business is one big family. Later Don would marry Sandy Duncan, from "The Boy Friend," and then we would all three work together in "My One and Only." Even later still, he and I became golfing buddies.

Having just settled into my apartment, Canadian chauvinism reared its "ugly head." In Canada beer could not be purchased in a grocery store, you had to go to a special package store that sold only beer and spirits. Not knowing anything about Canadian beers my simple question to the man behind the counter was, "What kind of beer would you recommend?"

"What do you drink in the US?" he asked.

"Well, do you have anything comparable to Budweiser?" I queried.

"Yes," he replied, "water." Oops. Soon enough the delights of the wonderful Canadian beers were discovered.

Right after we opened, management asked me to read for the understudy for Zach. It worked out. Good thing I learned the script quickly. Eivind Harum, the actor playing Zach, was suddenly taken ill and I was on in the role in a baptism by fire. After playing the part several times, the powers that be were satisfied. Now we come to one of my more stupid moves - playing tennis one afternoon. It is really not a good idea to engage in other strenuous physical activities when you are in a dancing role. I reached up to serve the ball and felt like someone had hit my right calf muscle with a hammer. I could barely hobble off the court. It was diagnosed as an inner contusion of the plantaris muscle, in other words a big bruise on the inside of the calf muscle. No dancing for two weeks. The management was not too happy to hear that. They gave me a couple of nights off then had me limp in every night to sing in the off-stage chorus that augmented the production numbers. It took two weeks of rehab to get back in the show. That stinging lesson was certainly learned in a very painful way.

One of the dancers in the show, Steve Bauman, casually mentioned that he was going to see one of the pioneering doctors in the field of hair transplants, Dr. Walter Unger, right there in Toronto. That was interesting. Let's get more information. Ok, Ok, I confess. One of my mottos in life has always been, "Vanity is a terrible thing, unless you're really into it!" Bret and I had been talking about my receding hairline and if anything should be done about it. We decided that at my age, mid thirties, and given the roles that were possibilities for me, it would probably be a wise move to address this burgeoning problem. My consultation with Dr. Unger was set.

After checking my scalp, he affirmed, "You are definitely a candidate for hair transplants."

"I'll call for an appointment when my run in 'Chorus Line' is over. It will probably be another nine months." Even having to travel to Canada for the procedure would be cheaper than having it done in the States.

Then it was on to London. The next six months were very eventful. First the hype for our opening was staggering. Michael had strong-armed the English Equity Association to get his way. Normally when a show "crosses the pond" in either direction one or two performers are permitted to go with the show. Michael let it be known that if the entire cast, including understudies, weren't allowed to come to England, the show would not be seen in London. Whoa, talk about a power play. He knew what kind of a hand he was playing. They let the whole cast open and stay for the entire six months. Michael was right in his assessment of the talent pool of English dancer/singers. When he cast the show to replace all of us at the end of the run, the all-English cast, with the exception of the Frenchman Jean-Pierre Cassel as Zach, lasted only about three months. Back in the seventies the training for musical performers in London was not on a par with the States. That has since changed, but at that time there was a big discrepancy.

We all found "flats" in London. David Harris, a friend of a friend, found me a flat in the Sloane Square area, paid the security and one month's rent, and had the fridge stocked for my arrival. Talk about British hospitality. Sloane Square was one of the many delightful areas in London to explore and my stay there lasted for two months.

The hoopla surrounding our opening was massive. On our first night in London we were given a party by the English cast of "Side by Side by Sondheim." It was there that I met Fergus Montgomery, a Member of Parliament, who was a huge theater buff. He and his wife, Joyce, became friends. Later on when he was knighted for his service during Margaret Thatcher's term, I was able to claim a "Sir Fergus" in my address book. He was very generous with his connections throughout my stay.

The opening night at the Theatre Royal Drury Lane was a screaming success, literally. We developed our own "groupies" who saw the show multiple times. Being 35, and a little older than the average age of the rest of the cast, gave me a better overview of what was really happening. It was very easy to get caught up with all the attention,

My finale shot from "A Chorus Line." Woody Shelp, the hat maker, made me a copy of my original hat, that now resides under Plexiglas in my house in Oklahoma.(Photo by Martha Swope)

the autographs at the stage door, the celebrities coming back-stage, the parties. I was able to step back and realize that the stars of the show were Michael and the white line. The rest of us were cogs in the machine. If a dancer was right for the role, knew the steps and could hit the lighting marks on stage, he or she could fill the slot. Later, when multiple companies would be out on the road, a dancer from one company could be moved to another company at the drop of a hat, with a minimum of rehearsal. This didn't register with most of the other members of the company. They thought that this was going to be the big step to stardom. From what has been written about the original company, that was really the brass ring they all grabbed. How could it not be? ACL was the most colossal change in the course of musical theater history. It was, however just a gig, A very good gig, but still just a gig.

Two events happened shortly into the run. The first is a little complicated. Robert LuPone, the original Zach who was now playing in LA, wanted to leave the show to try to make it in the movies in Hollywood. So Michael then wanted Joe Bennett, the Zach in New York and originally from LA, to move to the LA company and bring Eivind from our company to New York. This was all dependent upon my being able to take over the role in London. I was put on to play the role in a couple of shows for the powers that be, once again, to check me out. Could I cut it? Evidently so, management offered me a new contract as Zach for the remainder of the 18-months. This was very exciting to finally claim the leading role as my own. Little perks, like a bigger dressing room with a refrigerator to keep champagne for guests after the show, came with the bump up to the leading actor in the show. There was even a glowing telegram from David Niven, the veteran screen actor, sent to Zach that was on the company bulletin board. After an appropriate time elapsed it became mine. After all, it was addressed to me. It now hangs on a wall in my home in Oklahoma.

The other was happily simple. One evening there was a note backstage from Bud Hamilton, a Sigma Chi fraternity brother, and his wife, Sandy. They were seeing the show that night and wanted to see me afterward. Great. Little did I know just how great this was going to be. "Hey, Ronnie, we are stationed in London now. Bud's company has rented us a house in Hampstead Heath, with a separate flat upstairs. Would you like to have it?

Oh, by the way, we aren't allowed to let it out, so it would be rent-free."
Sandy managed to say this with a straight face. I couldn't believe it. Hampstead Heath was another delightful section of London. Eureka! That was my home for the last four months of my stay.

There was always something to do after the show. One night Bud and Sandy were bringing some friends from the states to see the show and asked me to join them for dinner afterward. So following drinks in my dressing room we went out on the town to this fancy private club. There turned out to be a minor snag. That afternoon I had purchased a Harris Tweed sport coat and a cashmere camel colored turtleneck sweater. This new outfit was really very spiffy.

Cut to the maître d' at the club. "Excuse me, sir, but a tie is required to enter." This was said in high British and with a slight look down his nose.

"But I don't have a tie with me," I countered.

"We can provide you one from the cloak room."

"What?" I'm thinking, "you expect me to wear a tie over a turtleneck sweater, when I look sharper than most of the men in the restaurant." "It will look a little silly over a turtle neck sweater," I pled.

Bud even jumped in, "I'm a member here. Is there anyway you can overlook the rule for my friend? He is playing in 'A Chorus Line' at the Theatre Royal Drury Lane"

"I'm sorry, sir, but the rule is the rule," he superciliously intoned.

What to do, sit in the car while my friends have dinner? No way! So into the cloakroom to sort through the few ties and pick out the one that I thought would be the least offensive. Who was I kidding? Was there ever a tie designed that would not look offensive with a turtleneck sweater?

So we took our seats at a prime table for dinner. Everyone was being kind. "Oh, it doesn't look that bad." "The color goes with your jacket." "No one has even noticed." Who were they kidding? I was ready to crawl down a hole. Wait! The best (or worst) is yet to come. After dinner, there was a little stage show.

During the show the Emcee said, "We are very fortunate to have a star from the West End with us tonight. Ron Young from "A Chorus Line" is here. Ron, stand up and take a bow."

I stand, the light swings over and I seem to remember turning to the side to minimize the tie. The bad dream goes on.

"Ron, we know you are a singer as well as a dancer. Come up and give us a song."

You've got to be kidding me. I was not only going to have to sing for my supper, I would have to look like a doofus as well. Not since the 4-H Club pledge with Phyllis Diller, have I felt this mortified. So once again I summoned the old adrenalin rush, went up to the microphone and unabashedly faced the audience with the new look of the day: foreign hand tie on a turtleneck sweater. "If Ever I Would Leave You," knocked their socks off. "Thank you again, Robert Goulet," was in my mind. It would be nice to think that several of the men in the audience went out the next day to buy their matching turtleneck sweaters and ties, but that's doubtful. It was probably more like, "Oh no, another ugly American." That is, until my song won them over. It was a night to remember.

Fergus invited me to the opening of parliament that year and Sandy was able to accompany me. He immediately dubbed her "Lady Hamilton." The big day arrived and *voila* there was Queen Elizabeth in all her jewels and robes. It was pretty impressive. There was also lunch in the House of Commons and a visit to the House for the Question and Answer session with the Prime Minister. The latter turned out to be a little like watching "Family Feud" on TV. Fergus told me that it was just the nature of the beast. That is always how it had been done in the House of Commons.

The Speaker of the House at that time was George Thomas, who was also a friend of Fergus. Sir George, Fergus and Joyce were invited to see the show as my guests. Sandy offered to do a late sit down supper for everyone after the show. It was another magical night, champagne after the show in my dressing room, limos up to Hampstead, and the relaxed dinner. Sandy had developed into a hostess extraordinaire in her years as a corporate wife. The food and wine were superb and she had even drawn individual place cards with a picture of Parliament on each one. Sir George was a former Welsh minister and regaled us with countless anecdotes from his life. Another moment was indelibly etched in the patchwork quilt of my life.

This was my first time in Europe, so it had to be explored. Once a month I would leave early Sunday morning for some coveted destination and return Monday afternoon in time to do the show that evening. My English friends said this was a bit "cheeky" of me, but that was OK. Not knowing if, or when, this opportunity would ever be there again, it became an all out sprint every four weeks. My first trip was to Paris. Bret's partner, Paul Reich, was studying there at the time, so there was a place to crash. Of course everything couldn't be seen in that short of a time span, but inroads were made. The Eiffel Tower, the Rodin Museum and Sacre Coeur were favorites. However, it was outside Notre Dame Cathedral that the most unusual thing happened. In the plaza someone stopped me with, "Excuse me, but didn't I see you in 'A Chorus Line' in London last Tuesday?" Talk about a small world.

The fountain where Gene Kelly had danced in "An American in Paris" became another photo op. I jumped up on the edge of the fountain with arms outspread for my homage. That snapshot, with the caption of "Just Another American in Paris," became my Christmas card that year.

Another trip took me to Brussels to see George Bright, a college chum who was working there with IBM. That also included a side trip to the delightful town of Bruges. Then there was a trip to Amsterdam to visit a friend of Beverley's. My most memorable visit, however, was to South Wales to visit a friend of a friend. Yes, networking pays off. That Sunday evening

On a trip to Paris I found the Place du Concorde fountain where Gene Kelley danced in "American in Paris."

119

concluded with a visit to the local church where the women's choir was rehearsing for an upcoming competition. They knew there was going to be a visitor from the "West End" at their practice. They ranged in age from about 18 tp 70 and most were wearing hats in pastel colors, even though it was well into the fall season. The sound they made was remarkable. When it was over I was introduced as a "celebrity" from the West End.

"I have always heard about the male singers from Wales, but now I know who the real singers are," was my greeting to them.

They all beamed upon hearing that. As we left the church headed toward the village at the foot of the hill an extraordinary thing happened. It was fairly dark except for the starlight, so I never saw any signals of what was to happen. I started walking with a woman on each of my arms. At some undetermined time they would be replaced by two others, until by the time we reached the village each member of the choir had been arm in arm with me. How do you top that?

For the Christmas holidays Bud and Sandy were going back to the states and told me to use the house while they were gone. This was perfect. I invited the folks to visit me in London. They quickly got their passports as this was to be their first time out of the States and I arranged their travel. There is a wonderful photo of them arriving at Heathrow, looking a little like the proverbial deer in the headlights. Their time was all planned with side trips to Scotland, Spain and Paris. I even drove them, on the wrong side of the road, to Windsor Castle and Blenheim Palace. One day driving through Trafalgar Square during rush hour it dawned on me that if I could drive there, I could drive anywhere. Of course they saw the show a couple of times and had the thrill of seeing their son in the lead role.

Even though it was wintertime it was important for Dad to visit the famous golf courses at St. Andrews, Troon and Carnoustie. On their visit to Scotland he was able to go into the pro shops at each course and introduce himself as a visiting PGA member, which I will explain later. This was a highlight of the trip for him. A trip to the south coast of Spain was planned to visit another friend of a friend. I traveled with them on Sunday and when I returned to London on Monday, they went on to Paris. It was a little difficult to be on their own, without a tour guide and not speaking the language. The first night they found a restaurant where the waiter spoke English and they went back for every meal. So much for sampling the French cuisine. It was all a bit of a whirlwind for them, but quite an experience for their first trip abroad. It was a thrill to be able to share it all with them.

As the time in London was winding down and we were preparing to come back to the States to tour, as another national company of the show an abrupt snag occurred. It seems that Robert LuPone had not liked the Hollywood scene and wanted to come back into the show in New York. Michael was OK with that and wanted Eivind to come back to our company. That meant he wanted me to go back into the line as Don. Oh, this was like a blow in the solar plexus. What to do? I talked it over with Bret. After all, my new contract was for Zach for the rest of the 18 months. We decided to decline the offer of going back to play Don in the line, and that I expected my current contract to be honored. What did I really expect? Michael always got what he wanted. The next negotiation was to buy me out of my contract. Even with the $20,000 buyout it had the feeling of being fired. This was a first in my career. As you might guess closing night in London was a very emotional experience. Not only was the show closing in London, I was also leaving another close family with no job in my future.

Fortunately there was a little buffer. Before the "snag" I had planned a quick tour of Moscow with about five other members of the cast. At the time I was seeing a wonderful English girl, Liz Robertson, who would come with me. Later Liz would marry Allen Jay Lerner after meeting him when she played Eliza in a West End revival of "My Fair Lady." This was a connection that would surface later in my career. You might be thinking, "Didn't he just state earlier hat he was gay?" You're right. But it wasn't until my fifties that there was total acceptance of that fact. Up to that point, I kept looking and hoping.

The tour in Russia occurred in January 1977, while the cold war was still going full force. There were a few dicey moments when we were escorted in the airport by soldiers with rifles, when our passports were taken at the hotel and when we had to check in with the floor matron upon leaving and entering our hotel rooms. It was a wonderful experience as well, with a troika ride in the snow, the Moscow State Circus, the Bolshoi Ballet, Gums department store and much more. Local Muscovites kept trying to trade us out of our blue jeans. The one regret is not having had enough time to include St. Petersburg.

After, it was back to the States and uncertainty. What would be the next step along this chosen path of mine?

LESSONS LEARNED

- **Be Ready For Any Chance to Take a Step Forward**
- **Use Setbacks to Encourage Change**

EXPLORING NEW VISTAS

Back in the states there was an empty feeling that was very new. The old "Pollyanna bounce-back" was a little slower to kick in gear. They hadn't really fired me. Why did it feel like it? Michael didn't think I was good enough to keep me in the role of Zach. That's what it felt like. This was an unforeseen turn, because nine more months of work had been in my plan. "OK, here's some lemons, let's make some lemonade!"

First, it was off to Toronto immediately for my first set of hair transplants. This was much earlier than originally thought possible, because of my early release from the show. Dr. Unger was able to work me into his schedule fairly soon after my return to the states. The preparation started a few days before the actual surgery. Vitamin E and any other blood thinning medications were stopped to lessen the bleeding. I arrived at the office and was given a valium. The procedure then began with me face down on the table and local anesthesia applied to the "donor area," a space on the back of my head, above the hairline that had been trimmed to two millimeters in length. Then with a small electrical device, not unlike the manual tool used to dig the holes on golf course greens, plugs are removed, containing 8 to 20 hairs and placed on a sterile surface. The number of plugs had been predetermined by Dr. Unger's evaluation of the front surface of my head that was to be treated. Then the area was sutured. Flipped over on my back, that same little machine was used to remove plugs of skin in the "non-hair" (OK, "bald") area. Then the little plugs with the hair follicles intact were just inserted in the empty holes with pressure. My head was cleaned up and a white turban-like bandage applied. The next morning the bandage was removed and my head shampooed lightly in the office before going back to the states. The transplanted hair would then actually fall out, go into a dormant stage for about six weeks and then start growing just like the rest of my hair. It was such a success that over the next fifteen years the procedure was performed an additional six times. Dr. Unger's work was so good that often a barber giving me a haircut couldn't tell that transplants had been done. Hope this hasn't been TMI (Too Much Information).

Wearing a white turban for the first 24 hours was a surprise that first time. Dinner that evening had been planned with Sandra O'Neil, a friend from industrial show days, who was living in Toronto.

I called her, "Sandra, I don't know if you want to be seen having dinner with a man in a white turban. That's what my bandage looks like."

"It doesn't matter a bit to me," she replied. So, we met in the hotel dining room. Perhaps the other patrons that evening thought they were dining with a gentleman of Eastern descent. After all, Toronto is a very international city.

There was a short recovery period in New York, and then it was back home to Oklahoma to spend some time with my folks, which was good. Several years back Dad had made a big shift in his career. A new resort called Shangri-la had been developed on the tip of Monkey Island on Grand Lake. He was hired to help the golf course designer in building the golf course by laying the water lines and digging the sand traps. When the job was completed he apprenticed himself to the PGA (Professional Golfer's Association), and became an Assistant Professional at Shangri-la. Later, he moved up to the position of Head Professional and retained that position until he retired. He made this monumental change in his mid fifties to return to his first passion in life, golf. This was why it had been important for me to enable him to see the birthplace of golf in Scotland when he came to England.

The owner of Shangri-la had built a development of houses around the golf course. It seemed like it would be a good investment to take some of the money from my buyout from "A CHORUS LINE" and purchase a unit. It could then be rented out for me and become a source of income. There was one available right across from the first tee of the golf course. It was a small two bedroom split-level, with a fireplace and terrace. This was more than a big step for me, who had always rented and never owned anything. Dad was willing to look after it, with my being in New York most of the time, so I took the plunge. It felt good to have that little house, plus the extra income from the rental. In the two years of ownership, I probably stayed in the house a total of two weeks. One of the unique aspects of this setup was being able to call the room service department of the resort and have a van deliver my meal. Neat.

Back in New York a new challenge was presented to me. One of the most important steps in my development as an artist was joining a performance class with no teacher. How did this work? Initially we met in the penthouse apartment of Carole Demas. There was a pianist and we each had about a half hour to work on material, after which the rest of the class critiqued the work. The core of the class started with Carole, Kurt Peterson, Pamela Shaw, Larry Moss, Susan Slavin and myself. Others would join the class including Donna McKechnie and Jane Summerhayes. Here's what made it work. We were all at a certain level professionally and there was no hidden agenda to our comments about each other. We all were there to be supportive and to grow. We could work on audition material, songs for a club act, music that allowed us to explore other aspects of ourselves, whatever. There was a very protective atmosphere. At one point the class strongly encouraged me to go back to my roots, Oklahoma.

What was the impetus for this change? As a kid I could take or leave country music. It was always around, but didn't really pique my interest. In college it was definitely in the backseat to Broadway, classical and pop. Well, it was a time to revisit this genre. With this encouragement I began to write music and lyrics for my version of country songs. Maybe my composition class in college was leading up to this, who knows? Over the course of the next three years I wrote about seven songs and recorded them. A real exploration process began. My first song, "Oklahoma Man," was my life. Then there was my beer drinking song, "I'm Guilty of Hurtin' Overtime." "Outside Looking In" came from my feelings of always being in the B group, never the A group. "This is My Love Song To Donna" was a birthday gift for Donna McKechnie

There was a lack of faith and a big dose of fear on my part that kept me from going to Nashville, just to hang out and try to sell my songs. There was also the fact that my voice had a little too much of the sound of a trained singer to be accepted as authentic country. As a result I just whiled away the hours in my ivory tower. Still, the discovery process proved to be an invaluable use of my time. It gave me access to parts of myself that hadn't been touched before.

Performing the "Manson Trio" from "Pippin."
(Photo by Vincent Prestia)

During this period of concentrating on composing and the self-directed class there were two other shows offered to me that made me jump back into performing, "Pippin" and "The Music Man," both at Coachlight Dinner Theatre in Connecticut. Ben Vareen had originally played The Leading Player in "Pippin" on Broadway. My being cast in the role was one of the first times a white actor had played the part. We were fortunate to have a choreographer who had been a performer in the original cast, Lynne Gannaway. In "The Manson Trio," a number for the Leading Player and two female dancers, she staged us in the original Fosse choreography. Not ever having had the opportunity to work with Bob Fosse, this was a real gift. There was a second production of "Pippin" on a summer tour with Maxine Andrews, one of the original Andrews Sisters. Over the years my list of famous leading ladies continued to grow.

Being asked to play Harold Hill in "The Music Man" was a bit of a dream come true. This was one of the quintessential roles for a male in the musical theater repertoire, having been established on Broadway by Robert Preston. My Marian was Joy Franz, another friend from my first days in stock at Kansas City. This was a delight to do and was a role that would be reprised later in my career. This was my first "mustache role," which stayed with me until it later blossomed into the full beard and mustache of my country music period.

Here's a little aside about the "biz." The billing in a show is always a bone

Playing Harold Hill in "The Music Man" with Joy Franz as Marian. (Photo from Coachlight Dinner Theatre)

126

of contention in contract negotiations. The star is the one who has the best shot at selling tickets. So the producers want to cast that role with a high visibility rating. After that the billing depends on several conditions: your visibility and past accomplishments, your track record with the producers in previous productions and the tenacity of your agent. Bret was always very good at these negotiations. Even though not a household name from TV or the movies, I had a pretty good reputation as a musical performer. So it became sort of a standard practice that my billing would be "Also Starring" in a box at the bottom of the billing page. There were exceptions when it would be top billing in a smaller theater. This seemed an ego-driven exercise to me, and I'll admit I participated hook, line and sinker in the process many times. On a practical note there was the dressing room situation. The better the billing, the better the dressing room. So billing was always worth the fight.

Being a prolific composer was not my strong suit, but perseverance was. This became a full time pursuit, meaning there were not many auditions, just composing and classes. Along the way it seemed natural to grow a beard with the mustache, let my hair grow long and get it curled. It was definitely a look, a little like Kris Kristofferson. It would become a little game for me, walking down the street, passing someone I knew and seeing if they recognized me. It was almost like wearing a disguise.

It wasn't particularly right for a role in "Little Me," but the director, Lucia Victor, allowed me to keep it. This was another summer stock production that starred two Hollywood stars of the past: Donald O'Connor and Eve Arden. These two veterans were a joy to behold. At times Eve would have trouble remembering lines. I just wanted to say, "It's OK. Just say anything. The audience just wants to hear your voice." She had developed that distinctive sound over the years that was totally hers and very recognizable, from "Our Miss Brooks." My role was George

Yes, this is me with full beard and hair permed. Would you buy a used car from this man? Photographer Unknown

127

Musgrove, played by Swen Swenson in the original Broadway production. My big moment in the show, "I've Got Your Number," was a pseudo-strip number where the only items I removed were my hat, vest and arm garters. However, John Sharpe, the choreographer, had worked with Bob Fosse and staged a version of the original number for me. It was a challenge and a treat to do every night. We played several different theaters across the country that summer and there were hopes that it might come back to New York as a Broadway revival. Didn't happen.

Here's another failure of guts. In class I had been working on "High Flying Adored," Che's song from "Evita." With the full beard and the vocal chops that role was very much in my ability to perform. Paul Gemignani, the musical director, had nixed me after my first audition for the role. So there would be no chance for me to see Hal Prince, the director. The word was out that Hal was in Chicago, rehearsing the national company of the show. There was a fantasy about flying to Chicago, dressing as Che and hanging out at the stage door until he appeared and then pleading my case. What would have happened? I'll never know, because I was too chicken to try.

By not working as often, money, mostly the lack of it, was becoming a problem. After owning my house for two years it was sold for a profit. This helped my cash flow and eased the pressure. Still it didn't just get spent "willy-nilly." There was always a sense that this was finite and needed to be watched over carefully.

Every summer my voice teacher, Beverley Johnson, taught at the Aspen Music Festival. She had invited me out several times, but the timing was never right. Our schedules finally meshed and I was able to make that visit. A couple of memorable events occurred.

The first was meeting and spending some time with one of Beverley's students, Renée Fleming. This incredible artist was just at the beginning of her career. One day while Beverley was teaching we drove to the top of the Continental Divide. During the trip Renée spoke of her hopes and dreams of becoming a professional opera singer. She has since gone on to become one of the most sought-after musical stars in the world. It has always made me feel like her "Uncle Ronnie," just watching her career skyrocket.

The other special moment was a once-in-a-lifetime experience, plane glid-ing. The plane, just holding the pilot and me, was towed aloft by another plane and then released to just glide for an hour on the wind currents. This was a majestic feeling, to be soaring among the Rocky Mountains. The most amazing part was the landing. The plane only had two wheels, aligned from front to back. So the landing had to be judged so that two assistants would be there to catch each wing as we rolled to a stop, to keep from tipping to one side or the other. This was another "do it, it might never happen again" moment. There was also a little side trip of white wa-ter rafting down the Colorado River. Being a daredevil is really not in my DNA, but these two experiences were truly thrilling.

Bret had opened a branch of his theatrical agency in California, so we thought it would be good for me to spend a little time in LA since things were fairly slow in New York. So, Westward Ho! As luck would have it Pam, one of my cohorts in the "teacherless class," and her husband, Victor, needed to have a house sitter for the place they had just rented in Beverly Hills. Their busy lives had taken them in another direction. Work didn't pan out, but it provided a time in LA to reconnect with friends who moved out there from New York.

A surprise occurred in the fall of 1979. "Broadway Musicals," a large coffee table book by Mar-tin Gottfried was published with a photograph of "A Chorus Line" in finale costumes on the cover. What's so surprising about that? The show altered the course of musical theater. Why shouldn't it be on the cover? True, but the cast in the picture was the London cast, not the original cast! We were all shocked, but there I was look-ing out in my champagne colored

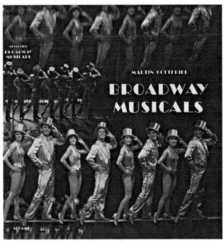

The cover of Martin Gottfried's Broadway Musicals. (Photo by Martha Swope)

satin suit with top hat. This book was in all the bookstore windows and was a big seller. Hey, that could be my Christmas present that year for all my family and friends. Done. Everyone loved it.

During this time there was also the opportunity to do two movies, both in New York. The first in 1979 was "Hair," directed by Academy Award-winning Milos Forman. My character was that of a concert singer who sang "An Old Fashioned Melody," dressed in a white tails outfit in Central Park. This little cameo was interesting on several levels. My "Johnny" song at the audition won me the role. Then the vocal prerecord was done right away, only to find that the video portion wouldn't be shot for about six months. The costume fitting put me in both the white tails and a black tails outfit. The first day of the shoot came with no rehearsals. This was not like a stage production when rehearsal was always possible. What would be required of me on screen? An assistant director finally materialized.

"Would it be possible to speak to Mr. Foreman before my camera time?" was my nervous query. He was found, introductions were made and he then told me in his charmingly-thick Czechoslovakian accent, "Ron, you are concert singer."

OK, that was doable. The tape of my audio had been listened to ad infinitum on the way out to the Long Island location. It's a good thing, because there were two sound technicians listening for the accuracy of my lip sync. The filming was a little complicated with the camera zooming down a trolley during my vocal. I had been ending the section with both arms flung open wide. On about the fourteenth take only one "heartfelt" arm was used.

"Cut, Cut. No Ron, use two arms. Two arms are so beautiful," was the extent of my direction from Milos Forman.

When the final cut came out the reason for the zooming camera was clear. Claude, the John Savage character, has just taken LSD for the first time and was hallucinating. At the premiere at the Ziegfeld Theater my face so filled that enormous screen that it pushed me back in my seat. I was big! An entire pier along the Hudson River had been transformed into Central Park for the party. Live the moment! I rented a limo and walked the red carpet into that premiere.

My second movie was the 1982 version of "Annie," with Albert Finney and Carol Burnett, directed by another Academy Award winner, John Huston, and produced by Joe Layton, my director in "GEORGE M!" As a dancer I was one of the butlers in Daddy Warbucks' estate who showed Annie her new home during "'I Think I'm Gonna Like It Here." During the number I helped set the dining room table by doing a cartwheel over the place setting and leaving silver in place. Then with another dancer, Terry Eno, I did a series of butterflies, an acrobatic trick, with a mop handle between us, down the length of the hall. That evening we watched the trailers and discovered that every time Terry was doing the trick with his legs in the air and his head below the mop handle, he was looking at the camera. We had to shoot the segment again the next day with those acrobatic tricks. Result, I threw my back out. There was no more strenuous dancing coming up, but it felt like it knocked me out of being asked to stay for another scene. Bummer.

The upshot of my only two movies is that residuals on their worldwide showings still arrive. It has dwindled to about $100 a year per movie. Hey, we don't knock that over twenty-five years later. My Hollywood career had a chance to expand when Cliff Robertson was casting for a sequel to his critically successful movie, "Charly." I read with him for a small role that would be in at least three or four scenes. Bret received the call that Cliff had decided on me for the part and we would start shooting on a certain day in Boston. Bingo! Hollywood, here I come. But not so fast. The day before the Boston shoot the call came that the movie had been canceled. It seems that Cliff had been involved in exposing a major studio fraud, and the way the good old boys network thanked him was to arrange to have the funding pulled for his movie. That turned out to be my last brush with the world of celluloid.

My modus operandi was in high gear during this time period. Don't get beaten down, always flip the coin over and try a new tack, keep exploring all possibilities and continue to be open to where your past endeavors will lead you.

Could another big show be on the horizon?

LESSONS LEARNED

- **Never Forget Your Roots**
- **Practice Fiscal Responsibility**
- **Keep Learning**

MY ONE AND ONLY

During my 33 years of working in the world of musical theater there were just a handful of real luminaries. Tommy Tune was one of those elite few. He has won a total of nine Tony Awards, so far, and is the only artist ever to win in four different categories: Best Director, Best Choreographer, Best Actor in a Musical and Best Featured Actor in a Musical. That record will probably never be duplicated. In case you don't know, Tommy is a tall drink of water. His actual height is 6'6", but when asked he always replies 5'18". He's probably just a little tired of being asked that question so often. The first time I met Tommy was at a party and immediately had to sit down. At 6'2" myself it was a little unnerving being around anyone taller than me. That soon passed. Tommy is delightfully quirky and an immense talent.

He called me one day after he had started rehearsals for his new show, "MY ONE AND ONLY." "Ronnie, would you come and audition for my stand-by in my new show? I think you would be just right and it would be a good job for you. There is a lot of tap in the show and some great Gershwin music."

"That would be great, Tommy. We have always wanted to work together. Maybe this is the show," was my excited reply.

He was co-choreographing with Thommie Walsh and was starring in the show opposite Twiggy, the iconic fashion model in the 1960's. The director was Peter Sellers, a rather avant-garde director from the world of opera. After auditioning for Peter the job of stand-by for both Tommy's role and the role of the villain, Prince Niki, was offered. The second one really wasn't right for me, but it could be done. Here was my dilemma. Alan Jay Lerner, the composer of "My Fair Lady," had written a new musical for Broadway, "Dance a Little Closer," for his wife and my friend from London, Liz Robertson. Recently he and Liz had seen one of my operetta concerts with Jack Lee and taken me out to dinner afterwards to convince me to take a supporting role in their new show.

It might have been his way of wooing me, but he told me. "You have one of the most beautiful voices I have ever heard." That coming from the famous Alan Jay Lerner stuck in my mind. (Wish I had had a tape recorder under the table at that dinner!)

The role in his show required that the actor ice skate. So ice skating lessons began. Then came the offer from Tommy. Which job to take? Bring out that "Pros and Cons" paper again and start writing. The result was that I took the stand-by job this time. Another lucky choice? Not really, not after doing the "Pros and Cons" paper. "Dance a Little Closer" closed shortly after it opened and "MY ONE AND ONLY" had an almost two-year run on Broadway and then an international tour.

One of the big "pros" was a chance to work with one of the gods of the tap dancing world, Charles "Honi" Coles. At one point he and Tommy had what turned out to be a show stopping number with the title song, "My One And Only." Rehearsals had been in progress for about a week already, so bring on that killer work ethic. I began to inhale everything about the show, learning steps and lines very quickly. This was a good thing. Midway into the Boston tryout Peter Sellers and the conductor, Craig Smith, were let go. Tommy took over as director and Jack Lee, my friend and operetta conductor, came in to replace Craig. The only way this new set up was going to work was for me to perform Tommy's role in most of the rehearsals and for Tommy to stay out front directing. Then before each preview performance, I would teach Tommy what had been done in the afternoon and be in the wings for his entrance and exits. At the first rehearsal after Tommy took over directing the show, I was going through the opening scene on stage with Roscoe Lee Brown. We came to a break and Roscoe took me aside, "Young man you are quite remarkable to do this with no rehearsal."

That was a good feeling, coming from someone who had such a lengthy résumé in film and stage. Later in the second act of that rehearsal it was the tap dance duet with Honi. The choreography was quite complicated and hadn't been completely learned by the dance captain, who was teaching me, but the first half of the routine was down pat.

When we came to a break Honi put his arm around me with, "Man, you've definitely got the chops for this." By the end of that day there was a feeling of being on cloud nine about this job.

Tommy allowed me to fill several slots during those weeks in Boston. One day the conductor had to be in another meeting when a rehearsal was taking place on stage. The pit pianist could not see the stage, so I served as the conductor to allow the pianist and performers to remain in sync. Then there was the time when Tommy and Twiggy had a separate rehearsal scheduled to learn their harmonies on "Little Jazz Bird." There was no rehearsal pianist available, so I played piano and taught them the number. I would also vocalize Tommy before each performance and give him some of the Paul Draper tap exercises to get his feet loosened up for the duet with Honi.

The biggest learning experience occurred when Mike Nichols came in to "doctor" the show. We had opened in Boston to less than stellar reviews and Mike was brought in, unofficially, to help. Tommy asked me to sit in on the brainstorming sessions with the two of them, Jack Lee and the book writers, Peter Stone and Timothy S. Mayer. This was like auditing a graduate class in professional theater. I took notes and would give Tommy a written synopsis of each session. That time in Boston utilized a lot of my skill sets. Remember, even the most distsnt lessons may become useful at some point.

When we came back to New York it was decided that the show was not in shape to open on Broadway. So we went back into rehearsals with a completely revamped book. There was a time when it was doubtful that we would even open. After a run-through of the new Act 1, the producers made the decision to proceed and an opening date was set. As we were frantically putting together the new Act 2, someone realized that contractually Honi was not going to be available for the first few previews. Before he had even signed his contract for this show, he had committed to dance with his group, "The Copacetics," on the West Coast. Tommy auditioned several older black tap dancers for Honi's role and no one could learn the Second Act routine fast enough. There were just a few days to go before our first preview.

The next day at rehearsal Tommy looked at me with a strange look in his eye, "Go home tonight and create a character. I want you to read for Mr.

Magix to go on for Honi while he is out."

"OK, but I don't want to audition with the rest of the company around," I cautioned.

"We can do it during the lunch break tomorrow," he said.

It seemed like a stab in the dark, but I did already know the tap steps in the "My One and Only" number. My thought was how to pull this off, not being 70 years old and definitely not black. At home that night the clothes came flying out of my closet. Let's put together some outfit that would give me a sense of being a version of that character. So the next day it was time for my "debut." The look that gave me the closest feel to the character was a black tuxedo with a white frilly shirt, a silver lame belt, red patent leather tap shoes, a cowboy hat with a feather headband and sunglasses. Yes, this was all from my closet. Don't ask.

Dressed in my costume I came in to read with Tommy just as Twiggy was leaving. She actually didn't know who that alien looking fellow was. After reading, Tommy said, "That's it. You're on."

What? Quickly, to wardrobe. Honi wore a black tails outfit with sequined lapels and a top hat. We needed a different look. There was a white suit Honi had worn in the "Cuban Ballet" that was cut after the Boston run. That works and it fit. We're about the same size. We'll keep the red tap shoes and sunglasses. Add a red tie, white gloves and a white fedora. Done!

But wait. Mike Nichols saw the final look, "Ron you have to put on a dark make-up." "I can't do that. It's against Equity's rules." He responded, "Just put it on."

I searched the theatrical makeup store and found Bob Kelly's "Suntan" makeup and put it on with a trowel. A thin penciled-in mustache completed the final look. Oh, one other thing. Mr. Magix started the duet with Tommy's character by snapping his fingers. That meant my right hand had to be made up, so that when I took my glove off to start the number everything would match.

We were ready for the first preview in New York at the St. James Theatre, which felt like home from my "Hello, Dolly" days. I'm sitting in a barber chair, waiting to be pushed on stage for my first entrance, wondering what the hell I was doing! There was one other ace up my sleeve. The past year I had been working on a psychological acting technique called Voice Dialogue with Anna Ivara. In that work you learn to find the "Voices," universal personalities that live hidden inside you. They are like all other people you can imagine though unexpressed in your personal life. As an actor you pick the "Voice" or sub-personality that most suits your character. This can give an added color to your work. (No pun intended). In this instance I found a sub-personality, which gave me that little extra something it took to make my character believable on stage. The audience bought me as Mr. Magix. Over the course of the two and a half years with the show I played the character about 80 times and was told that people in the audience thought that Mr. Magix was either black, Puerto Rican, Creole or Quadroon. That last designation came from Ann Rice, the author of "The Vampire Chronicles." The night she saw the show I was on for Honi and afterwards was introduced to her out of costume as the actor who had portrayed Mr. Magix. "Oh no, that man was a Quadroon," she declared, with her extensive knowledge of New Orleans culture. So, the joke backstage became that if it was a bit of an off night for me, which can happen to anyone, I was an "Octaroon," not a Quadroon.

Just a note about the Mr. Magix stand-by. During those first previews of my performing the role, a representative from Actor's Equity came to see what was going on and why a black performer had not been hired in this position. They were evidently satisfied that the producers had held the necessary auditions without finding someone to fill the bill and that I was not performing in "black-face." In my two and a half years with the show in that capacity there were never any complaints registered, that I knew about.

Back to the previews. Honi returned and wasn't quite up on his lines. So they had him watch me do the role for two nights. That was a little unnerving. Even with Honi's reputation in the dance world there had been a ten-year period when he couldn't get work as a dancer and had to take a job as manager of the Apollo Theater in Harlem. This was to be his big shot on Broadway. So just imagine what went through his mind, watching someone play his dream Broadway role and get a big audience reaction before he had the chance. He was thrown on a little too early and had a shaky first couple of performances. Backstage he was a little cool to me. Then he hit his stride. He got glowing reviews, won a Drama Desk Award and a Tony for Best Supporting Performance in a Musical.

Cut to one of the cast parties a couple of months into the run. Honi was sitting at a table by himself and when he saw me come in beckoned me over. "I saw you up there doing my part," he started. "Yes, sir." I replied. Pause. "And I thought 'that black motha-fucka is BAD!'" Well, from that moment on we became friends.

The Broadway opening was approaching. Previews were going well and the show was coming together. It was hard work for everyone. There was a little glitch. Tommy asked Michael Bennett to come in and look at the show and be a second "doctor." He was only there for a couple of performances and then was gone. What transpired behind those closed doors? Who knows? The result was that Michael didn't stay.

We were to open on a Sunday, and during the previous Friday night performance it was evident that Twiggy was having a little trouble vocally and that Tommy just sounded a little tired. I alerted Twiggy's understudy, Nana Visitor, that she might be on the next day. I came into the theater early on Saturday to rehearse with her, only to find out that we were both on for the matinee. The producers didn't want to take a chance by having their stars do two shows the day before the opening. We quickly had costume fittings and rehearsed tricky spots. My entrance was from a suspended position upstage center, as if flying in on a parachute. While hanging in that harness, there was the added pressure of hearing the audience groan when it was announced that both of the stars would be out. Then the overture started and we were on. It was like being shot out of a cannon. Later we were told that when some of the audience members walked up the aisles to get their tickets refunded the ushers tried to get them to stay, telling them how wonderful we were. The show went extremely well with just a couple of minor glitches. Nana and I couldn't believe that we had gotten through it. The next day my friend, Paul Phillips, called to tell me he had been in the audience for the matinee performance with Gwen Verdon. She had asked him to call specifically to tell Nana and me how much she had enjoyed our work. Wow! Gwen Verdon, the quintessential Broadway performer, liking us! (Dang, where was that tape recorder?)

There were two incidents with Honi over the next two and a half years that were treasures. "Waiting in the Wings" was a showcase for all the stand-bys and understudies on Broadway. When I was asked to appear on the show as Tommy's stand-by, Honi offered to introduce me on the show. My medley of songs from the show was very well received. That would have been enough, but along with Honi's introduction, a memorable night transpired. The second incident took place during the tour of the show. I was on for Tommy in Louisville, Kentucky for a week while he was on vacation. My folks drove up to see the show and brought friends. After the show they came backstage to meet Honi, his words to my Dad were "I sure like dancing with your boy." Does it get any better than that?

During the run on Broadway I continued to sing in the operetta concerts with Jack Lee. It worked out great because being in the same show our schedules matched. One of the shows we put together was on American operetta. Jack always chose material that was very right for each performer to sing. "Kismet" by Robert Wright and George (Chet) Forrest was on the program and my number was "Stranger in Paradise" from the score. The composers were friends of Jack and came to one of the performances.

After the show they came up to me, "We were just discussing at intermission how we wished you had been around to introduce each new song as we had written it," said either Bob or Chet, can't remember which. Can you imagine? (TAPE RECORDER!!!)

Working on music with Jack Lee was a unique experience. He had the ability to help a performer "lift the music off of the page." In other words, make the music your own by infusing it with your life's experience and point of view. It helped me bring my performing to the next level. A very telling incident occurred. One day in my coaching session, he stopped playing in the middle of a song and slammed down the lid on the keyboard. "Stop singing so pretty!" he yelled. It finally dawned on me what he had been trying to get through to me for all this time. When I didn't do the necessary work on a song to connect to my inner life and make it real, I would rely

139

on my sound to get me through. Many listeners wouldn't know the exact difference. Jack of course did and wouldn't let me get away with it. He has become a dear friend and years later I've told him that he is the only one who could ever have slammed a piano lid on me without my walking out of the session. I knew he had my best interests at heart and wasn't just having a diva moment. He was also capable of that as well, but not that time.

After the show had been running for a year Tommy and Honi were each going to take a week's vacation. It just so happened that they were back to back, which meant that I would be on for Tommy for a week and then step right into Honi's role. Our press representative at the time was the very creative and feisty Judy Jacksina. She was incredibly helpful in putting together a brochure for me advertising my two-week coup. It was a tri-fold leaflet with pictures of me in both roles and the dates of my performances. What made this feat unique was the diverse nature of the two roles. It showed that my skill levels as an actor/singer/dancer had zoomed up the charts to be able to pull this off. It was a sublime two weeks.

as
Captain Billy Buck Chandler
(January 10th - January 15th)

and as
Mr. Magix
(January 17th - January 25th)

The flyer that advertised my back-to-back weeks of going on for Tommy Tune and Honey Coles in "My One And Only." (Photos by Ken Duncan & Martha Swope)

Sometime during the second year management asked me to become co-dance captain with Niki Harris. This meant learning all the choreography and staging in the show, taking notes on the show and running clean up rehearsals. One of the reasons was that not being in the show every night I could be out front to keep tabs on the show. In any long running show certain "improvements" creep into the performances. Some are unconscious and some are planned. They had to be weeded out, and sometimes the guilty performers were not too willing to take the notes. That part of the job was not to my liking, but it had to be done.

It was also during the second year of our run that "A Chorus Line" became the longest running show on Broadway. To celebrate, Michael Bennett brought all of the dancers who had ever performed in any of the companies back to do one performance and an invited dress rehearsal. Since the Schubert Theater was just across the street from the St. James it was easy for me to participate. The gala was the theatrical event of the decade. Michael had outdone himself in devising ways to utilize all of us. The climax was the finale, "One," when he filled the stage and then had performers streaming down the aisles of the orchestra and both balconies. The roar from that audience was unlike anything that had ever been heard in the Shubert Theater. Then after the show Shubert Alley, the block long space between 44th Street and 45th Street, had been tented over for the party. We each got one ticket to the performance. I gave mine to Bret, who was so overcome that he couldn't even stay for the party, but just had to go home to rehash the whole event.

Tommy had been asked to be the headline performer at the Latin Quarter nightclub on New Year's Eve that year and asked me to assist him with the production. Lillian Montevechi, fresh from her Tony Award-winning performance in "Nine," was on the show with him. She would come back into my life a little later. It never ceases to amaze me how small the "show biz" world really is. The best part of that whole evening was getting to spend time with Tommy's mother, Eva, and his sister, Gracey. They both loved to dance. I would just alternate whirling them out on the dance floor after Tommy's show. Even though Gracey lives in Ft. Worth, Texas, she has remained one of my close friends.

Close friends fill my life. Here is the place for me to talk about my relationships and lack thereof. For whatever reasons, I don't seem to be capable of a real one-on-one intimate relationship. However, I am able to maintain deep lasting friendships. Pollyanna rules once again. Is my glass half full or half empty? It is definitely half full! I treasure my close friends like precious jewels. Some of them I don't see on a regular basis, but I know they are there. When I do see them it is just like bringing a jewel out into the light. They bring such a sparkle into my life.

During my vacation in 1983 I was asked to participate in the Roy Clark Celebrity Golf Tournament in Tulsa, with just enough visibility to make it as a minor celeb. This was the first of two years that I was invited. The format was a scramble, where you have a five-man team and you play the best ball on each shot. That tee shot on the first hole was more nerve wracking for me than any time on stage performing for thousands of people. The second year my team placed 7th, out of about 50 teams, and we each won a chaise lounge chair. That was the only time to ever win anything in a sporting competition. Should have had it bronzed, but instead gave it to my folks for them to use on the porch of their home on the lake.

One night when I was on for Tommy, Twiggy slipped in the water dance and fell flat. I could tell her foot or ankle had been hurt, so I just scooped her up in my arms and carried her crying off stage. It felt a little like something out of an old Tarzan movie. It was just unthinking. She fell. She needed help. Me Tarzan, you Jane.

When Tommy and Twiggy left the show Sandy Duncan and her husband, Don Correia, replaced them. So rehearsals were a little like old home week and great fun. Tommy was just out for a few months before he and Sandy would go out with us in the international company. At first it was a disappointment that I was not allowed to take over Tommy's role after all the accolades I had received for performing the part. However, reality is reality. Don had starred in "Singing in the Rain" on Broadway and by being married to Sandy brought an added element for advertising the show. The object is to have someone in the starring role who would sell tickets. Don could. I couldn't. I jumped in to help him learn the role in rehearsals.

Georgia Engel had also come into the Broadway company as Mickey the Mechanic and as the understudy to Edith Herbert, the Twiggy role. She had played Minnie Faye in "Hello, Dolly" with Phyllis and Ethel in the 1970 production with me. Our understudy rehearsals became like a reunion with another dear friend. This would pay off later when we would star in two companies of "MY ONE AND ONLY." Georgia was an alumna of the Washington Ballet and had a close relationship with Mary Day, the director of the company. Because of this and her national reputation from the "Mary Tyler Moore" show, she had been asked to perform for a benefit at the Kennedy Center. Jack Lee was going to be her musical director and she asked me to stage it for her. It was a wonderful number by Hugh Martin, "I'm the First Girl," and was suited to Georgia's delicate comedic touch. When we were in DC rehearsing the show she got a little uptight, thinking she might be out of place. The bulk of the show was made up of stars from the ballet world. She was the only comedy in the entire evening. I tried to reassure her that with a whole evening of just serious dance the audience would be dying for a little fun. She just didn't seem convinced. It wasn't until she brought the house down with laughter and applause that she believed me.

Now we started the tour of "My One and Only." Touring had always been fun for me, seeing new places and exploring the unique areas each one had to offer. Also, with my large network of friends, many times I would stay with someone while in a particular city. This led to accusations from fellow cast members of being cheap, by not having to pay for hotels in the various cities. That wasn't the case in Japan.

The five weeks spent there were an incredible experience. The Japanese producers had booked our show into a different theater every week, which meant that it was a killer schedule for our crew, moving the set into a new theater for each new venue. For the cast it meant a couple of days off to visit the sights. Don Amendolia, who played Prince Niki in the show, was my fellow explorer. We took full advantage of that time off, visiting as many of the wonders of Japan as we could. One of those planned trips also included Sandy and Jack Lee. We stayed in a famous Japanese ryokan (inn), Tawaraya. We arrived, took our shoes off in the hall and were taken to our rooms. By the time we got there our bags had already been delivered and a hot bath had been drawn. It is the custom in Japan to soap up and wash on a little stool by the side of the bathtub, rinse off and then get into the tub to soak and relax. Don and I knew this. Sandy and Jack didn't. They soaped up in the tub. Oh, those embarrassing "gaijin." We had arranged for a private room for dinner and all came down in our yukatas, the Japanese robes that had been provided by the inn. We all sat on the floor with little individual tables to lean on and our own brassieres to cook the famous Kobi beef to taste. After a little saki Sandy gave us an interpretive dance, much to our delight and the bemusement of the two women who were serving our dinner. A little more sake and we all retired to Sandy's room to play Trivial Pursuit that Jack had brought along. We might have been a little rowdy for the staid atmosphere of the inn, but we had a good time. Now comes the really fun part. Don's room was fairly close to Sandy's, but Jack and I had rooms upstairs. There were no lights on, but we had one little flashlight. For some reason at night the staff repositioned the shogi screens and we couldn't find the stairs. So here you have these two slightly tipsy men in long robes, Jack being a little short and me, the taller one, stumbling around trying to get to our rooms. It probably had the look of Mutt and Jeff in a Laurel and Hardy movie. After much giggling and "Ssh, everyone's asleep!" we found our rooms. The hospitality of the ryokan extended through our departure with the entire staff standing on the street and waving *sayonara* to us until our car was out of sight.

Back at our hotel in Tokyo, who should get on the elevator but Hulk Hogan, the professional wrestler. I couldn't sit down in the elevator, so I just sort of shrank up in the corner. If that wasn't enough, at the desk the next morning the even more gargantuan Andre the Giant showed up. They were in Tokyo for a wrestling show. Boy, were those guys big!

Higashi Hoganji, the Buddhist Temple in Kyoto, Japan, where I felt so at home.

On one side trip we had taken the bullet train from Tokyo to Kyoto just for the day. Very close to the train station in Kyoto was one of the stops on our list of "things to see." This was Higashi Honganji, a famous Buddhist temple. Shoes were left at the door as we entered. We were then allowed a brief tour before being taken into the main part of the temple. As we knelt down in the vast expanse, the most unusual feeling came over me that this was a familiar place. The longer we stayed, the stronger the feeling be-

144

came. After a few minutes Don said, "Come on, let's go." "I can't just yet, give me a minute." This was something never experienced before in my life. What did it mean? There was no logical explanation. Had I been there in a previous life? Was it the oneness in my inner life that I had been longing for in my own spiritual journey? It was simply overwhelming at that moment. As we left, it was with a sublime feeling of calmness that remained with me for some time. An explanation never materialized for me. It simply reinforced my acceptance that there is some force in the universe that is bigger than this small infinitesimal "dot" called Ron. Yet, by the sparest Herculean unseen thread, I am as one with that force. That moment was worth my entire time in Japan.

But there were still more memorable situations to come. Anyone at 6'2" stands out in a crowd in Japan, especially at some of the tourist attractions. There would be groups of school children that would just throng around me looking up with these smiling faces. It would become an expected occurrence when we were sightseeing.

Standing out in a crowd of school children in Japan.

Another incident occurred at the health club where I had signed up for a massage. The ritual is to undress, put on a robe and meet your therapist in a communal room with many tables. You bow to each other and then get on the table. My therapist did not speak English and my Japanese was practically non-existent. I had given up after asking for a glass of water in a restaurant, only to be brought the check. Now, the massage was going well until she indicated for me to sit up. She then crawled up on the table, put one knee in the middle of my back and was attempting to roll my shoulders with both her hands. My shoulders were evidently more than a little tight, because suddenly her hands slipped off and she fell off the table. There was a hush as all other massage activity stopped. Then after ascertaining she wasn't hurt, there was much giggling with hands covering mouths throughout the room, everyone greatly relieved that an international incident had been narrowly averted.

A unique quality of the audiences in Japan was silence during the show, no laughs and very little applause. It was at the end of the show that they let loose. The first night Tommy and Sandy had taken prolonged applause on stage, gone back to their dressing rooms and then had to come back on-stage to acknowledge the continuing applause. The show was a big hit in each theater. The Japanese hospitality extended to the airport when we left. Many of the crew that had been with us for the five-week run came to see us off and say a tearful *sayonara* as we returned to the states.

In my Japanese garb for the opening night party in Los Angeles.

Our first stop back in the states was LA. At the opening night party I decided to wear some of my finery from Japan. It included a black kimono with a gold samurai jacket. These were worn over black pants and wooden getas (Japanese platform sandals). Then the hairdresser for the show tied a little topknot of hair on my head. It was a striking ensemble. Several people commented and gave me looks, but finally Margot Kidder, from "Superman" movie fame, came up and said, "Who are you?"

It would take several more years for me to grow out of my prolonged costume period. There had even been a time back in the seventies when a black English bobby's cape became my winter coat. That, coupled with a black wide brimmed hat would bring comments of "Hey, Zorro!" on the street.

Sandy was scheduled to leave during the LA run and Lucie Arnaz was going to replace her. That meant I would be teaching Lucie a lot of the show. There was one number that required belly dancing and finger cymbals for her character. We were rehearsing this number one day when she stopped and said, "I just hate it. You look better than I do!" During some of the rehearsals her mother, Lucille Ball, would sit in the back of the theater to watch.

Later, after Lucie had opened, I was on for Honi and her mother came to see the show. She asked to meet me after the performance and had very nice things to say. Cut to our run in San Francisco. She came to see the show and I just happened to be on for Honi. Afterwards she asked to see me again and greeted me with "I was telling the driver on the way here, that I hoped you were going to be on tonight." (Oh, that tape recorder was just never handy!)

We happened to be spending Halloween in San Francisco and Lucie and Tommy gave a big party for the cast. Aha! A chance for another costume! At a costume house I found a white Indian loincloth and a floor length feather headdress. That night both Tommy and Honi were on, so during the last half of the show I started applying body make-up and was in full war paint in time for the party. Would this prolonged exhibitionistic period ever come to an end? Maybe it was going to be a prolonged lime-light love affair. Oh, please. NO!

In full war paint and headdress with Lucie Arnaz at our Halloween party in San Francisco. (Photo by Kevin's Photograph Service)

My intrepid fellow traveler from the show, Don Amendolia, and I decided that we just had to try a hot air balloon ride while we were in San Francisco, near Napa Valley. The flights were at dawn. So on our day off we found a bed and breakfast close to the balloon site and went up the night before to be up bright and early for the ride. The basket we were to ride in was a fairly confined space for ten people. We took off and the pilot started his instructions, "Keep your hands and feet inside the basket, don't lean out and above all else... (just then he gave a long blast of the gas that inflates the balloon to take it higher and completely drowned out the rest of his instructions.)...Did you get that?" It was of course his standard spiel, but it had the desired effect of putting us "newbies" just a little on edge. The flight itself was memorable, being several hundred feet above the ground and moving along with no sound, other than the occasional gas blast. How the support people and the pilot could coordinate where we would land was amazing to me, but they pulled it off. Each passenger received a certificate and we all had champagne. What a way to start the day!

New Orleans was a highlight on the tour. Through a friend of a friend (networking is a wonderful thing!) an apartment was available on the corner of Jackson Square, across the street from the Café du Monde, for the entire eight days. It was on the second floor with a wrought iron balcony overlooking the square. What a joy to get up in the morning, sit out on the balcony and watch the square come to life. Of course I had to have some beignets from Café du Monde. Beignets are those powdered sugar confections that just melt in your mouth. Unfortunately, coffee didn't appeal to me at the time, so the full experience of beignets with coffee wasn't enjoyed. The week could have been spent in a hotel with the rest of the cast, but for a little more money New Orleans became a hands-on experience. This was another time when I said, "Go for it!" I happened to be on for Honi for one of the matinees that week when Eva, Tommy's Mother, came to visit. She came rushing backstage after the show with "At last I got to see my two boys dance together!" She was a special lady.

This show continued to be an important part of my life. The summer after touring with the international company, I was asked to star in a production

of the show with Georgia Engel at Kansas City Starlight Theater. As stand-bys in the New York production we both knew the roles. It was a good thing because there was only a one-week rehearsal period.

Georgia Engel and I in "He Loves and She Loves" from "My One And Only" in the production in Kansas City. (Photograph courtesy of Kansas City Starlight Theatre)

This was the place where, exactly 25 years ago, I had earned my Equity card in my first summer stock job. Can you imagine I was now coming back to star in a production? It was memorable. First it was a very good production that even included fireworks on the hill behind the stage during the finale. My folks got a little theater party together of about seventy-five friends to come up to see the show from Oklahoma, including all my family. The night they attended the show I threw a big catered party for the cast, the crew and all my friends and family from Oklahoma. I even hired a pianist for the evening and asked him to play "S'wonderful" when Georgia and I made our entrance. Let's just call it a magical evening, made even more so by my father. He had always made it very clear that he was proud of me, but that night he said words I had been longing to hear for many years, "Son, you were really good tonight."

Remember, life is not a rehearsal. You only get one shot at making memorable moments. Take it!

Later that fall we starred in a production of the show at the Claridge Hotel in Atlantic City. Mr. Magix was to be played by another icon in the tap dance world, Bunny Briggs. It was my suggestion to the producer that someone start teaching the big tap number to Bunny early, because it was a little complicated. Did anyone listen to me? No. So by opening night Bunny still hadn't learned it completely. Since he was the teacher in our big number and I was the student, I assured him that if he went up on the steps I would just follow whatever he did. It worked and he eventually learned the routine and was just a charmer in the role.

The Claridge Hotel always had a billboard to advertise the current show on the highway coming into Atlantic City. Bret had negotiated that my name was to appear on any advertisement where Georgia was featured. Well, my name would never appear on a highway billboard again. Had to get a picture of that!

During the run it was my routine to always stop by Bunny's dressing room before the show, to pay my respects and see how he was doing. One night I found out his anniversary was in the near future. On the big day, Bunny and his wife, Olivette, were my guests to celebrate. At the brunch they said something that stunned me. "We were afraid you were going to have Bunny fired because he couldn't learn the number by opening night."

The billboard outside Atlantic City announcing "My One And Only."

"What?" I was in disbelief. "You're Bunny Briggs, one of the Gods of the tap dancing world! That never crossed my mind for one second." We remained friends and later when Bunny was on Broadway in "Black and Blue" I went backstage after seeing the show. He immediately took me down the hall to meet Jimmy Slyde, another biggie in the tap dance world. "Jimmy, you've got to check out this guy's feet!" he said as he started me into the routine from "My One and Only." Jimmy seemed impressed, but he was possibly just being polite.

About this time there was another show at the Ford's Theatre in DC where Tommy and Sandy were invited to perform for President Reagan. They had asked Tad Tadlock to stage the number and for me to assist her. Tad and I had worked together on several Oldsmobile industrial shows and two Miss USA pageants. (Those two Miss USA pageants could take up a whole chapter, but I digress.) Tommy and Sandy sparkled in the number and were an audience favorite. Backstage was a trip with all the secret service detail present and an ambulance right outside. After all, it was the Ford's Theatre, you know. Remember what happened to Lincoln? Thank goodness it wasn't needed that night.

My entire time with "My One And Only" was one of the most rewarding, both professionally and financially, of my career thus far. Thank you, Tommy! It was during this time that a vast range of my skill sets came into play. Many aspects of my gifts and talents that had been honed earlier were utilized. Pursue those interests! Learn new skills! You never know when they might come in handy and propel you to new heights.

With continued expansion in my life could I also be a Director and Choreographer?

LESSONS LEARNED

- Capitalize on Your Unique Skill-set
- Jump in "Where Angels Fear to Tread"
- See the World

LET'S TRY DIRECTING AND CHOREOGRAPHING

Branching out into choreographing and directing was beginning to happen. My first show doing both was "GEORGE M!" at the Fireside Theater in Wisconsin. Having been through so many auditions as a performer, I was determined to make every audition as painless as possible, treating everyone with the respect they were due. The preproduction work was behind me, and opening day of rehearsals arrived. In the opening scene every actor was in place in the opening tableau, the action unfolded and they each performed what they had been given to do. It was a magical moment for me. I can do this! The show was very successful for the theater, so much that the producer would ask me to stage "Funny Girl" for them at their sister theater in Ohio.

About this time, Tommy Tune was developing a club act with the Manhattan Rhythm Kings, a very talented trio of musician/singer/dancers.

He approached me, "Ronnie, would you like to choreograph a couple of numbers for me and the Kings for our new act?"

"You bet. When do we start?"

This was challenging and exciting work. One of the numbers for Tommy, "I'm building Up To An Awful Letdown," was staged using a standing microphone as a dance partner. It was a very Fred Astaire take on the use of props in a dance number. It turned out to be an eye-catching routine and Tommy did it beautifully for that first gig in Atlantic City. He kept it in for several incarnations of his show. The Kings were quite competent tappers as well, so choreographing for all four of them was a pleasure, especially in their film noir spoof, "Shanghai Lil."

Tommy had directed and choreographed "Stepping Out" on Broadway in 1987. This was a delightful import from England in which ordinary people come to a church basement once a week for a tap class. The class was all women except for one shy man, played by Don Amendolia, my inveterate sight-seer from "My One and Only" days in Japan. This was a real crowd-pleasing show, topped by the cast performing a dynamite number for the finale.

The Little Theater in Greenville, South Carolina called and asked me to direct and choreograph a production of "Stepping Out" for them. Tommy allowed me to use some of the original choreography, which I adapted for the local performers, and then I created the rest. In a community theater situation you can't always find actors who are perfect for each role. Concessions have to be made. Once again this proved to be an audience favorite and Greenville would ask me to return for another show. Of course I went back. The people were wonderful to work with and I loved the unlimited refill of your ice tea glass in all the restaurants.

My next assignment was mounting "My One and Only" for the Dutch Apple Dinner Theater in Pennsylvania. This proved to be a challenge. My rehearsal space for a tap show was carpeted! We did it. Don't ask me how. An interesting side note here. One of my male dancers had to drop out just as rehearsals were starting. On the phone that night Kay McLean, a friend from high school, told me that her son, Lance, had just completed a stint in Busch Gardens, Virginia, and was now free and looking for work.

"Put him on the phone," I said. "Can you dance?" was my first question. "Some," was his response. "Can you tap?" was next. "A little," he replied tentatively. "Get here as soon as you can!" And he was hired.

When Lance arrived he was a little behind the other dancers, but we worked outside of the regular rehearsals until he caught up. Remember, no one in the audience knows, or cares, who learned it first. Opening night Lance's parents, Kay and Angus, were sitting very proudly with me in the audience: a Kodak moment. That young man has gone on to become a nuclear physicist. Not bad for a little old tap dancer from North Carolina.

For several years running Gracey Tune had asked me to be the guest artist to celebrate National Tap Day on May 25th with her dance company in Ft. Worth, Texas. This was always a very fulfilling time performing with her and teaching classes. After a couple of years the "real reason" surfaced for which she kept asking me back: I was the only one tall enough to clean the ceiling fans in the dance studio, and they definitely needed a good cleaning once a year.

One evening over a margarita at Joe T. Garcia's Mexican Restaurant Gracey and I delved into the subject of "dreams." One of us wondered how we could introduce tap around the world. Maybe this was after two margaritas. Well, why not just tap around the world? That night the idea of "Tap Ambassadors" was born. Over the next few months we kept developing this concept, with a brochure and short video. We had the idea of presenting the history of tap, with each of us speaking about and demonstrating the different styles. Wardrobe was even thought out and purchased. The problem arose, as it so often does with a new idea, about how do we get this lecture/show/demonstration booked? Since neither of us was a "name" this was going to be a major problem. Some contacts were made. Dead ends. With the two of us living in Ft. Worth and New York, and with unique schedules and responsibilities, our enthusiasm waned and we simply let the idea fizzle out. It was still a heartfelt dream for us whose time just did not materialize.

It was during this time that my father had a serious car accident. He was driving home from working at Shangri-la and didn't stop for a stop sign close to his home. He was broadsided on the driver's side by an oncoming vehicle. He was clearly at fault, running the stop sign, and should probably not have been driving. He ended up with a broken hip and a frozen shoulder that would transform him into an invalid for the rest of his life. It was here that my mom, LaVon, showed her true colors. She became an angel of mercy in caring for him, rarely leaving his side. She was a constant caregiver, and by so doing enabled me to keep my career going.

Work was continuing to expand and my reputation as a choreographer who could work with actors was developing. Austin Pendleton was directing Michael Weller's "Spoils of War," and called me to stage a dance sequence for Kate Nelligan. It was to be off–Broadway at the Second Stage Theatre. Kate Nelligan was already an established screen actress and you could see why. She had a mesmerizing presence on stage. She took my steps and direction and soaked them up like a sponge. Her little dance turn in the show definitely added a zing to her performance. Also, in that first cast was Annette Benning who went on to become, well, you know. The reviews were so good that it was decided to move it to Broadway after an ou-of-town run at my old stomping ground, The Royal Alexandra Theatre in Toronto. After the tune up time there we moved to the Music Box Theatre on Broadway. Working with actors who moved well but were not trained dancers was definitely a plus. Once they were able to get over trying to do the steps correctly, they could infuse the movement with a deeper meaning from the particular point of view of their character. It was that first step of getting over trying to do the steps perfectly that was the difficult part. Once that was accomplished it was smooth sailing. The whole experience with "Spoils of War" was very fulfilling.

Don Amendolia and I in a rehearsal shot for "Stepping Out" at the Pasadena Playhouse in California. This is one of my favorite pictures. (Photograph by Craig Schwartz)

"Stepping Out" resurfaced. Don Amendolia had been asked to direct and be in the show at the Pasadena Playhouse in California. He asked me to choreograph. This was a step up to a bigger theater for me and the cast was quite extraordinary. Tommy allowed me to use some of his choreography, giving him credit in the playbill and once again adaptations were made for the individual performers. It was a love-in working with Don and there was a publicity photo taken that makes that quite evident.

During the rehearsal period my housing was in a near-by apartment complex. At about 5:00 AM one morning I woke up thinking, "Oh that damn subway is making the building shake." Wait, I was in California! There were no subways in Pasadena. It was an earthquake! Yes, it was a small tremor, but very unnerving for someone who had never been in one before. I survived. After that, the show opened to mostly good reviews with my winning a Dramalogue Award for best Choreography that year.

The summer of 1988 Susan Schulman, the director of "My One and Only" in Kansas City was going to direct "42nd Street" at Artpark, a large outdoor venue in upstate New York. The role of Billy Lawler required a tenor who could tap dance. Hey, do you think that role would be a possibility for me? It was back to being a performer for a while. The cast was very strong for a summer stock production, with Karen Ziemba reprising her Broadway role of Peggy Sawyer. Randy Skinner, one of Gower's original assistants on the Broadway production, was recreating the choreography. In the big tap ballet at the end of the show Karen and I teamed up very well and had a blast. Cast members would sometimes be in the wings just to watch the number. In later years when I would go backstage to see Karen after seeing

With Karen Ziemba in the "tap ballet" from "42nd St" at the Art Park Theater in upstate New York. Photographer unknown.

her in one of her Broadway hits, she would bring up what fun we had tapping that "ballet" in "42nd Street."

What else could increase my chances of employment with a 25-year resumé in the business? How about a one-man show? That might take some work. You have no idea how much work it finally did entail. Sheila Smith, Angela's original stand-by in "MAME" and my cohort from industrial shows, was also a writer. Together we came up with a concept of doing a history of the leading man in musical theater. Dennis Buck, my vocal coach at the time, agreed to be my musical director. We had a performer, a writer and a musical director. Now all we needed was a show. That was going to take a little longer.

After much research we started with the operetta period and progressed through a Jerome Kern medley and a Ray Bolger number, "The Old Soft Show." Somehow we unearthed a videotape of his performing this number on TV that enabled me to recreate the original dance. Then it was on to "I've Grown Accustomed to Her Face" from "My Fair Lady," "Trouble in River City" from "The Music Man" and ending Act 1 with a "GEORGE

NINETY YEARS OF THE BROADWAY MUSIC MAN

RON YOUNG

In Residence

| Bret Adams Limited | 448 West 44th Street | (212) 765-5630 |
| Artist's Agency | New York, NY 10036 | (212) 265-2212 FAX |

The cover of my advertising flyer for "In The Limelight."

M!" segment. That act was first performed in 1989 at the Southwest Theater Conference in Oklahoma City with Dennis at the piano. It must have gone well. The Conference awarded me a plaque with the designation, "Oklahoma's Favorite Son" for that year. The second act was more complicated with a puppet section, audience participation, a Stephen Sondheim medley, a pre-recorded section, "Music of the Night" from "Phantom of the Opera" and the closing "My One and Only" medley.

This ambitious program meant learning some new skills. So, a concertina was purchased and conquered to play the opening for the puppet section. Puppets? A friend of a friend made puppets for a puppet company, Pegasus. Who knew? Networking is a wonderful thing! Not being a puppeteer by training, it was again a "learn by the seat of your pants" endeavor. Margaurite, one of my puppets, had a permanent fan in one hand. When the puppets were talking or singing, a little scheme was devised where her fan was in front of my mouth. After all, I wasn't a ventriloquist. The skill to throw my voice and disguise where it was coming from couldn't be learned at that point in my life. Certain limitations had to be recognized. So, let's use the fan. When it came to the end of the number with three of us singing, the two harmonies were prerecorded. It was a nice effect for the audience to suddenly hear three voices.

When it was ascertained that Dennis would not be available to accompany me each time I might be booked, we worked very hard on prerecording the piano. It was especially tricky to be as "in the moment" as possible. Stuart Allyn, a wonderful sound engineer who was by now married to my friend, Carole Demas, worked tirelessly with Dennis and me to get the sound track in working order. Sheila wrote a script that was warm, instructive and laced with humor. The title was "In the Limelight: Ninety Years of the Broadway Music Man." The show was a bit of a tour de force and it was a challenge to pull it off. In fact, it took much more effort than you can imagine. Here was this one-man band who had to gather the props, get the puppet screen made, type the script and mark all the lighting and sound cues, bring the audio tape and teach the technicians how it worked each time. When it was show time my wardrobe had to be set out and checked - a costume for each act. Then the props had to be preset, the sound and lighting checked out, and the time set aside for me to warm up for the performance. Oh, by the way, I still didn't drink coffee.

A performance shot taken during the "My One and Only" number from "In The Limelight." Photographer unknown.

The first booking was a six-week session at The University of Texas Pan American in Edinburg, Texas. I was to teach classes, direct the students in "Stepping Out" and open the season with my show. It just so happened that the only night the video department was available to videotape my show was on opening night. This would be my very first time going through the entire show with an audience. Well, at least it's preserved, even if there was a fly buzzing around my face for one number. It played for four performances and the audiences built each night as the word got around. Several students came every night.

The work with the students was very fulfilling. We had a tap class every morning for the cast of "Stepping Out," but any of the students were welcome. On opening night of the show the cast gave me an engraved watch. One of the professors even wrote me, extolling my work for the summer session and stating how well I fit in and adapted to the academic setting.

One of the reasons this gig at a university was possible had to do with my three college degrees. To teach at a university level it was important to have at least a Master's Degree. This was one of three different stints at universities. Earlier there had been a booking at the University of Georgia with just the First Act and a question and answer period. All that dedicated hard work in college was worth it. A word to the wise, stay in school and get that education. The world will always be out there for you to conquer and you never know when the degrees will come in handy.

"In the Limelight" was presented in other venues across the country. The first time was at a fundraiser for the Circle Theatre in Ft. Worth, Texas. Next, Gracey Tune invited me to perform the show at her studio for a fundraiser for the Eva Tune Tap Scholarship Fund. Then Michael Hurdle, the nephew of my college mentor, presented the show for three performances at a theater in Richmond, Virginia. This was very exciting, but disappointing as well. My name was not a big draw and tickets did not fly off the shelf. After all the work that was put into creating this show, it became an impossibility to book it anywhere. Unless you're a known name to the public and they are interested in seeing you, it really doesn't matter how talented you are. Reality had spoken, loud and clear.

Soon after, an opportunity came at the University of Santa Fe. Donna McKechnie called, "I have a schedule conflict and have to bow out of directing and choreographing a production of "On the Town" at the University of Santa Fe. Could I recommend you? Would you be interested in doing the job?"

"Do you think I could do it? It is a very complex show," I hesitated.

"I think you could and it would be a great experience for you," she replied.

Jump in! Take a chance! Thank you, Donna. The University of Santa Fe had a unique set-up. The drama department, the dance department and the music department worked very closely together. Often in a divided system there is an on-going sense of competition among departments that leads to a lack of cooperation. Not so here. This was a complicated show and that cooperation was vital. It also allowed me to be involved in all aspects of the production, in addition to directing and choreographing. The auditions seemed to be a little different for the students because of all the encouragement given each one during the process.

Here is an observation about theater on a college level or a community theater level. Occasionally, there will be a director or teacher who puts down the students and amateur performers with caustic comments, for whatever reasons. That was not in my arsenal of techniques. In fact one of my actors in Greenville told me that after working with me in two shows he would never allow anyone to verbally abuse him again, because he saw how the work could be done in a positive way.

My housing in Santa Fe was a few miles outside of town and it was wintertime. So, waking up to the beautiful sight of snow-capped hillsides was a pleasure every morning. On opening night my cousins, Mary Ann and Jack Yonke, and a friend from college, Charlotte Heth, were all in Santa Fe and attended. It is always an added treat to share these experiences with friends and family.

That second show at the Greenville Little Theater was "42nd Street." It was a big production for a community theater. Here again, directing and choreographing were just the beginning of my tasks. Helping design the sets, select the wardrobe and coach the new musical conductor were now part of my job description. With the increased scope of my job it was vital to have an assistant that could really function in this situation. B. J. Koonce was a jewel. B. J. was extremely active in the Greenville Theater scene, becoming the Executive Director of the Centre Stage Company. A few months later her husband, Don, would hire me to return to Greenville for a big industrial show for his company. There was a feeling of pulling together on "42nd Street" that was quite extraordinary. It seemed that my being so prepared to lead, so involved in every aspect of the production and so approachable made everyone want to work harder. Also, humor never left me. If anyone ever had a little snit during rehearsal, they invariably received my three little words, "Get over it." It usually worked like a charm. It was also necessary to laugh at myself at times.

"I Do! I Do!" was being done at the Dallas Summer Musical, starring Sandy Duncan and James Naughton. Don Amendolia had been asked to direct, Jack Lee to conduct and me to stage the musical numbers. It was like old home week again. As the standby for James as well, the producers got me as a "two for the price of one" deal. In addition, Sheila Smith gave me a quick lesson on playing the violin. In one number Sandy had to play the violin and James the tenor saxophone. Now you had this choreographer/stand-by who was a band instructor. See, you just never know when all the little skills that you have accumulated over the years will be used. Be a sponge. Learn everything. It also brought in another member of our little family. Connie Coit, who had sung in Jack's operetta group with me, was now living in Dallas and stood by for Sandy. This little familial production was a knockout.

Performing was co-mingling with directing and choreographing by this time. Jack, Connie and I were asked to do a cruise to Alaska. We were to be, as in my last cruise, the culture on board. We put together some of the songs we had used in our concerts and took off. Jack would accompany us and join in the singing at times. It was an adventure. One morning I woke up, looked out the porthole and saw blue icebergs! What?

Call Jack in his room, "Jack, look out your window. There are blue icebergs. Did we have too much to drink last night?" It turned out that it wasn't really ice. These icebergs had "calved" off of the glaciers, and being made of compacted snow, had that blue color in the water.

During our free time on the cruise an on-going gin rummy game was started between Jack and me. One of us ended up owing the other one hundreds of dollars. Did anyone ever collect? Not in this lifetime. Stopping in all the ports and seeing the glaciers along the way made for another magical time.

After returning from the cruise, along came "Wizard of Oz." First it was the role of The Tin Man in the production at Civic Light Opera in Pittsburg, starring Cathy Rigby, the Olympic gymnast. Don't ever play the role of the Tin Man role with a long technical rehearsal. You can't sit or bend over in the costume. It is excruciating. The good part was a photograph taken between scenes with Christmas ornaments draped over me. Yes, another Christmas card had materialized for that year.

Later the Scarecrow was added to my cast of characters. This was for a production at Theater Under the Stars in Houston, and we turned out to be a feisty cast. Phil McKinley directed, and being the good old boy that he was, set the tone. We had way too much fun. One time when he had to go

My Tin Man Christmas card.

Playing the Scarecrow in "The Wizard of Oz." (Photograph by Susie Works, Property of Theatre Under the Stars, Houston, Texas)

back to New York, we got into his room, short-sheeted the bed, hid his stuff and put saran wrap over the top of the toilet bowl. He got us all back when he returned. When we were all on stage, he got into our rooms and wreaked havoc. Jeanne Lehman played Glinda, the Good Witch, in both productions. She had the quintessential cascading soprano laugh. It was perfect for her role. Toni DiBuono was the Wicked Witch of the West. Her significant other at the time played way too much golf for her taste and she hated it. Hmm, let's make hay with this one. So golf tees started appearing in her props and dressing room for her to discover at inopportune times. Who could have done that? She and Jeannie got me back. As Auntie Em in the beginning of the show, Jeannie had to serve the farm hands, played by the Scarecrow, Tin Man & Cowardly Lion, some cookies. One night the cookie that I had to take had this golf tee sticking out underneath. I had to eat it without letting the audience know anything was different. The last laugh had to be mine, although it was impossible to know. I snuck into Toni's dressing room and worked a tee into the bottom of her large jar of face powder. It would take her forever to use enough powder to get down to that level. Did she ever find it? I never heard. By the way, I was just never able to gain enough weight to play the Cowardly Lion to round out my "Ozian Trilogy."

During a performance of "Cabaret" as the EmCee. (Photograph by the late Richard C. Hallinan, Downtown Cabaret Theatre)

What show is about 180 degrees from "Wizard of Oz?" How about "Cabaret?" The role of the Emcee proved to be qjuite a stretch for me. The Downtown Cabaret Theatre in Bridgeport, CT, surprisingly hired me. Usually a shorter actor plays this role. Joel Grey was the original Emcee on both Broadway and in the movie version. My white make-up actually morphed into a death mask by the end of the show. My accordion was also used for an eerie effect during one scene. There was one number where the Emcee was discovered dancing in the girls' chorus line. This could always work with a shorter actor. Put this 6'2" guy in heels, a blond wig and a Nazi helmet and there was no way to hide me in the chorus line. The girls came out and did a few steps, then here came this creature charging out of a beaded curtain with a high kick. Now this had to be a sight. I was also dressed in a black lace corset with black fishnet stockings. I was told that it was one of the more frighteningly unattractive drag appearances of the year. My reviews, however, were uniformly good for this performance, and the Connecticut theater critics nominated me for Best Actor in a Musical that year.

A tour of the perennial favorite, "Annie," was announced. Bob Fitch, a friend from the original Paul Draper tap class, was directing. Remember, Show Biz is one big family. His wife, Polly, had even worked with me as a dresser in the original "Hello, Dolly." He cast me in the role of Rooster, his original role on Broadway, over several well-known younger dancers who had auditioned. Bob was also a magician and taught me his disappearing knife trick to use in the show. With his encouragement I found another trick to use during my bow. My curtain call started with shackles on my wrist. Then it was my bow and *Voila*, the shackles were off. Once again it was that little extra something to get attention. Sometimes it worked, sometimes it didn't. The tour had started out with JoAnne Worley, from "Laugh In" fame, playing Miss Hannigan. Marcia Lewis later replaced her. The tour ended prematurely, by popular demand, and it was back to living on unemployment and savings. It was always part of my plan to save some during a show, knowing that eventually there would be no income. It was my own version of a

Playing Rooster during "Easy Street" from "Annie" with Jennifer Smith and Marcia Lewis. Photographer unknown.

"fail safe." No matter how many shows close on you, it is always a little bit of a shock not to get the weekly paycheck. *C'est la vie.* This was my chosen profession.

There was to be a production of "MAME" at the St. Louis MUNI, a large outdoor theater. My friend, Diana Brill, was directing and choreographing with Oona White, the original choreographer, supervising. Now here's where the Show Biz family gets to be even more connected. Gretchen Wyler, a fellow Okie, from one of my productions of "The Boy Friend," was playing Vera, and Georgia Engel, from "Hello, Dolly" and "My One and Only," was playing Agnes Gooch. Diana asked me to play Beau, the brief love interest of Mame, before he falls off the Matterhorn on one of their exotic excursions. The cheapskate in me surfaced again, when Gretchen and Paul Ross, a college chum and her husband, invited me to stay with them. Georgia stopped the show so cold with her number on opening night that the conductor just had to put his baton down and wait out the applause. This was a fun production and very easy for me, not having to carry the show.

You take a job for different reasons. Bret heard of a small revue, "Take 2," that was going to be done in Hawaii. Let me at it! The job was to choreograph the numbers and be one of the four performers in the cast. The show was another vanity production, where the writer acted as the producer. It wasn't the best of shows, but it did get me to Hawaii for the first time. It was another family affair, with Bonnie Schon and Diane Findlay from "Hello, Dolly!" and David Chaney from "MAME." Naomi Buck, from the Kansas City production of "My One and Only," served as the stage manager and Bick Goss, a friend from my first days in New York, directed. How's that for an enlarged show business family? A good time was had by all of us, though I'm not so sure about the audience. Hawaii was definitely worth it for me.

Meanwhile, dad was not recovering from his physical setbacks. When I returned to New York, LaVon called to tell me that Dad was fading fast. I rushed back to Oklahoma and went to see him in the hospital. By that time he was so weak that he couldn't speak, and his eyesight was failing. As he heard my voice, his face lit up. It was as if he had been waiting for me. We sat with him for the rest of the afternoon then went to dinner. That evening alone with him was time spent just holding his hand, talking to him about our lives together and telling him how much I loved him. Going over all our fun times together, he would give my hand a little squeeze as if he were reliving those memories with me. Finally, "Dad, it's OK to let go. You don't have to fight anymore." Then I kissed him and went home. The next morning we had just entered the hospital when Dr. Cotner told us they had been trying to call us. Dad had passed away early that morning. Sometimes a gravely ill person just needs permission from a loved one to let go of this life. Not that any of us have any control over life and death. It is sometimes the simple fact of knowing that they had been loved and that it is now alright to move on, that can allow one to pass.

It was difficult at the cemetery for me. For some reason it hadn't crossed my mind that Dad would be buried next to Mother. Seeing her headstone next to his casket hit me hard. I was now an orphan, a 53 year old orphan, but a little child inside with no parents. It was almost too much for me to bear at that moment. Then suddenly there was a hand on each of my shoulders. It was my niece, Beneé, and her husband, Rami, standing behind me and sensing my emotional pain. Their touch, sending their love to me, steadied me and helped me get through the rest of the service. I will never forget them for that moment.

Emotional losses ripple through your life, causing you to think about your life choices. This is when the question began to arise about what to do with the rest of my life. Having been performing for over thirty years and not making it to the "star" level, was it important to keep pursuing this? What else was possible? I began working with my last therapist, Richard Soll, on the problem. However, this line of thinking would have to be put on hold for a while.

Bret had made a contact with a German producer, Karl-Heinz Stracke, who was presenting a touring production of Maury Yeston's version of "Phantom of the Opera," throughout Germany. All of the principals were from the United States, with the chorus and orchestra made up of artists from Poland. My booking was for six months in the role of Cholet, the husband of Carlotta, the opera diva. The interesting challenge was that the production required the performers to speak in German and sing in English. OK, let's recall the skill that was used in recitals that had German selections. A German coach was found to help me learn the script. Arriv-

A dressing room shot with Connie Coit during "Phantom of the Opera" in Germany.

ing in Germany with all my lines learned, my sound was intelligible and convincing. It was still a bit of a shock, going on stage the first time speaking in German. Mine was a comedic role, so it was even more fun to get laughs in German. My problem started off stage.

After seeing me in the show sometimes people would speak to me in German. Oops! *"Langsam, bitte,"* "slow down, please." Then if I was still unable to pick up a few words, my confession would come out, "Sorry, but German and I aren't compatible."

Many of the Germans spoke English so it was fairly easy to get by. Halfway through the tour Connie Coit came over to play Carlotta. She joined me in my tradition of seeing everything there was to see in any place where we had a little time off. I kept a big map of Germany and highlighted each place we performed. The map was almost entirely green by the end of the six months.

It was a bus and truck tour and we literally played a different venue every day, from theaters to sport halls. One of the performances was in the most eastern part of old East Germany. So before the show several of my Polish friends from the cast walked me across the border river, to have the experience of having dined in Poland.

Once the cast found out about my tap dancing, they begged me to give them tap classes. So a tradition started. We did a class every day when we had a little extra time. Sometimes they would be held in parking lots, tennis courts or carpeted hotel lobbies, with as many as twenty people in the class. There were three men from the orchestra who were especially dedicated. At the end of the my stint in the tour they performed a special routine for the rest of the cast. They then presented me with a beautiful book on Poland, as my "Three Musketeers."

Teaching a tap class to the cast of "Phantom of the Opera" in a parking lot on our tour of Germany.

At one point the show went on hiatus for eight days. The other cast members from the states were going home. My thought was "This is a once in a lifetime opportunity." So a holiday was booked to Italy, going from Venice to Florence to Rome. Walking about ten to fifteen miles a day allowed me to see all the art treasures that up to now had only been photographs in

books. Remember my little catch phrase, "Life is not a rehearsal?" It paid
off in spades that time.

The producer and his assistant/partner, Ingrid, were colorful characters.
We were paid in cash, hundred dollar bills. It was the only time in my life
where a money belt was part of my daily wardrobe. On our last payday
it seemed that they had forgotten to pay us, when Ingrid's gold Cadillac
pulled the bus over. One by one the American actors were called out of
the bus to be paid by Ingrid, sitting in that gold Cadillac, counting off the
c-notes from her large wad of bills.

Being paid in hundred dollar bills sitting in a gold Cadillac on the last week of my tour in Germany.

Another interesting event occurred right before my six months ended. The
percussionist in the orchestra was desperate for a set of steel drums and he
couldn't purchase them anywhere in Europe. His English was not so good
and my Polish was practically non-existent. With one of our mutual friends
in the orchestra translating, he asked me to purchase a set of drums for him
in the States and ship them to him in Poland. With no idea how to find the
drums, it seemed like a long shot. He trustingly gave me $1,000 in cash. It
took a bit of searching, but the drum set was found, purchased and sent to
him at a cost of just slightly over what he gave me. Mission accomplished.
At one point I heard that he had put them to good use by becoming a
street musician in Paris.

The entire six months were most memorable in my life. Never again will I
tell a Polish joke. My new Polish friends were so warm and endearing that
it is just no longer appropriate. It is also important to keep challenging

yourself. Who knew there was a German performance in me?

After the tour it was back to Oklahoma to visit LaVon, who was living in Miami, Oklahoma, now. With Dad gone, she had more friends there, than in Grove. One night after dinner we were sitting at the table and she opened up to me, "Ronnie, I have felt so guilty all these years. I keep thinking about that time when you brought René home and I got a migraine headache. If I hadn't reacted that way, you would be married by now."

What was I hearing? This was in the same vein as when Mom died. One more visit from me during her radiation treatments and she would have lived. "LaVon, it is not your fault. I won't ever be married because I'm gay."

She sat in silence for a moment and then said, "Well, I don't understand it, but I love you anyway." What more could be said? We embraced and changed the subject.

I was now moving on with my life. Then one day my first grade dancing partner, Suzanne, called, "Ronnie, I wanted to check something out with you. Jim and I want to start a community theater in Grove and wondered if you would be interested in helping us. We want to put on a production

of "The Music Man" with you as Harold Hill on the high school auditorium stage with all the other roles played by local performers. I would direct and choreograph and Jim would be the music director. What do you think?"

No hesitation. "When?"

Everyone was excited for me to come back home for this project and worked extremely hard to put this complicated show together. There was a challenge for me. The actress playing Marion opposite me was twenty-three.

Here's 54-year-old Harold Hill with his 23-year-old Marion, Shannon Ailey, in "The Music Man. (Photo by Gibson Studios)

My age? Fifty-four. How to not look like a dirty old man in our love scene?

170

Hmmmm…. Well, I always looked a little younger than my chronological age, but this was a stretch. Aha, makeup! Also, at that time there was my little secret called "Just For Men," to keep the gray hair from showing. It all came together to make us a believable couple on stage. At least nobody snickered.

After each show there would be a receiving line to speak for the members of the audience. Sometimes the names came with the faces, but more often than not the name would just escape me. Lots of memories flooded over me every night. This turned out to be a most incredible experience. It also provided bookends to my theatrical career, from that first chorus job in the Kansas City production of "The Music Man," to this. And, fifteen years later the Grove Area Community Playmakers are still going strong.

If this were to be my last theatrical job, what would my future hold? Why not continue working in theater, since the jobs still seemed to be available to me? Did I have any skills besides singing, dancing and acting that could earn me a living?

Help!

LESSONS LEARNED

- **Create Your Own Opportunities**
- **Make the Most of Networking**
- **Life is Not a Rehearsal – Do it Now!**

TRANSITION IS A PROCESS

There are many lives to be lived in a lifetime. At age 54 it was a scary process to even contemplate making any drastic change. This feeling of unease had slowly crept into my life, but what was it specifically that was drawing me into this vortex that cried out for change?

First, though work was still available, the "biz" part of show business was finally getting to me. Over the years one learned to differentiate between "show" and "business." This was an essential tool for survival. When you auditioned, it was expected that you give 100 % of yourself for the powers that be to make their selection. Then if you didn't get the job, it was hard not to take it personally, because you had given your all, right? The reality was often that you were too short, too tall, too old, too young, too thin, too fat, had blond hair, had dark hair, had the wrong voice type, or the director had worked with one of your competitors and wanted to hire him or her. So, do you see the catch-22 here? If you held something in reserve and didn't quite give it your all, you lessened the hurt when the job went to someone else, but you also lessened your chance of making an impression. By giving 110% and then not getting hired, the result could be quite devastating.

Realizing that it was usually not personal made it a lot more palatable to accept the many rejections that came with the territory. An example of this happened back in the 70's at an audition for the small role of Eros in "Antony and Cleopatra," a new opera by Samuel Barber that would be the first production in the new Metropolitan Opera House at Lincoln Center. The audition had gone well and Franco Zeffirelli, the director, and Thomas Schippers, the conductor, seemed to like my voice. Then I was asked to stand next to Justino Diza, the basso playing Antony. Guess what? Oops. The star was a little under six feet. Then there was the "giant" at 6'2" next to him. That just wouldn't do. See? The results were rarely personal.

Now here's the part of the "biz" that was beginning to fester inside me. After 33 years of earning a living in a very difficult environment and never taking a job outside the world of entertainment, my résumés were strong, both as a performer and as a director/choreographer. Yet, when submitted for a job, the interview would often be with someone half my age, who didn't have a clue about me or my accomplishments. This meant starting from the top, proving myself once again. It was beginning to wear on me. The inappropriate scream was stifled, "Don't you know who I am? I've been doing this for thirty-three years!"

There was also a deeper more personal reason that had to do with my long-time friend and mentor, Leon Shaw. Leon was a brilliant comic actor from Nova Scotia, Canada, who had played the father in "The Boyfriend" with me back in 1970. We became good friends and over the years he had invited me to visit him in Canada and had come to Oklahoma to play golf with Dad and me. We had many a meal together at Monte's, his favorite haunt on MacDougal Street in the Village. Toward the end of his life he would tell me about sitting by the phone in his apartment, hoping that his agent would call, telling him that he had a job, say, playing the butler in a show for two weeks in summer stock in the Poconos. My heart broke when this happened over and over again. Observing this my resolve became steely. That point would never be reached in my career. This was a big part of the engine that was driving me toward the precipice of change. Yikes!

Beating a tom-tom in my head every day was the very real fear that I didn't have any other skills with which to earn a living. The drive to succeed in theater had been so front and center in my life, was there any other possible way to pay the rent? Just when I needed it, a lifeline turned up in Career Transition For Dancers. This was a non-profit organization founded to help the professional dancer in the career transition process. The following essay was written in 1996 to document my year of making a successful transition. It was written out of gratitude and for others to use as a guide in their search for another vocation.

MY CAREER TRANSITION PROCESS

In the spring of 1995 I made the decision to search for a new direction in my life. After a 33 year career in musical theater, I felt that I wanted to do something else. As all of the current media tell us, this is a time of downsizing in many businesses and instability in others. How to approach even beginning to find out what else I might want to do loomed as a large problem. Having been so singularly focused, I didn't have an inkling of what else might interest me. There was just this very strong feeling inside that told me I needed to change my life.

First, I bought *What Color Is Your Parachute*, a book written for the individual who is thinking about a new career. This is a great start for someone contemplating a career change and is published yearly in an updated version. Then at the suggestion of Diana Baffa Brill, a choreographer friend of mine, I made an appointment with Suzie Jary at Career Transitions For Dancers. I began one-on-one consultations with Suzie, plus noontime conversation seminars she ran for dancers. One of my first tasks was to write a skills based résumé. There are many books written to help you do this, and I bought one. After eight drafts, I came up with mine. It took that long for me to realize how many skills I had from the theater that were cross-over skills. During that time I took the Holland Self-Directed Search Test that Suzie provided for me, and it was very helpful in narrowing down my possible career change choices. In the Assessment part of the search my interests were most visible in social, enterprising, & artistic. Then, going through the Dictionary of Holland Occupational Codes, the two areas in which I felt had distinct possibilities were fundraising and public relations. This led me to find a writing class in fundraising at NYU that CTFD funded with scholarship money. It had an unexpected result. Halfway through the class I realized that it was an area that I would not like to pursue. The good part was that it led me to volunteer at God's Love We Deliver in the fundraising department for six months.

Soon, I started attending a focus group at CTFD with like-minded dancers, headed by Suzie Jary and Elizabeth Campbell. This support group was helpful in many ways, from feedback on my latest endeavor to helpful suggestions on positive actions to take. I also took the Myers-Briggs Type Indicator, which determined that I was an ESTJ (Extraversion, Sensing, Thinking & Judgment). People of this type are usually fact-minded, practical organizers. This test was helpful in assuring me that I was still going in the right direction. It was during this time that I bought my first computer. CTFD provided me with more funding for computer training. I followed many other avenues in searching for a new career, including attending seminars on job-searches (like The Five O'clock Club), networking seminars in several church basements, the NYTimes Want Ads, the unemployment office job-search computer, a meeting of NSA (National Speaker's Association), and a meeting of NAPO (National Association of Professional Organizers). NAPO gave me a real possibility. For years I had been helping friends organize their garages, homes, closets, etc. Now I began to work in this field. I had business cards made for my new business, Order Out Of Chaos, and also began to work part time for another organizing business, Task Masters. These jobs were of an independent contracting nature and took me mainly into offices and home offices.

Then I sent a résumé to Fredrick Wodin (a CTFD Alum) at Merrill Lynch in reply to a job search that he had sent to CTFD. Before my first interview I went to the Mid-Manhattan Library and researched Merrill Lynch, reading their Annual Report and their Annual Philanthropic Report. During my three interviews I was able to talk in a very informed way about Merrill Lynch. On the same day, after each interview, I wrote a thank-you letter to the person who had taken the time to speak with me. I put time and thought into these letters, making them as personal as possible and addressing any questions that the interviewer might have expressed about my qualifications for the position. This proved to be a very important part of my job search. Although I did not get this job, my thank-you letters were kept on file in the Marketing/ Communications Department of Merrill Lynch. Six months later I was called again to interview for another position. One of the Vice Presidents I had spoken with previously remembered me and my letters, and suggested me as a candidate for this new position. After two more interviews I was hired as a long-term consultant to Lee Roselle, First Vice President/Director of the Corporate Heritage Programs, in charge of installing a museum on the Legacy of Merrill Lynch in the lobby of the North Tower of the World Financial Center. At my final interview my new boss noted that on my résumé I had listed as one of my qualifications that I "... communicate well with a good sense of humor." Being a creative person with a funny bone himself, he picked up on that. So it is important to really take stock of yourself, assess all of your qualities and let them be known. You never know....

This career change process took about a year for me. There were many low periods of doubt about what I was doing. What kept me going was my commitment to the process, and CTFD. I could not have made my mid-life move without the work that I did with this group. The scholarship money made available to me gave me needed training. The individual counseling with Suzie Jary and the focus group headed by Suzie and Elizabeth Campbell were the catalysts that kept me on the right track, always exploring every avenue. My own thoroughness in approaching this task was constantly encouraged. My main discovery was that a new career will not just happen. I approached this process as a job that I was creating. Therefore, there were no limits on what I could do to make it happen. The times of flagging energy and discouragement had to become springboards to help me focus on what I really wanted. For me, one of the key ingredients for finding a new job in a new career happened to be my thank-you Letters. It could have been any one of the many specific things I did while on the job of "finding a new career."

After reviewing this year of career transition, I want to thank CTFD with all my heart for helping me make this leap from theater to the corporate world. When I started my search I didn't know if this type of change was possible for me. Now, I have proof that it is.

My essay included how difficult it was to write a skills based résumé. Remember that for theater my résumés were just a listing of shows and roles. This was the 8th draft of my new résumé.

RONALD YOUNG

OBJECTIVE

- A career change to a responsible and challenging position that will utilize my people skills, communication ability, and strong work ethic.

QUALIFICATION HIGHLIGHTS

- Capable of assimilating information quickly, communicating well, and keeping a good sense of humor.
- Proficient at assessing and formulating highly organized approaches for establishing and completing goals.
- Able to apply both a common sense and creative approach to problem assessment.
- Attentive to detail and able to follow detailed instructions with punctuality.
- Open to change, new ideas, and willing to meet any challenge.

EXPERIENCE

- More than 30 years performing experience as an actor, singer, and dancer on Broadway, Off-Broadway, and in international theater and film. Also worked as a director, choreographer and teacher.
  - Participated in the record-setting 3,389th performance of A CHORUS LINE on Broadway.
  - Received Los Angeles Drama-Logue Award for Choreography in STEPPING OUT at the Pasadena Playhouse.
  - Performed at the Kennedy Center inaugural presentation and recording of Leonard Bernstein's MASS.
  - Created and performed solo musical concert piece, IN THE LIMELIGHT, throughout the United States.
- Task Masters—6/95 to Present
  Professional organizer providing needs assessment, implementation and maintenance to various companies (e.g., retail, entertainment, non-profit, and insurance).
- Order Out of Chaos—4/95 to Present
  Professional organizer for private clients and start-up businesses, including both home and office spaces.

SKILLS

- Typing—50 wpm
- WordPerfect—Windows 6.1

EDUCATION

- University of Tulsa
  - Master of Music
  - Bachelor of Music (with honors)
  - Bachelor of Music Education (with honors)

There were many times when this career search felt like a hopeless pursuit. Hey, wait a minute. My dad had made a big transition back to his passion, golf, in his mid fifties. Bingo, a role model! This could be accomplished. Then discovering the world of professional organizing was like hitting a jackpot on the slots. Working with the clients became a passion for me. This could be pursued part time with private clients, or with Julie Morgenstern's Task Masters, and fit very nicely with my new corporate job at Merrill Lynch.

CTFD even made me the "Poster Boy" for a while, with interviews for newspapers and magazines and speaking to groups. But the best way for a little payback was to invite individuals in the process of transitioning down to lunch at the World Financial Center, answering all their questions about the process, reviewing their résumés and giving them encouragement. Hey, "If I can do it, you can do it." Suzie Jari would call about a client who was stuck and the invitation to "come on down," was the next step.

My leaving the theater surprised and shocked my friends. They all knew how gung-ho my enthusiasm had been throughout my career. There were different reactions.

"You'll still continue singing, won't you?" "No."

"You'll still do shows occasionally, I know you." "No."

"If a great part came along, you would do it, right?" "No."

It has taken time for some of them to really get that my transition was complete. Now here comes my selfish confession. Just like the athletes who know when it is time to hang up their spikes while still at the top of their game, I wanted to stop before my abilities started to slide. There are many performers who can grow gracefully into those wonderful character roles. That's not me. This was a recognition process that helped me move on.

Remember, this is not a "how to" book. It is simply my journey. It is commonplace for many people to have multiple careers in this day and age. For other actors it might work to have an additional part-time career and still stay in the "biz." Everyone has to find the path that is the one they can follow with a passion. Mine was practically a 180-degree turn from the theater to the corporate world. Others will not be that drastic. You might be thinking, "How can he have a passion for work in the corporate world?" Once again passion was combined with a pragmatic approach. My real passion was my part time work in the field of organizing. My practical side reveled in the weekly paycheck, the ability to start saving money and the freedom to plan ahead.

In my essay earlier in this chapter you can see the extent of my exploration. No stone was left unturned. Every possible avenue was followed in my search. Many were dead ends, but they were explored. "What am I doing?" "This is crazy!" "Nothing seems right," just seemed to spur me on.

The most important concept to gain from reading this book is that you are in charge of your own life. You create your world. You never need to play the role of the victim of your circumstance. You might have enormous challenges to face, but with creative thinking you can always learn a lesson or make your life a little fuller by dealing with the problem at hand. Being single without any family responsibilities gave me a certain freedom. Others with those concerns will need to factor them in when making transition decisions. Nothing is easy in this process. Identify your skills and your passions. Then find a workable mix. You can do it.

LESSONS LEARNED

> - **Dive into the Deep End – Trust That You Can Swim**
>
> - **Approach a Major Life Change From All Directions**
>
> - **Use Low Points as a Springboard to Get You Back on Track**
>
> - **YOU ARE IN CHARGE OF YOUR OWN LIFE!**

STARTING MY CORPORATE LIFE

Going to work at the World Financial Center in New York was like going to another city. It was located on the west side of the southern tip of Manhattan in Battery Park City on the Hudson River. It consisted of four office skyscrapers directly across the Westside Highway from the World Trade Center. There was a ten-story glass atrium with sixteen giant palm trees rising 45 feet in the middle of the complex, with many restaurants and shops on the ground floors of all four buildings. There was a landscaped boardwalk along the Hudson River for noontime strolls. It was an incredibly easy 15 to 20 minute commute on the subway from door to desk, never having to come above ground. The World Trade Center station was two subway stops for me and then it was a short walk to the enclosed bridge over the West Side Highway to the World Financial Center. You can imagine how envious some of my co-workers were when they compared their own commutes of an hour and a half to two hours, each way.

It was on April 29, 1996 that my new life in Corporate America started. The same old feeling in the pit of my stomach that was always present when taking my first class with a new teacher was again present that morning. This nervous roiling in my solar plexus had been with me since childhood. It was always, "Will I be good enough? Will they like me?" It had the feel of being on the edge of a precipice and being shoved off without a net below. What was going to happen?

My desk was right outside Lee's office. The first challenge was organizing my desk area with the necessary supplies. Organizing? OK, that's a go! But right in the middle of my first task, one of Lee's associates asked me to type a business letter for him, his assistant was out for the day. Oh no, this was a first! Jump in. Guess how many spaces to come down for the letterhead. Type it. Let him proof it. Finish it. Whew! First assignment completed. Notice how casually "type it" was mentioned? Here again is another case of "you never know…" Typing class in high school gave me the touch typing skill for a lifetime. You would be amazed at the number of people in the corporate world who still use the "hunt and peck" method.

181

With Lee Roselle, my boss at Merrill Lynch, in my "costume." (Photo from Lee Roselle Archive)

Other challenges were dealt with that first week: learning the phone system and setting up voice mail, handling travel arrangements, changing the toner on the fax and copy machines, making purchasing orders, reserving a car service and the most difficult for me, answering the phone. Answering the phone? Yes. You see, multi-tasking had never been one of my strong suits. So when a call would come in, it always felt like an interruption and the tone of my voice tended to convey that feeling. Answering the phone with a neutral voice was probably the biggest skill to perfect in my new position. Hey, it was learned… eventually. Those were just a few of the tasks that presented themselves to me and were conquered. Computer classes were offered and my name was first on the sign-up sheet.

Lee's desk and office could have been an advertisement for disorganization, piles of paper all over his desk, drawers bulging and Rolodex out of control. Aha, here's where my organizing skills could come into play again. Right away this became my priority. His office became a model of functionality. Files that had grown out of control were tamed. He could now actually write on his desk and open his drawer to find what he needed. This had an unanticipated side effect. He liked his newly organized life, and took it to the next level with his label machine. Everything now had a label, both in his office and his home. "Godzilla the Label Monster" had been created!

During the first two years my work continued with Richard Soll, my therapist who had helped me during my transition period. This was to ferret out any pockets of hidden resistance that still lurked in those hidden recesses of my psyche. There were a few, but mainly the work helped me gain confidence in my new profession.

A notice for a meeting of "Dancers Over 40" came in the mail one day. Maybe that group should be checked out by this dancer, who was definitely over 40. At the first gathering I bumped into a friend from the original company of "Hello, Dolly," Nicole Barth. She had married while in "Hello, Dolly," had a daughter, divorced, moved to California and was now back in New York. She had been one of the most beautiful dancers on Broadway and even though she was out of the business now, still took three ballet classes a week. We had an instant connection that went beyond "Dolly" and soon became fast friends. So much so, that as the years went by and with her red hair, we became known as the "Senior Will and Grace."

This was still a time when office attire for men consisted of a suit and tie every day, no casual Fridays, yet. OK, that was a change, but doable. During that first summer of work, CTFD asked me to speak to a group of Broadway dancers meeting between shows on a Wednesday at Sardi's Restaurant. In responding to a question about my transition I said, "My way of adapting to the dress code is this. I get up every morning and put on my costume for my role as a businessman," That got a big reaction. Nicole was in the audience and later told me, "What a great idea. I never thought of it that way."

When the Merrill Lynch museum opened in the spring of 1997, Lee asked me to be one of the docents, giving tours to student groups, high-end clients and VIPs from around the world. Here again past skills came into play. Speaking to groups was no problem for this former "State Champion 4-H Club Timely Topic" speaker, and making history interesting with a bit of humor became my modus operandi.

Lee had designated Yvonne Umpierre to be the director of the museum. We soon became very compatible co-workers and good friends. Another important member of Lee's team was Betty Hope, a brilliant researcher and writer, who also filled in as a docent at the museum. Betty was a constant with her "can-do" attitude and buoyant personality. She was the

As a docent in "The World of Merrill Lynch" in front of the Timeline. (Photo by Lee Roselle)

183

treasure on our team, and most aptly named. It soon became evident that this museum was really quite unique in the world of finance and we quite proudly presented it to our guests.

Many of my friends had difficulty comprehending my adapting to the corporate way of life so quickly. Let me reiterate my gratitude for a weekly paycheck and a regular schedule! Plans could be made without the fear of last minute changes necessitated by a new show that was just booked. It's a little complex to explain the "freedom within a framework" this new scheduled environment gave me.

"I think I'll go home for Christmas." Dates could be set and plane reservations made with no fear of changes. This was something unheard of for me.

My new life was great and it even got better when Lee pushed for me to become a full-time employee. This was a big step that included health coverage and my being able to work toward being vested in the company. It also made me eligible for a bonus at the end of the year. This happened May 1, 1997, almost a year to the day after my start with Merrill Lynch.

Following my mantra of "More," organizing jobs were scheduled on weekends and occasional evenings. In addition Julie started booking me for seminars, based on the material in her first book, "Organizing From the Inside Out." There was an initial fear that the "Question and Answer" period at the end of each seminar would pose questions that would stump me. That was soon conquered.

I was lulled into a false sense of security with the success of these seminars. The content of each script was literally memorized, with never really any speaking "off the cuff." What a mistake that was! Jump ahead about two years. Julie was preparing a new seminar for the corporate world. "Ron, would you be interested in co-presenting with me?" "Sure," was my immediate response. There was a little nervousness about the short time frame before the first show, er, I mean presentation, but it was exciting to be on the ground floor of a new endeavor. Countless hours were spent memorizing my part of the material, but there just wasn't enough time. The words needed to be in front of me.

Came the morning of the seminar. Julie opened with the introduction and goals for the day, then introduced me for my first section. The difference in our presentation was quite evident from the get-go. Speaking from memory and needing to refer to the text made me look unprepared, even though I knew the material. When my section finished, Julie came up to continue and then kept going for the rest of the day with just an occasional assist from me. After the painful process ended, Julie and Jerve Joulicur, from her office, took me to dinner. They must have sensed my feeling of failure. At one point Julie pointedly noted, "We wanted to see if the material was arranged correctly. Now I see that if you, of all people, couldn't make it work, it needs to be overhauled." That was meant to soothe, but it felt like salt in a wound. Nothing was mentioned of my "memorizing" approach.

Why do some failures affect us more than others? Julie didn't see it as a failure. It was to me, and the feeling stung. From that time there were no more seminars. Oh, she asked, but there was always an excuse, or the time was inconvenient with my day job. This was a failure on my part. The challenge wasn't met. This was so unlike how other adversities had been met in my life. Why this, why now? There wasn't a good answer. It might have been the feeling that now in my 50's I didn't want to do anything I wasn't good at. Maybe someday this unmet challenge will be conquered.

My living situation remained unchanged. Those five flights of 75 steps were still there and no elevator had been installed. However, there was a change on the main floor. The owner of the building, Charlie Duross, had sold it. One or the conditions of the sale was that he and his wife, Judy, would have the first floor apartment and put in a staircase to the basement to make a duplex. Oh, the envy! We became friends and had many a dinner together. Unfortunately, Charlie became ill and passed away. The first New Year's Eve after his death was approaching.

"Judy, what are you doing on New Year's Eve? Do you have any plans?"

"I had just planned to take Charlie's ashes down to the World Financial Center, toast him with champagne and throw his ashes in the Hudson River. That's what he wanted," she confided.

"Would you like some company?" I asked. "Sure," was her reply.

So off we went with our splits of champagne and Charlie's ashes on a cold New Year's Eve. Now here's the part that Charlie would have loved. We got down there, found a nice spot along the railing of the promenade and brought out the splits. We were being a little covert, because there was supposedly no drinking of alcoholic beverages in that area. The champagne popped, we toasted and tossed the ashes into the river. One little mistake. We hadn't taken into account the direction of the wind. The ashes blew right back in our faces. Charlie was always such a jokster that we figured he had just planned that all along to have the last laugh.

We remained friends and when she married Peter Just a few years later, becoming Judy Just, she asked me to join them at City Hall as their witness. In the waiting room they both looked a little lost and forlorn.

"Where are your flowers? You have to have flowers to get married," I said. "We didn't think about getting flowers," was her semi-stricken reply.

After checking with the clerk about how long a wait they would have before it was their turn, it was off on a frantic flower search. About four blocks away there was a Korean grocery with a fairly large selection.

"Could you combine these two bunches into one bouquet with a ribbon?"

Next a disposable camera was found. Now to get back in time for the ceremony. Picture a tall guy in a suit and tie, with a bouquet in his hand running down Chambers Street. No one even noticed. Remember? It's New York City. Returning with just minutes to spare, we were then called into the magistrate's chamber. If you have never witnessed a wedding in a city hall, you might not have any idea of the sterility of the occasion. We were in and out in about two minutes. However, all the while pictures were being snapped that would become her wedding album. That was a very eventful lunch hour.

Back at the corporate world I began to look toward my own future. After one year at Merrill Lynch a full time employee was eligible to open a 401(k) and receive matching money from the company.

"Enroll me and take the maximum out of my salary."

This was a wise decision that would pay off when on retirement. Then a colleague, Shawn O'Connor, suggested a very skilled financial advisor, Jackie Knoll. She guided me through my years at ML with good fiscal planning and as of this writing remains my financial mentor.

"Keeper of the Bulls" was also added to my growing list of assignments. About 20 years ago an artist had been commissioned to design a bull statuette for Merrill. One hundred small and twenty-five large limited editions were cast in bronze. Each bull was signed by the artist and numbered for a limited edition. These commemorative gifts were given to retiring executives and VIP friends of the firm. By the time the project was given to me all the large ones had been distributed and there were about 40 of the small ones left in a secure storage unit. The paper work was so unclear that my first step was to combine it all into one cohesive document that listed who had been given which numbered bull.

When a request would come through for a bull, the department in charge of storage had to be contacted and the bull delivered to me. After the signage for the plaque on the bull was approved, it had to be hand-delivered to the vendor to create and attach the plaque, then picked up and delivered to the executive who had requested the gift. This process was eventually shortened when the remaining bulls were delivered to me to keep locked in the Archive Room. This is the saga of my "Keeper of the Bulls" title.

Each employee was encouraged to donate to the United Way Campaign in the fall of each year. This fit with my own practice of charitable donations. Over the years, contributions had regularly been made to God's Love We Deliver, Save the Children, Disabled American Veterans, Broadway Cares/Equity Fights AIDS, Habitat for Humanity and various theater groups. Giving back had just always seemed the right thing for me to do. Evidently my commitments were not always fully considered.

One day on a phone conversation with my old college roommate, Don Doss, I brought up the subject.

"Doss, I keep getting these requests for donations from the University of Tulsa and I just keep throwing them away. What do you do?"

"Well, I usually send in a donation. I figured that I was on a scholarship for those school years and now that I can afford it, I can give something back," was his arrow-to-the-heart reply.

Duh! What had I been thinking??? My entire college career had been funded by scholarships! Regular donations began immediately, with a little extra to try to make up for my lengthy stupidity.

There were other ways of participating to give back. In the 1998 First Revlon Run/Walk for Women, about $2500 was raised, with 75 friends sponsoring me. Also, in that year before my trip to visit my cousin, Beverly, in Mexico, used clothing and donations were collected from my co-workers for the children in the village where she lived. With the money raised we purchased 50 pairs of shoes to go with the clothing. She wrote back that sometimes this clothing made the difference between a child being able to go to school and not being able to go. Later in 1997 for the AIDS Walk in New York City 40 friends had sponsored me with a total of over $1300..

Vacation time was set aside for a very special trip with my cousin, Beverly. We decided we wanted to travel together. Where did we want to go? After we both made our "want to" list, we discussed all the possibilities and came up with a tour of Spain, Morocco and Portugal. We booked a 16-day tour. On bus tours your lodging and travel were provided for a certain price. From there the company offered additional tours, each for a fee. We did a lot of research before the tour, so that we were able to explore on our own, rather than sign up for those side trips. Oh, we took a couple, but for the most part we would just take off and then meet up with our tourmates for dinner.

The experience of wandering in the old cities of Fez and Marakesh in Morocco was extraordinary. You had to take a guide or end up hopelessly lost. Shopping was unique. If you went into a shop and the keeper felt you were a good prospect, you were served mint tea. Then you were expected to bargain. It was a cultural pastime. One instance stands out. There was a beautiful velvet gown in royal purple that would have looked beautiful on LaVon. There was a problem, a long row of tiny buttons down the front would have been difficult for her to handle.

"Have another cup of mint tea. I'll be right back," said the proprietor. He returned with a zipper installed down the front, right by the buttons, so it would still have a finished look.

What could I say but, "I'll take it." It was beautiful and LaVon loved it.

Another highlight occurred in Lisbon, Portugal. I love port wine and with a little sleuthing, what should turn up but the Port Wine Institute. It had the look of a gentleman's club with soft leather chairs. The menu of port wine was fairly extensive so that you could try just one glass of many different vintage ports. Cheese and crackers were provided to cleanse your palate between ports. Beverly didn't drink any, but managed to take a photo of me after my third glass, looking a little askew.

But the best part of Lisbon for us was finding a little restaurant off the beaten path with Fado singers. Fado is one of the national styles of music of Portugal and the singers were usually older. At times the women's voices were lower than the men's.

The entire vacation was very special for us. One of my mottos was put into play once again, "Do it. You might not have the chance again." That credo has been a part of my life and has paid off more than once. It was always tempered with being able to afford it and not compromising my fiscal responsibility.

Back from vacation my corporate life continued to run fairly smoothly until the beginning of 1999. Lee called me into his office, "They have offered me a package and I have decided to retire and take it." Oh, no! Change was never my best friend. The idea had always been to get life "right," and then just live it. Never happened, and probably never would.

"Are you sure? Is this the right time?" I queried. "Yeah, but don't worry, you'll be fine," he assured me.

Lee had set me up for success before he left. First, in the previous year he had saved my job when there had been a round of layoffs, by convincing the powers that be that I was fulfilling a necessary slot. Then, he had put me in charge of the Merrill Lynch Archives. What? There was no archival training in my background. OK, I'm an organizer and the Archives had files, photos, memorabilia, audiotapes and videotapes that were stored in an organized way. Assisting the previous archivist had given me the knowledge of how the system worked, but to be in charge was a big step. It worked out very positively, with my eventually becoming the "go-to" person in the firm for Merrill Lynch historical information. My organizing capability, coupled with a burgeoning knowledge of ML history, made this work. Membership in The Archivist Roundtable in New York was even part of this new job. Other of Lee's responsibilities were also assigned to me. I became the Liaison with the Retired Partners and compiled an end-of-the-year press book for the current Chairman of ML. This started with Dan Tully and continued with Dave Komanski and Stan O'Neal, until my retirement. So my position was gaining some solidity in the firm. Thank you, Lee!

Lee's retirement dinner on February 4, 1999 was enhanced by Eggroll the Clown. That's right; thanks to me a clown entertained Lee at his corporate retirement dinner. Being a funny man himself, he loved it.

With Lee gone my direct report was Fredrick Wodin, who had gone through Career Transition For Dancers and was my first interview at Merrill. Logic would say that we had so much in common that it would be a good working relationship. Wrong. Things were never quite done right for Fredrick. Lee had essentially spoiled me and now there was a big-time adjustment. So why not just leave? With the change of careers also came the realization of one day possibly retiring with the need of financial solvency. So a little more elbow grease was applied to this new manner of working. Luckily Lee's phone number was handy and he could be called anytime for advice. It just wasn't the same, but now my retirement goal kept me keyed into keeping a positive attitude. My passion could still be fulfilled with my organizing jobs.

Friends would still hit me with, "Don't you miss performing?" My standard reply became, "Not for a minute. When I work with an overwhelmed organizing client and we get to the end of a session, the look in their eyes is my standing ovation. I have helped someone do something that they can't quite do by themselves."

There was also the discovery of a definite weak area, managing another worker. With all my experience as a director and a choreographer telling others what you to do, this should have been a no-brainer. Wrong! This is how the scenario went down. It was decided that an assistant was needed in the archives. Fredrick and I both interviewed several candidates and decided on a very bright, personable young woman, who would report to me. It started off well. She was taught to enter new items into the archives, fill the requests that came in for information and photographs, and give tours. She was very ambitious and I didn't pick up that she needed "more" to be fulfilled in her job. Small glitches began to occur. She began to create little frictions in the office environment and then my impatience with her would surface. It finally came to a head and we had to let her go. She had other issues besides her disliking my managerial style. However, her final act was to write a letter to Fredrick detailing all of my failings as a manager. After she was gone he showed me the letter and said it would go no further. Thank you, Fredrick. That episode was painful. Managing another worker in the corporate world was not in my skill set at that time. Remember, I just don't like to do anything that I don't do well, or can't learn to do well.

One of my co-workers, Leigh Henderson, was quite helpful with her computer expertise. One of her corporate responsibilities was to offer courses to upgrade the employees' computer skills. My name was always on the sign-up list. One day we were talking and she mentioned, "I've written a biographical piece and was thinking about doing it as a one-woman show. Would you listen to it some time and tell me what you think?" "Sure, I'll be glad to."

Here's where you never say, "Never." I volunteered to direct her piece at a small off-Broadway theater. She had never been on the stage before, and with my theater background the piece could be made production-ready. It was also my way of thanking her for all her computer tutoring that had helped me so much. We both put a lot of work into the project and she was quite pleased with the reaction to her theatrical debut.

Confession time again. Remember that motto of mine, "Vanity is a terrible thing, unless you're really into it!" Well, because of many early attempts to be bronzed and beautiful with excessive sun tanning, regular visits to the dermatologist were now a necessity to remove the occasional keratosis and to check for skin cancers.

On one such visit Dr. Ronald Brancaccio, my long time doctor, was doing his usual body scan for problems, when he proclaimed, "You know you would be a good candidate for liposuction around your mid-section."

I smacked him, "What?"

"The rest of your body is in really good shape for a 58 year old, but you have this little 'extra' around your mid section," he pointed out.

"Let me think about it," was my deflated response.

To be truthful, that little "extra" around my mid section had not been responding to the exercises that had always kept me trim before. So of course this procedure had to be undergone. Dr. Christopher Nanny, an associate in Dr. Brancaccio's office had a good reputation in the field, so we scheduled the procedure for right after Christmas. With a week off, it would give me a chance to heal.

Here is a brief overview of the "wet liposuction" process. While standing upright about ten sites were marked around my mid section for incisions. These were the spots for the insertion of the cannula, a hollow stainless steel tube. (Think small version of a vacuum cleaner attachment.) First, a solution containing Lidocaine (a local anesthetic), Epinephrine (to contract blood vessels and minimize bleeding) and a saline component was inserted with the cannula, at the designated marks. This works to loosen the fat cells, to lift the skin away from the muscles and to reduce bruising. Then with the cannula connected to an aspirator, the fat cells, along with most of the solution, are literally sucked out. It even sounds a little like a small vacuum cleaner. There were no sutures done on the small incisions to abet the necessary drainage in the ensuing days. The next big step involved a spandex compression garment ... all right, girdle. This had to be worn day and night for about two weeks to aid the skin in adhering back to the muscles and inner tissue. Special pads also had to be used on the bed to absorb the drainage that would ensue. It was a little messy but the discomfort level was not too great. After three or four months the difference was quite evident.

Let's go back to my doctor. Several years later on a segment of "Entertainment Tonight" there he was with a high profile patient. He had moved to California a couple of years after my procedure. Now, here he was doing a complete makeover for Debbie Rowe, Michael Jackson's first wife! Get out!

During this time my friend, Rob Rees, and I discovered our mutual love of golf and decided that we had to find a place to play occasionally. This isn't easy in The Big Apple. He worked at Golf Digest Magazine and would run across ads for deals at different resorts. He discovered the Blackhead Mountain Resort in the Catskill Mountains about an hour and a half out of the city. They advertised "Golf and Schnitzel." The resort was operated by the Massman family and everyone in the family had a job, either with the golf course or the resort. There was a special offer right before the season started in May, so we decided to go up on a Friday evening and come back on Sunday afternoon. The deal included two nights lodging, meals and two 18-hole rounds of golf at a very reasonable rate. We took off one Friday after work in a rental car.

Finding the resort after dark was like a scene from a Three Stooges movie. "Turn left here." "No we should turn right." "You missed that sign behind the tree. Back up."

We finally arrived barely in time to eat dinner before the dining room closed and then found our rooms. This was an old resort, so the rooms had no phones and a small TV with bad reception. It could have been a summer camp before becoming a "resort." The next morning we were up early and out on the golf course. It was a beautiful nine hole course but very difficult. Almost every hole was on a hill. We would play it twice for our 18-hole round. The view from the eighth green was just breathtaking. It was the highest point on the course and you could see for miles around. That evening at our delicious German dinner we discovered Warsteiner beer. Ah, ambrosia! For the next few years we made this pilgrimage every spring and fall to get the off-season rates. Don Correia, from my Chorus Line time in Toronto, joined us a couple of times. It was always a great get-away.

For the previous few years Beverley Johnson, my friend, voice teacher and mentor, had been in failing health. With her latest hospitalization there was little hope for her recovery and she passed away. This was a great loss to many people. Most of us did not realize that she was 96 when she died. We all thought she was in her mid eighties. She had kept her real age a very guarded secret. What was remarkable was that she had continued to teach voice until shortly before her last trip to the hospital. There were two services for her – a church service and a memorial service at Julliard. Tony Griffey, one of her students, and I planned the service at her church, St. James Episcopal. Then, along with Renée Fleming, ten of us spoke at the Julliard service.

Ed Berkeley, a colleague of hers at Julliard, was the executer of her estate. That was not an enviable job. She had left a lot of wishes and bequests. One was that her ashes were to be buried alongside her husband, at a cemetery in Minneapolis, Minnesota. Ed asked me to accompany him on this journey and I did. The handling of her estate was to take over a year. In her will she had left me a small portion of her total estate. I am eternally grateful. It would come to change my life in an unexpected way..

The changes in my life had been fairly dramatic and Career Transition For Dancers still played an important role in that revolution. Four years later this was my follow-up essay.

CAREER TRANSITION ESSAY ADDENDUM

Merrill Lynch has now been my place of employment for four years. After working one year as a consultant, I was made a full time employee with full benefits. My current position is Assistant Vice President, Corporate Heritage Services, in charge of the Merrill Lynch Archives. Part of my time is also spent in The World of Merrill Lynch, the Merrill Lynch Museum at the World Financial Center, as the Interim Manager and as a docent, giving tours to private groups and handling open hours. On occasional weekends and some evenings organizing jobs through Task Masters will fill my time.

Some of my friends and I still find it strange that such a drastic career transition to the corporate world could find me feeling happy and completed. It is a little amazing. There wasn't anyone more "gung-ho" for show business than me. I loved it – the shows, the performing, the travel, the people, the adventure! Now, other things make me feel good. The meeting of new challenges; the interaction with others in the corporate world; assured vacation time, where I can actually plan ahead, knowing that I will not have to cancel the dates and that I will have a job upon my return; regular benefits and retirement plans; and consistent pay checks; all these things leave me grateful and a little in awe. In addition I have found a very satisfying freedom within the framework of nine to five workdays.

There have also been some creative sidelines during this time. I directed a one woman show off-off Broadway. Then the tango beckoned. My friend, Diana Baffa Brill, and I enjoyed taking classes and getting a taste of the Argentine Tango. I can also go to the theater and enjoy it without, for a minute, wishing that I were up on the stage.

The relief of not being judged is almost palpable. If I get a correction at work now, it is on a skill. It does not affect my gut and soul. There is a tremendous weight off my shoulders, coming from no longer worrying daily if I am measuring up to whatever is expected of me on that particular day.

Four years after writing My Career Transition Process, I am filled with gratitude for my good fortune. CTFD played such an instrumental part in my successful transition that I want to continue being a part of this meaningful organization and helping in any way that I can.

Another opportunity came along to practice what I preach – "Life is not a rehearsal." My 60th birthday was approaching. Oi Vey! How to deal with this milestone? Mary Ellen Ashley, my friend who was having a birthday on the same day, and I decided to throw a big bash at her duplex apartment. It would be big enough to hold all our guests. We formed a little planning committee, consisting of Mary Ellen, Louisa Flaningam, Leigh Henderson,

Gracey Tune and myself. We hired the Bread and Circus Catering Company run by my friend, Judy Gibson, and her husband, Bob Van Pelt. Then Dennis Buck, the musical director from my one-man show, volunteered to be the entertainment.

The invitation to my 60th birthday party bash.

For all my friends who attended from out of town, theater tickets were arranged to two different Broadway shows on Friday evening. Then all 14 of us met for a bite at Joe Allen's after the shows. Saturday, the out-of-towners were left to their own devices until the party in the evening. It was just the best! The best!! We all had nametags with either Mary Ellen or my picture as toddlers, so that guests would know who were friends of whom.

The invitation had gone out with the dress code listed as "a touch of red." This proved to be great fun for everyone. In addition, red hats could be made from material available at the door as each guest entered. It was beautiful weather and the party flowed out to the terraces on both levels. The food was outstanding, the wine flowed and the interaction of the guests, just priceless. We had indicated no gifts on the invitation, but my friends surprised me with a scrapbook where each guest, or couple, had made a page with photographs and writing to honor me. That book is a keepsake. Sandy Hamilton, my friend from college and my time in London, made another scrapbook for me, chronicling those times. Another jewel to treasure.

The next morning, before my out of town guests had to leave, they were all invited to brunch at the revolving restaurant atop the Marriot Marquis hotel in midtown Manhattan. It was a perfect ending for that special weekend. It is with such joy that I recall this event. Never regret living your own Big Moments!

This was a singular time in my life that held many lessons and surprises. Skills were found that could earn me a living and I found more could be mastered. A beloved career could be left without regret. Limitations were experienced. No one can be 100% functional in all areas. Accept it. This doesn't mean you should just "give up," but be selective about where you put your desire and energy to work. Continue to plan ahead. Producers had been contributing to my actor's pension for every job over my 33 years of performing, but now with the career change, saving started in earnest for those upcoming "golden years." You will be amazed when you contemplate the entirety of your skill set at how you can mix and mold them for different jobs and tasks. Being up for new challenges is paramount and having a keen interest in the unknown is a necessity.

If this song and dance man from Oklahoma can morph into a corporate archivist, just imagine what you can do!

LESSONS LEARNED

- Be Adaptable
- Give Back to Your Community
- Be a Mentor

THE DAY THE WORLD CHANGED

September 11, 2001, was a beautiful autumn day. I dressed for work, took the subway and crossed under the World Trade Center to my office in the World Financial Center, just across the West Side Highway. This was shortly after 8:00 AM. Sitting at my desk at about 8:45, I heard and felt a terrible explosion. Of course the others who were in the office experienced it was well. No one had any idea what had happened. After a few minutes I looked out of an office window and saw the top part of the North Tower of the World Trade Center in flames. Again the earth shook, the time literally, but this time, my feet were not leaden. I turned to my nearest

In 1998 Jackie came to New York for the 30th year reunion of the cast of "George M!" and I took her to the top of the WTC. Photographer unknown.

co-workers and said, "Let's evacuate!" Worried about Yvonne, whose office was in the North Tower of the World Financial Center, I quickly called. No answer. As I left to go search for Yvonne, Vinnie, Mr. Komansky's driver, was running down the hall. All he said was "God damned terrorists!" Upon reaching the North Tower of the WFC, Yvonne's office was empty and she was not in the museum. She must be out of the building and safe.

The exodus had already begun north-bound along the Hudson River. Arriving at one apartment complex, someone had a car radio playing the news loudly. It was then we all first heard that a plane had struck the North Tower. Looking back at the site of carnage, we were all frozen in place as a second plane hit the South Tower, a little after 9:00 AM. Then the unimaginable happened. People were jumping out of windows. One can only imagine the horror and the titanic heat from the explosions that forced those victims to take their final course of action. It was later documented that over 200 people had jumped. Not able to stand witnessing this unimaginable sight, I continued walking away from the mass destruction. No cell phones worked. The telecommunications network had been centered on top of the WTC.

Marie Chinicci, one of my co-workers from the fifth floor, was walking away as well. We tearfully embraced. "I've got to get hold of Tim, to tell him I'm OK," she choked out. Tim Everitt was her husband and a colleague of mine who was on assignment in London at the time.

"If I hear from him, I'll let him know," was the only solace I could give just then.

We both just continued walking away. At one point I turned east to begin wending my way to my apartment on W. 13th Street. It was then that I looked back and saw the South Tower collapse, sending up that mushroom cloud of debris that overtook so many who were trying to escape. I just stood rooted in one spot, again mesmerized in disbelief. What was happening? Was the world, as I knew it, ending? Was this also going to cause the collapse of the World Financial Center? Like a zombie I continued home. There is a vague remembrance of stopping at a Deli and picking something up to eat, as if that was the primary action to take in the current crisis. Nothing in my past had prepared me to deal with a tragedy of this magnitude.

My apartment seemed like a much-needed haven, and thankfully my telephone was working. The rest of the day was spent on the phone, contacting friends and relatives, to assure them that I had survived.

Tim called me from London, "Ron, have you seen Marie?" His voice was frantic with worry.

"Yes, I ran into her as we were walking up by the West Side Highway. She is alive and unhurt," I assured him.

He literally heaved this huge sigh of relief on the other end of the phone as he thanked me for the welcome news. We rang off. From my window the WTC had always been visible. By now the North Tower had also collapsed, leaving this discernable mushroom cloud of ashes blowing north towards my apartment. I closed the windows and continued to watch, too stunned for action of any other sort. For the next few days the police barricade for no admittance into the "Ground Zero" area started at 14th Street. An ID had to be produced just to get to my apartment on 13th Street.

Not knowing if a loved one was alive or dead was the most excruciating period for the families of those missing. Immediately flyers with photographs and names began to appear. They were on street corner stop signs, walls, fences, all over the city, asking anyone if they had seen this person to please call. Small memorials would spring up on a sidewalk or street corner with a photo, candles and flowers. The way the people in the city came together and supported each other was astounding. No one wanted to be alone. Comfort and solace became necessities just to make it through that nightmare. My friend, Nicole, and I heard about the memorials being created at Union Square and one evening walked over. There was a hushed stillness as we passed from one candlelit remembrance to another. There were photographs and flowers at each one. Some illuminated with a few candles, some with hundreds. The grief was palpable, but a sense of survival was paramount. Yes, life would go on, but in a forever altered way. When the final accounting was complete almost 3,000 people had lost their lives in this unfathomable tragedy.

I watched way too many news reports. I had to, still trying to make sense of the unimaginable. Coupled with my first-hand experience, this had the unfortunate consequence of leaving me with too many images of the destruction burned in my mind. Sleep became elusive. I called Richard, my therapist, for an appointment. We found that the classic symptoms of post traumatic stress disorder were present. The flashbacks and being unable to sleep were there immediately. A strange feeling of guilt accompanied me constantly. Why was I spared? I didn't die. I wasn't caught up in the cloud of debris, trying to breathe, when the towers imploded. Why me? The eerie feeling just wouldn't leave. There was also a feeling of being emotionally numb, as if it would just be more than I could bear to actually feel the enormity of the catastrophe. The work with Richard slowly eased me back to normalcy, or as normal as life could be after the seismic event. One result was that from that point on, anytime a movie about the event was previewed, I would just lower my head and close my eyes. If the images were being shown on TV, I changed the channel. No more! There were already too many images seared in my memory that will never ever leave.

Merrill Lynch gave employees a daily call-in number for each department. After an initial evaluation it was determined that we wouldn't be allowed back in the World Financial Center for over six months. The Marketing Communications group was called to a meeting about two weeks later at the Westin Hotel on Union Square. We were told that starting on September 26th we would have temporary working quarters at Burson Marsteller, a public relations firm connected to Merrill Lynch, located on 19th Street and Park Avenue. The next day was to be the start of my vacation to Australia, which had been planned for several months. Management decided that it could proceed as scheduled, because not much could be done with the inaccessible Archives at this time.

Here is one time when Fredrick really came through for me. Earlier, when planning the trip, it was apparent that I was short about 25,000 miles for a frequent flyer business class ticket to Australia.

When Fredrick heard this he called me into his office, "How many miles would it take for you to get a business class ticket?"

"A business class ticket to Sydney would take 125,000 miles," I responded.

"How many miles do you have now?" he wanted to know.

"Only 100,000 at this point."

He had a suggestion, "Let me buy your ticket on my account. Then you can purchase four round-trip tickets for me and my family, at 25,000 miles each."

He was essentially giving me 25,000 miles. This was going to make a huge difference on that long flight. As tall as I am, sitting in coach that long would have been a killer on my legs. Thank you Fredrick.

This get-away couldn't have happened at a better time. Getting on that plane to Los Angeles, was like having a huge boulder lifted off my chest. Finally, a deep breath. Call it running away, but it worked for me. The reason that Australia was my destination was that Pam and Victor Syrmis had been inviting me to visit them for years and the time had finally been carved out of both our schedules to actually set the dates. Pam and Victor were based in New York City, but by dint of Victor's Australian heritage, kept a place in Sydney as well.

The first surprise occurred while waiting in the VIP Lounge for my connecting flight in LA. Who should be sitting across the room but Phyllis Diller, looking a little frail, but with that world-famous smile in place. We spoke for a few moments and she seemed to remember me from her "Hello, Dolly" appearance on Broadway, but who knows? The next surprise was getting on the plane to Sydney and realizing that business class was upstairs on the plane! This would be a first. Immediately the stewardess offered me a glass of champagne, which I proceeded to knock over in my excitement. That had to be a good luck omen, right? It was to be an overnight flight and, best of all, the seats fully reclined! Did it get any better than this? Yes, it did. Arriving at the Land Down Under.

Australia was to be a much-needed healing time. First there was the beauty of the country and the people. The Aussies simply embraced me. Halfway around the world utter disbelief of what had happened was expressed by everyone I met. There was human warmth and empathy given to me that literally felt like a life jacket keeping me afloat. This was a constant for my entire visit. Pam and Victor were the perfect hosts. Most days were spent sightseeing on my own and then meeting my friends in the evening. In addition to seeing the Sydney Opera House, the Toronga Zoo, and the Blue Mountains, the Syd-

Sitting on the edge of a cliff in the Blue Mountains of Australia.

ney Harbor Bridge climb was high on my list of "to-dos." It turned out that Victor, a native Australian, had never made this climb. He was interested, Pam, was not.

On the morning of the climb Victor and I arrived for our instruction. First, everyone in our group watched a training video of what to expect. Then

With my good friend, Victor Syrmis, on top of the Sydney Harbor Bridge in Australia. (Photo by Bridge Climb Sydney)

we were given matching jump-suits to don. All watches, jewelry and anything that might come loose were checked and stored in a safe place, to be returned at the end of the climb. Needed glasses had to be attached to a lanyard around your neck. We would be walking on a metal grillwork, so that if anything did fall off, it could possibly strike a car windshield with great force, from the height we would be walking. We started off by attaching a lead line on our belts to a cable along the walkway. There was really never any danger of falling, but this was a safety precaution. The walk was so well planned that rest stops were given at strategic points while our guide continued a running monologue of the history of the bridge and Sydney itself. The highlight was reaching the top and having a photograph taken with the Sydney Opera House in the background. It was just spectacular and one can only imagine what the climb must look like at night! That photograph became my Christmas card for 2001. However, the requisite jumpsuit was not explained and several friends commented on my very retro taste in clothing that had developed in my sixties.

There is an interesting side bar to my visit. Prior to this time in my life the taste of coffee was just not appealing, with the exception of an occasional cup of espresso with sambuca after an Italian dinner as dessert. Suddenly, down under, coffee began to have an enticing aroma. One cup with a little cream and sugar every morning got me hooked. Now I am an inveterate coffee drinker and can hardly wait for my two cups of black java every morning. Go figure!

There were dinners with Pam and Victor's friends planned for almost every evening. One night after seeing a performance at the opera house, Anthony Wong, an actor friend who was just completing work on one of the "Matrix" films, joined us. He had asked if he could bring along one of the other actors on the film, who just happened to be Lawrence Fishburne!

Our conversation took an interesting turn during the dinner. We were sitting next to each other and he politely asked, "What do you do, are you in the business?"

"Not any more," I replied, "I used to be in musical theater, but left it about eight years ago to work in the corporate world."

"Oh, what were some of your shows?" he wanted to know.

I gave him a brief résumé and when I said, "In 'My One and Only' I stood by for both Tommy Tune and Honi Coles," he stopped eating and intently began to quiz me about Honi. The fact that I had worked with him and gone on in his role fascinated him. He wanted to know everything I knew about Honi . This was only to be topped later in the evening by Ian Thorpe, the gold medal winning Australian Olympic swimmer, entering the restaurant with his entourage. Normally, being star-struck is not part of my modus operandi. However, these two in one night totally perked up this partially jaded former thespian and long-time fervent Olympics follower.

Another highlight was a Sydney Harbor brunch cruise that Pam and Victor had planned for me to meet more of their friends. We boarded on a sunlit, cloudless Sunday morning and the occasion was just spectacular. Victor had also arranged for us to play golf here and in Melbourne. Melbourne?

After about a week in Sydney we flew down to Melbourne for a few days on our way to Port Fairy, Australia, for an arts festival, where Pam was to be performing. This charming little town is on the very southern tip of Australia and hosts an Arts Festival once a year. Pam was to perform in two separate events, one being a reading with an orchestra. She was dynamite in both presentations. However, there was a little learning curve with the orchestra. It was her first time and so I was able to help her with the protocol of being a soloist: when to acknowledge the conductor, when to shake hands with the concertmaster and to always precede the conductor when entering and exiting the stage.

This was evidently helpful for Pam, because a few months later, when she was reprising the piece at Royal Albert Hall in London, I got a call from her backstage, "Now what did you tell me? When do I acknowledge the conductor and when do I shake the concertmaster's hand?" I talked her through it again and she was fine.

We drove back to Melbourne and flew back to Sydney. On the driving segment Victor asked me to take over for a couple of hours. Not since London in 1976 had there been any driving on the "wrong side of the road" for me. My time behind the wheel was staggeringly adequate.

Departure time arrived. It was simply impossible to put words to my feelings of gratitude to Pam, Victor and all my new friends in Australia. "Thank You" was said, but seemed so inadequate. These few days in their presence and in their homeland had lifted me to take those important healing steps after the unspeakable had occurred.

Back in the States and back to work. It was very strange. Fredrick, Yvonne and I were all three working in the same small office. There was not much for me to do, being unable to access the Archives. There had been some damage on our floor in the World Financial Center and quite a bit of the Winter Garden Atrium had been destroyed. Tim Everitt had been allowed to go in with a video camera to check out the damage. The Archives had thankfully survived intact and we would be allowed in at some point to pack everything for offsite storage. The Marketing Communications Department would be relocated from the 6th floor to the 5th floor when we returned.

The day was set for packing up the Archives. Here again my organizing background paid off in spades. There was just one little problem. There were two large rooms to empty, filled with record boxes, photographs, videotapes and memorabilia. We were given one day to complete the job. This did not seem like enough time, after my initial needs assessment.

I went to Michele Coniglio, the person in charge of the move from our department, "Michele, there is no way we can get everything packed and ready for storage in one day. I need extra time."

"That's all the time you can have," she responded.

"What do I do about the items that are left at the end of that day?" I pled.

"Just throw them out," was her final edict. What? Toss historical artifacts? They are the magic mirror which reflects time rather than space, the past rather than the present. That couldn't happen.

The day arrived for the move. The maximum number of workers from the moving company was assigned to me. Three was the magic number. Then two more from our group were recruited. That was my army – six, including me. A plan was drawn up and everyone given jobs to do as the day started. Still not knowing if this was going to be possible, I really pushed them. By the end of the day we were all pretty beat, but after an hour or two of overtime all the important parts of the Archives were packed and ready for storage. Mission accomplished, thanks to all my organizational training. I don't know that Merrill Lynch ever knew, or cared, that they got "two for one" when they hired me.

Word finally reached Yvonne and me that the museum would not be re-opening when we returned. That was devastating news. The reasons were never given, but of course the bottom line had to be that it was not a moneymaker. The sad part – it was. There were several instances where a guest switched their brokerage accounts to Merrill Lynch after their visit to the museum. These could not be verified on a balance sheet, so therefore were never factored into the decision to close. The worst part would occur later when it became my responsibility to supervise the dismantling of all the artifacts on the Timeline.

It gets worse. One day Fredrick called me into the office, alone, to talk. "Your position is being cut. Here are your two choices. You can stay on three days a week at 60% salary, or we can let you go and you can collect unemployment. At the end of that time you can come back as a consultant."

I was too stunned to immediately reply. Lee had always saved me from this situation. Some little voice inside me spoke up, "Is this negotiable?"

"What do you mean," he countered.

"How about staying on at four days a week, 80% salary," I proposed.

"I'll check and get back to you," was the end of the conversation.

Fredrick's approach to this situation was always a puzzlement to me. It wouldn't have seemed like such a slap in the face if he had said something like, "We 're going to have to restructure part of the department. Let's see what will work out best for you." That was not the way it played out.

The waiting was a little tense. Finally, the next afternoon he called me back into the office, "We can do what you requested," he offered. So it was set.

"This is the end of November, could we start the new terms the first of the year?" I had thought out my final request.

"That will work as well," he concluded.

Whew! Whatever possessed me to negotiate? It goes back to my basic change of emotional status upon leaving show business. Previous to that, every question and every answer had additional emotional baggage, "Will they like me?" In the corporate world it was my skill set that was the basis for dealing with any situation. Of course I still wanted to be liked, but it wasn't the deeply held "have to" feeling that was present in the "biz." So, something inside told me that if they wanted me back as a consultant, my skills could still be usable. The negotiating request had practically been blurted out. The result, my status would be as a full time employee with limited hours and full benefits, still eligible for vacation time and a year-end bonus. Friday was to be my day off, so there was another plus of being available for organizing jobs that would take me out of town on a three-day weekend.

Once again the coin had been flipped over to make the best out of a not-so-good situation. This Pollyanna part of me that causes laughter and de-rision sometimes among my closest and dearest had worked magic once again. Why? How? I don't know. It just leaps out of the depths at times and saves me. My hope is that it never deserts me and will continue to take over when needed.

With the reassignment of duties Yvonne had been put in charge of the Midtown Conference Center where Merrill executives booked rooms for meetings. This was located on Lexington Avenue on the east side of Manhattan. Part of my interim assignments was to be part of her team that manned the reception desk. It meant learning another system and working at something outside my comfort zone. Done. Another mission accomplished.

My reaction to 9/11 seems paltry alongside the devastating losses that so many others experienced. Mine is just one of the thousands of first-hand chronicles of how the events of that day have forever impacted lives. There has been so much documented on the repercussions of the hatred that fermented into the life-altering actions of that day. Will these two sides ever be able to understand each other and co-exist in any sense of harmony? We have known throughout history that the majority of wars have been religious in origin, "My God is better than your God." This might be a simplistic explanation to some, but couldn't the possible solution simply lie with tolerance of our differences? This is probably the dilemma that will never be resolved in the lifetime of humanity.

This time, this event, will forever be embedded in our nation's psyche. All our future actions will be based to some extent on our reactions to 9/11. Healing will be slowly attainable and never quite complete. We can, as individuals, do everything in our power to acknowledge and allow differences to exist. We are all cut out of the same cloth, but different threads and different dyes were used. Yet this vibrant cloth is alive and every piece is useful material – a living being. We must hang onto this for the survival of the human race.

This is my story of 9/11 and its aftermath. I am gratefully alive.

LESSONS LEARNED

- **Reach Out For Support**
- **Be Unafraid to Negotiate From Your Strengths**

LIFE GOES ON

Returning to work at the World Financial Center was like living in a bad dream every day. The World Trade Center stop on the subway and the pedestrian bridge over the Westside Highway had both been destroyed. The bridge had actually been shoved into the Winter Garden Atrium of the WFC. The damage there was so extensive to the ten-story glass Atrium that it was not reopened until September of 2002. During that year it was meticulously restored with all broken windows put back, the 16 giant palm trees replaced, and large windows added on the east side looking out on the WTC site. The damaged marble throughout the Atrium was replaced from the original quarry in Italy. That quarry worked 24/7 to produce enough marble to allow the Atrium to reopen on schedule. That unheard of production timetable was their gift to the United State and all those touched by the tragedy.

Having to get off the subway one stop earlier at Chambers Street meant about a ten-minute additional walk to work. That route was constantly being changed due to the continued cleanup and construction work. This meant new areas of devastation to view daily. Going to work was not a pleasant experience.

Merrill Lynch employees who worked in the North Tower were allowed back to work earlier than those in the South Tower, because there was practically no damage to their building. There was an official ceremony to open the South Tower with the Mayor, the Governor and a video message from the President in March, 2002. However, we were not allowed back in the building officially until May. It had taken eight months to repair the damage.

The Archives had been stored at a warehouse in New Jersey. I was shocked when I finally got permission to go out and check on the manner in which they were stored. The warehouse had broken windows with birds flying around inside! Of course there was no temperature control. Getting the records and artifacts out as soon as possible, became a priority.

211

First, my new space had to be appraised and a storage system designed. Well, who could do that? An organizer? Here comes that "two for one" guy again. The two small rooms on the fifth floor assigned for the Archives had roughly one quarter of the previous space on the sixth floor. This was going to take some real imagination, along with my basic organizing skills. A plan was drawn up that could accommodate everything but the videotape and audiotape collection. Another small space in the art storage room in the sub-basement was assigned for those items. The plan devised was not exactly user-friendly. Practically every inch of space was utilized in a way that left the two aisles in each room so narrow that a slightly heavy person could not get through. No one ever called me on that misstep, probably because the space was so functional.

The shelving had to be installed, according to my plan. Taking into account the sprinkler system, it went as close to the ceiling as possible and covered every inch of wall space. Of course that didn't go smoothly, since the shelves delivered had different widths than had been ordered, but the rooms were eventually ready. All of the boxes in storage had been numbered on a master list. That list enabled me to request only certain boxes to be transferred that could be emptied and installed. It was still a lengthy process with the several hundred boxes being handled by that famous "one-man band." My co-workers would periodically drop by to check out the space and be fairly amazed at how everything was stored.

The same process was used for the space in the sub-basement. A plan was designed, the shelving set up, then the boxes brought back and the tapes installed. The process for these two projects was spread out over several months.

To commemorate the first anniversary of 9/11 twin towers of light were installed at Ground Zero. These lights were turned on every night for a month and could be seen for miles around reaching for the heavens. It was inspiring.

American Express then established Eleven Tears, another inspirational memorial, in the lobby of their building, World Financial Center #3. To simply describe it will not do it justice, but here goes. It was a shallow pool of water made of black marble and divided into eleven pie-shaped

212

wedges. There had been eleven victims that day from their company. In each wedge a victim's name was listed along with words describing them written by family and loved ones. From the ceiling of the lobby one drop of water fell into each wedge - tears. Also suspended from the ceiling, just a few feet above the water, was a large cone shaped crystal, which came to a point just above the center of the pool. The overall effect of this was a beautifully stark, yet loving, reminder of that day.

It was becoming increasingly more important for me to spend time in Oklahoma. On a trip there in June of that year a simple event took place that changed the course of my life. Bob, my brother-in-law, took LaVon and me out in an old car to drive through a field around a cove on the lake. Why? This entire area was covered in trees and underbrush so that one could barely see the lake. We really didn't know why we were looking at this area.

"I'm going to build a development of homes around this cove," he confided. This was not out of left field because he and his partner, Mike Long, had built other successful housing developments in the area.

"Then I'm going to build one model home, sell it to somebody and rent it back for two years to help sell the other lots," was his next pronouncement.

"Who's going to buy the model home?" I wanted to know.

"I haven't told anyone else about it yet," he allowed.

"What about me?" came out of his surprised passenger. This was so weird, because owning another house had never even been on my radar. Now, certain aspects in my life were aligned to make this a possibility. The money that Beverley had left me could cover the down payment. That age was approaching to consider all the aspects of possible retirement. There was a stronger pull to return to my "roots" and my family. Owning a piece of property was a deeply hidden dream that had been left behind, after selling the unit on the golf course over twenty years ago. Why not take the plunge? The house was completed and rented to Bob in April of 2003.

It was fascinating to be in on the building of the house from the very beginning. First the floor plan had to be determined. Then choosing the cabinetry, deciding on the hardware for all the drawers and cabinets, selecting the ceiling fans, choosing where the electrical outlets would be in each room, picking the paint colors, etc, were all new and fascinating activities. This was all done under the guidance and help of Linda, my sister. She was an artist and had done this many times before. Her special gift was using her artistic eye from my point of view and according to my taste. This selection process was often dictated by a short time frame, because of my being in Oklahoma for only a few days at a time. We agreed on almost every selection. The very rare disagreement was always settled after a short give and take of our reasoning.

This also meant an added mortgage payment to my monthly budget. Right away my standard practice was to pay something extra on the principal each month. After the initial two-year model home rental this was going to be a rental property for me that Bob's real estate company would handle, with my being able to use it during my vacation periods from Merrill Lynch.

This turned out to be a little dream home for me. It wasn't too big, but had three bedrooms, two baths, a great room with a fireplace that opened into the master bedroom, a garage and a deck on the lake. That meant about fifty feet of that over thirteen hundred miles of shoreline belonged to me! Unbelievable! This was the same Grand Lake of the Cherokees where I had water-skied as a youngster. Bob had named the new development "St. Andrew's Harbor." It gets better. It was located on Monkey Island, Oklahoma. You can just imagine what fun my friends had with that address.

Now came the tricky part. For those first two years as a model home, Bob had contracted Creative Designs, a local store, to furnish it. When that time ended and everything had to be removed, the house would be empty. OK, let's start buying furniture. This was a two-year process that took a lot of planning. First, what were my tastes? Well, let's look at a lot of magazines and catalogues, tear out the pages with possibilities and make a decorating binder. Then start buying and storing. Mathis Brothers Furniture in Tulsa allowed me to purchase items, and then set the delivery date for a day in April 2005, when the house would be empty. Some items were stored in the space above the garage, some under Linda's bed. Artwork from my apartment in New York was selected and sent out. Rugs were designed and made in Joplin, Missouri. A ceramic and pewter dining room light fixture

My house in Oklahoma with the lake in the background. Notice the cone shaped "safe room" in the garage. The Northeast part of Oklahoma is in "Tornado Alley," so that little "port-a-potty" looking structure is reinforced steel, bolted to the cement floor of the garage.

was carted back from Mexico. The dining table and chairs set had first been sighted in High Point, North Carolina. They couldn't be found anywhere in Tulsa, but showed up in a local store in Grove. How about that? They were purchased and stored there. The master plan for all of this was somewhere in the recesses of my mind, I hoped.

My friend Diana, from "MAME," commented, "I have to buy one piece of furniture at a time and live with it for a while to see how it feels in the space. How do you buy everything ahead of time, not knowing how it is going to look in each room?"

My answer was almost too simple, "Necessity. There will be one week when everything will be delivered and installed. Hopefully, all my planning and measuring will pay off."

It did. To jump ahead, that week in 2005 when it all came together felt a little magical. It began when I walked into an empty house, except for a gas barbeque grill with a big red bow standing in the middle of the living room. There was a card with it, "Welcome home from your grade school friends in Grove." My friends had chipped in for this one-of-a-kind "welcome home" gift. Deliveries started and unpacking commenced on that Monday. With all my planning there was only one table that didn't fit in the guest bedroom, but it did work in the great room. By Friday it was all in place except the dining room table and chairs. This was going to be tricky, because LaVon, Bob and Linda had been invited over as my first dinner guests. The table and chairs arrived about 5:30, so dinner was on the table by 6:30. See, things have a way of working out.

But 2005 was still a while away. Back in 2003, at work it almost seemed like we were moving underwater. The specter of 9/11 always loomed in the background. Soon, another big shift occurred. Fredrick resigned and went on to another job. Now my direct report would be Tim Everitt, who was in charge of the video network. This had an unexpected plus. His office was in the North Tower and the Archives were located in the South Tower. If you ever have a chance to be located in a different spot than your boss, do it! It had the effect of taking micromanaging out of the equation.

The Timeline in the museum before it was dismantled. (Photo by Lee Roselle)

The next big task for me to tackle was dismantling the Timeline in the museum. This was an emotional killer. There were decisions to be made on each item, whether it was to be returned to the Archives, put into deep storage or given to someone for safe keeping. Lee really couldn't be consulted, because it was just too painful for him. There had been so much loving care that had gone into the creation of this museum. The day came, the lift was brought in for those items at the top of the wall, and we started the demolition. That was exactly what it felt like - demolition. Slowly, each item was evaluated and the decision on its ultimate destination made. Talk about excruciating! There were the five major historical categories on the wall and each item had to be grouped with like items from each category. You can see from the photograph how many items could be placed on a wall that was over 70 feet long and 20 feet tall. The job was finally completed. The former museum was then converted into space for the video network.

My organizing business on the side was continuing with one very interesting job. Julie had called me to go with her and three other organizers to Chicago. Oprah's office had hired us to pack up the company offices in preparation for a renovation. This would be my second time working with Julie on an Oprah project. OK, I never met her, but I did work for her twice. That's about all that can be said. A confidentiality agreement had to be signed to work on her personal items in the office. It was nonetheless very exciting just to be on the spot where this extraordinary woman created her empire.

Another incident occurred where this skill set really came in handy. My friend, Georgia, called me one evening, "Ron, I'm in trouble. Can you come over?"

"Of course, I'll be right over," and I was out the door.

Her upstairs neighbor had left her water running and flooded Georgia's apartment. This happened just as she was about to go on tour with the 20th Anniversary production of "Nunsense." We proceeded to pack up everything for storage while the apartment was being renovated. She was able to "flip the coin over" and realize that she had wanted to organize all her belongings for some time, so now the opportunity had been provided. The bad news – she was going out on tour. The solution: I would supervise and work with the architect and contractor. We were very lucky to find Phil Consolvo, a very gifted and caring architect, and Tony Bartolotta, a very conscientious contractor. I later found out from other people that this was not the norm in The Big Apple. This was a big project for me to tackle. Decisions had to be made in Georgia's absence, but they were always made with her tastes in mind. The process took several months and was not without its dicey moments.

At one of our final meetings Tony told me, "I have done many renovation projects and I have never worked with anyone who was more tuned in to what the client wanted than you have been throughout this whole project."

Wow, my first supervising project and it was a home run! Mission accomplished. Plus, the end result - Georgia loved her apartment.

There had been a decision made at work to condense the material from the timeline into a traveling timeline of Merrill Lynch history. This was to be presented at recognition meetings of ML employees. Now who could be the logical choice to go out with this timeline as the expert to answer any questions about Merrill Lynch history that might arise? OK, twist my arm.

Explaining a bit of Merrill Lynch history from the Traveling Time Line at an event in Las Vegas. Photographer Unknown

These turned out to be great little jobs going to Florida, California and even the Bellagio Hotel in Las Vegas.

It just so happened that my birthday fell during the Las Vegas trip. What would be a present for myself that might never happen again? Let's see…. How about lunch at the Eiffel Tower (even if it was a replica in Vegas) and then a helicopter trip into the Grand Canyon (the real one)? That'll work. The flight was quite an experience. We're flying along and suddenly just swooped down over the rim into the canyon. There it was in all its splendor - just awesome. Then we landed to have some champagne and walk around. Experience those moments in life that you have dreamed about. They will stay with you forever.

Another one of those moments occurred on a trip to Costa Rica. It was taking a zip line in the rain forest. Once you're into the harness and attached, it is just a matter of trust as you jump off the platform and go skimming down the line to the next stop. For me it was a feeling akin to water skiing, with the wind on my face and feeling the speed of the movement. It's my version of a small adrenaline rush.

Unfortunately, life doesn't always continue on an upward course. Another loss came when Linda called to tell me that LaVon had died. We knew she was failing when I had just recently been home to see her. She was the last of my parents. The feeling of being an orphan can happen at any age. It first happened at Dad's funeral in my fifties. Now it returned in my sixties. The family had asked Jackie, my college sweetheart, to sing at the funeral.

Her singing had such emotional beauty and simplicity that it lifted us all to another plane. The church had told us it could make an audio recording of the service. Unfortunately the equipment malfunctioned and it didn't happen. Often the deeply held memory of an event can be the most personal of all remembrances.

LaVon had been a very frugal person and had always been determined to leave something for the three of us when she passed. She did. My portion went right onto the principal of my mortgage, helping me take a big step toward my goal of having my mortgage paid off before retiring from Merrill Lynch.

Back at work my boss's boss, Eileen Lynch, called me in to see her. "Ron, you are still doing your organizing work, aren't you?"

"Yes, I have my own clients and continue to work for Julie Morgenstern as one of her senior organizers," I replied.

"Would you have some time to come out and work on David's home office?" she asked. Her husband, David Sussan, knew me from working on the museum. His company had created the high definition movie that was shown there.

"Sure, just let me know what day would work for you," was my immediate response. This worked out so well that her garage was also tackled at a later date.

A few months later she had another request, "Could I recommend you to my sister, Claire? She and her husband, Dick, are downsizing from an eight-room apartment on Park Avenue to a smaller apartment and need help?"

"Of course, just give me her contact information," I confirmed.

Claire O'Brien, Eileen's sister, was a remarkable woman. She had an interior design company, was a published author and a master chef. All of this was almost an afterthought to her strong sense of family. My first appointment with Claire gave me immediate clarity about her situation. She was dying of cancer and wanted to go through all of her possessions to decide what was to be done with them. This was the act of a loving, giving woman, not to leave the endless job to her family. Through several sessions over a six-month period we were able to do that. Some days she would have to cancel, because she didn't have the strength to even sit and make decisions on items. There were days when we would talk deeply about life while we worked. I told her of my own mother's battle with the disease. About three months after our last session, Claire died. Eileen and her family wrote me a note thanking me for everything I had done for Claire in those last months and what it had meant to her. The truth was that she was an inspiration to me every time we had a session.

Later that year Eileen called me in again, "Ron, everyone thinks you're doing a good job with the Archives, but I'm afraid your job might be a little vulnerable, now that the museum is closed. I would like you to come and assist me, like you did for Lee, and continue your work with the Archives. This would make your position more secure. I want you to have a job until you decide to retire. Would you be interested?"

After thinking if over for about two seconds my response was, "Thank you, Eileen, for offering me this opportunity. Yes, I will do it."

If this was going to secure my job until retirement, there was no way to turn it down. My work methods were not an ideal fit for Eileen. She was much more multi-tasked and worked at a faster pace than I did. My belief has always been that she made this offer to me out of gratitude for my work with Claire before she died. I really tried my best all the time, but there were times when "overwhelmed" was my main feeling. Adjustments were made practically every day and there were times when the dreaded "Am I too old for this?" thought came to mind.

Here's where being goal-oriented paid off. At 64, retirement was a dream that was getting closer. "Hang in there!" "You can do it!" became my daily mantras. What was going to determine when that time would come? For me it was going to be anytime after my mortgage was paid off and Social Security had started. With LaVon's bequest being put right on the principal, that time was getting closer. So every extra dollar was now being moved in that direction. My actor's pension had been started at 62, but it was necessary to wait until my legal age to collect Social Security. That age was now on a sliding scale, mine being 65 years and 8 months. At that time I could collect full benefits and not be penalized for working. Any earlier and the government would have taken a dollar for every two dollars earned. With the two goals of paying of my mortgage and making it to Social Security age in mind, I buckled down.

That summer Georgia was going to have her apartment in California painted and new carpet installed. She was not looking forward to the prospect of dealing with moving out all the contents for the job.

"Georgia, I have some vacation time. Would you like me to come out for a week and help you out?" was my offer.

"You would do that?" she responded. "After going through all my stuff in New York wouldn't it be too much to do it again?"

"No, if it would help you, just give me the dates when you are going to be there, so I can arrange my vacation from work."

And so we were off for an intensive week of organizing work. Other than the new carpet and the paint job, it was not the complete renovation that was done for her New York apartment. When it was completed we had created a very warm, cozy place that was very much Georgia. Her New York apartment was her "jewel box" and her California apartment was her "nest." She was a very happy camper with both of them. There is also such a good feeling when you can share your gifts and skills with a friend to help them out. That week would really have been impossible to get through by herself. As it was, the two of us just barely finished in time for the car service pickup to the airport. Another mission accomplished.

Now it was time to concentrate on furnishing my own home. Stuart Allyn, the sound engineer for my one-man show, came back into my life. When he saw pictures of my home, he said, "Would you like me to design your entertainment unit in your great room for you?"

"Wow, it never even crossed my mind to ask you. That would be great," I responded. Later, after he had drawn the plans that included a 50" plasma TV, I happened to be out at his home in Irvington, New York to view them for the first time.

"Stuart, a TV that size seems too big" was my complaint.

"Come with me," was his only comment as he took me to one of his clients where he had installed the exact TV he was proposing.

"Sit down," he commanded as he turned on the TV.

It only took about ten seconds of watching it before I said, "Get it." It was just awesome and something that had never appeared in my wildest dreams. So, why not go for it? I did! The whole entertainment unit included spaces for all the electronic equipment, storage drawers and bookshelves. He was also going to arrange for smaller flat screen TVs to be installed in the upper corner of each of the three bedrooms. Now let's find someone to build that unit for me in Oklahoma.

Luckily, Suzanne had just had bookshelves built in her bedroom and highly recommended the skilled craftsman who had constructed them for her. This worked out great. After calling Alan Smith, introducing myself and explaining the project, he signed on. This got even better. He and his wife, Diana, live close to Monkey Island.

He did incredible work on the project and worked exceptionally well with Stuart, when he came out to install all the electronics. Diana and Allen remained friends after the project was completed.

The furnishings for my home just fell into place. Many years ago when PJ and Louisa had just moved into one of their new homes, I was working in Detroit. They were both performers but were into antiques, and even had a side business that featured antique clothing and toys. Walking around on my day off there was a craft fair to be explored. There it was! A little antique-looking pillow with a saying stenciled on the front, "Never mistake endurance for hospitality." Perfect for their guest room! All three of us have a slightly warped sense of humor, so they loved it. Cut to their garage sale, years later, in preparation for selling that house. Lo and behold on one of the tables in the sale was that little pillow. It was mine again for a dollar. There was a little embarrassment on their part when I pointed out, after purchasing, that it was a gift from me. They didn't want to take the dollar, but I insisted; a purchase is a purchase. There was a little glee with that

"Gotcha" moment, but it was all in fun. Now that pillow proudly hangs on the doorknob of my guest room closet.

That summer saw a dream vacation materialize. Angela Lansbury had invited Diana, Kathy (Wilson) Whitelaw, another dancer from the original company of "MAME," her husband, Rod, and myself to visit her at her home in Ireland! Can you imagine how excited we were? None of us had ever been to Southwest Ireland before.

From the moment we turned into the driveway of Angela's home on the cliffs of the Celtic Sea in the Southwestern part of Ireland the magic began. Her home was

A favorite photograph of me with Angela and Diana in front of Angela's home in Ireland on the Celtic Sea.

simple and simply beautiful! We stayed with her for three days, during which time she was tour guide, cook and hostess extraordinaire. It was three days of pure bliss.

After our stay in Angela's house, the four of us rented a car to see more of that beautiful country. I was the designated driver and that turned out to be an adventure. Driving on the right side of the road was OK. It was the narrowness of the roads, plus the vegetation that grew right up to the edge that made it a little harried. This was especially true when meeting one of the many tour buses that were seemingly everywhere. Sometimes the side rearview mirrors even had to be folded in to make it by the oncoming traffic.

We loved the food in the pubs, because of its taste and its price. Being the designated driver, my drink at lunch was always club soda, while the other three were slurping down their glasses of Guinness. However, for the evening meal we always found a bed and breakfast close to a pub so we could walk back and forth. That way I could make up for lost time in the Guinness drinking department. If you have never tasted Guinness, it has a different quality in Ireland than it does in the States. Here it is good. There it is delicious!

We toured all through the southwestern part of Ireland with Diana being the tour guide. She had always been a history buff and now regaled us with something at every turn. We learned more than we ever knew we needed to know about Ireland. We returned for one final night at Angela's before returning to the States. Of course we were profuse in our thanks, but I don't know that she will ever know what that trip meant to each one of us. Memories for a lifetime were stored during those ten days.

Back in New York another skill was added to my organizing, staging an apartment for resale. My first job was, or was not, a success, depending on your point of view. At the end of my work, the husband of my client walked in and stated: "Now I remember why I loved this apartment so much. I'm taking it off the market." And he did. It would be three years before he was willing to let it go. At that time we came in and helped them pack for the move. See what I mean by "success, or not"?

One of my jobs with Julie's office took me to a young family in California. On my first three-day session the husband was away on a business trip. We accomplished a great deal but did not entirely finish the house or get to the garage and office areas.

They hired me for another session in about three months to complete the project. The husband was present this weekend. At the very beginning I let them know, "I don't usually work with couples or partners, because you will try to put me in the middle to take sides."

"Oh no, we would never do that," they almost said simultaneously. Cut to the next day. It happened. One of them tried to get me to side with him/her (I don't remember which) against the other.

Backed into a corner the adrenalin kicked in again, "no hablo español, no hablo español," came out of my mouth. Why? Who knows, but it worked. We all laughed, they knew they had overstepped their boundaries and it never happened again. This is another instance that shows how far humor can go in situations where the overall feeling of being overwhelmed is present. The relationship with this client was so strong that it took a more personal turn a year later.

The wife called, "Ron, we are going to be travelling a lot this summer and we wanted to run something by you. Would you be willing to sign a document with our lawyer that if anything happens to us, you would come out to assist with the estate?"

This came out of left field, but not really. When someone trusts you with their "stuff" and you know where it is all located, it makes sense that you would be the one to come in and help settle the affairs.

"Yes I will do that. Just send me the document to sign and I'll make copies for myself and Julie's office." As of this writing the document is still in effect.

The diversity of my organizing jobs has not yet been fully explained. They run the gamut. Here are a couple of the more far-reaching jobs. Remember almost every client says the same thing in the first session, "Isn't this the worst you've ever seen?" I was always able to respond, "No, I've seen much worse that this," every time except for this one job. Luckily he didn't ask. It was a six-room apartment and the floor couldn't be seen in any of the rooms and possessions were piled to the ceiling. There was just a path through each room. My client was being evicted and had to have everything out of the apartment by a certain date. We began to work. Now remember it is very important to never show any judgment. This was actually difficult for the first time ever. I'll try to put this delicately. At one time one of the rooms was used to make adult films. So in going through everything certain items would be uncovered that would have been best left covered up. So I would always try to arrange for him to discover those items and handle them as he saw fit. Occasionally my dealing with the unsavory items was unavoidable, so humor was called forth many times on that job. More details will not be given in this memoir. Let's just end by saying that everything was removed by the eviction date and that my hands have never been cleaner, from their extensive washing every night, when I got home.

Another instance of someone being threatened with eviction as a fire hazard was called in to me. It was just a basic one-bedroom apartment, but once again the floor was not visible. This time I worked with latex gloves and a mask. The odor was almost overwhelming. The client's gratitude could be sensed that I wasn't there to judge, but to help. We managed to get the apartment in workable order in one weekend.

Earlier in my organizing career the call came into Julie's office to organize a barn. What? A barn? Yes, you read correctly. Who could do that? Better send Ron. A retired couple in Connecticut had a barn with wood flooring where they had been storing odds and ends for years. They wanted to reclaim the barn for a play area for their grandchildren. The husband picked me up at the train station and we had a very pleasant chat for the half hour drive to their house. The wife was like a cat on a hot tin roof when we arrived. What was going on? Unclear. So I said, "Let's just start in this one corner, identifying what you want to keep." They had designated an area outside for the items to be hauled off. We continued working until lunchtime. I am always very self-contained on a job, bringing water and a peanut butter and grape jelly sandwich.

She insisted, "You must have lunch with us. We have some homemade soup. Won't your sandwich keep?" What would you say to the choice between homemade soup and a P&J sandwich? Duh! After a delightful and delicious lunch the husband volunteered to work with me during the afternoon session. During that day we managed to sort and zone all the items in the barn, including the ones to be tossed, and cleared the floor. That evening when the wife was driving me back to the city she asked, "How did you do that? How did you win my husband over? Last night he was giving me nothing but grief for spending the money on this project."

What could I say? It seems that the rapport we had established in the ride from the train station carried over through lunch and the afternoon session. My being able to converse about subjects he was interested in probably helped. Another mission accomplished.

The attainment of my two goals occurred in 2007. My legal age to collect Social Security was reached in February and my mortgage was completely paid off in November. What a year! Life beyond Merrill Lynch was now a real possibility. When should that life begin? Books were read on retirement, all aspects were considered and the date was chosen: February 29, 2008. Looking back, it would appear that I left Merrill Lynch at just the right time. Many friends have commented how savvy I was to leave before the bad times at the firm started. It would be nice to be able to take credit for the wisdom of that decision, but the truth is a different matter. I wasn't smart; I was just hokey. February 29, 2008 was leap year. So I wanted to "leap out of corporate America," and the next day on March 1, 2008, I wanted to "march forward to the rest of my life." See what I mean by hokey? However, the end result was fairly perfect timing.

Our department gave me a retirement luncheon, with everyone giving me kudos and retirement gifts. Yvonne Umpierre and Sue Moccia gave me a

An updated version of the famous newspaper headline that Dewey had beaten Truman for the presidency, held by Harry S. Truman. This "send up" was courtesy of Judy Drake, my friend from college.

framed copy of the famous Christopher Bliss photograph of Central Park with a note stating, "We don't want you to ever forget New York." That photograph now hangs in my bedroom in Oklahoma, insuring that forgetting New York will never happen.

What's next on the horizon? Will retirement make me happy? What would occupy my time?

LESSONS LEARNED

- **Life Altering Events Can Move You Forward in Life**
- **Dare to Fulfill That Dream**

RETIRED?

Now what? Waking up the next morning was an "eye opener." (pun intended). Would there be enough income for me to continue my lifestyle with travel, dining out, seeing shows, etc.? What would fill my days? Was it possible to spend more time in Oklahoma and lose the income by taking my house off the rental market? Whoa, let me have that cup of coffee to help sort this out!

First, the books I had read and the research I had done on retirement gave me a sense of direction for the rest of my life. You don't retire "from" a career; you retire "to" something you are passionate about. For me it was "to" my organizing work. Now there would be no time constraints about scheduling a job anytime, or traveling anywhere. The appointments would no longer be limited to weekends and evenings. This opened up that world even more for me.

Life changed immediately. I retired on a Friday and traveled to Coconut Grove, Florida, on that Sunday for a four-day organizing job in the home of a young couple with two children. There were several challenging areas in the home, including the home office and the garage. The husband was traveling for the first two days and when he drove into his garage upon returning told me, "I thought I was in the wrong house for a minute. How did you do that?"

Both he and his wife had previously worked in the music business. So on my last day there he gave me an unexpected compliment, "You're like the 'Fifth Beatle' in our family. You can't leave now!" Another mission accomplished.

There was a huge realization that was dawning on me: that I could go anywhere I wanted to go, anytime I wanted without asking for permission from anyone, as long as I was fiscally responsible. Wow! What a revelation, becoming an adult at the age of 66!

Now it was time to try an extended stay in Oklahoma. My prime task during that time was to purchase my first car. Yes, you read correctly, my first car. Why does anyone who lives in New York City need a car? Having done research into cars and checked out a few in some showrooms, a Toyota

Matrix seemed like a good fit. Now wouldn't you know my nephew, Rami, had previously worked in a car dealership and still had some connections. On my second day in Oklahoma he made two phone calls and the following day we were on the road to the Toyota dealership in Stillwater, Oklahoma. So in March of 2008 I bought a 2009

My first car – at age 66 – looking like a proud high-schooler!

Toyota Matrix. That meant having a new car for a year and nine months! Sort of. It's hard to explain the feeling of driving home in my first car. When I stopped for dinner outside of Tulsa, that new car had to be parked in view of my table in the restaurant. When the people parked next to me were getting in their car to leave, it took all my restraint not to run out and say, "Please be careful opening your door and don't bang it into mine." Crisis averted. They didn't hit my door. Whew! My car now has its first ding, so that ultra-protective syndrome is over.

Later, back in New York during a discussion with my banker I mentioned, "I didn't retire from Merrill Lynch until the mortgage on my house was paid off, and I didn't buy my first car until I could pay for it in cash."

He stared at me for a moment and then with a bemused look in his eye said, "You don't think like other people." That's fine with me.

My new life was going to work in the following way, "Do anything you want to do, as long as you can afford it. If you can't, don't." Ok, how about a trip to Texas to visit friends? Connie and George lived in Dallas, and Gracey lived in Ft. Worth. Of course, visiting three friends on one trip, plus dividing my time among them, proved a little tricky.

Two days was the length of stay with each friend, keeping in mind the saying on my pillow. If you can believe it, the six-hour trip from my home in Oklahoma to Dallas was the longest I had ever driven by myself. It was great: listening to my CDs, stopping whenever to explore interesting areas. The two days also seemed just right with my friends. They all protested that my stay was too short, but the old show business adage is apropos, "Always leave the audience wanting more." I was able to help Connie with some organizing in her new home and Gracey organizing her office. George and I just hung out.

A new area of work was added with Julie's office. She called one day, "Ron, I'm doing a couple of seminars for a corporate outing in San Diego. Would you be able to come out and assist me? "

"I'm available. What would this entail?" I asked.

"You would be checking out each room to make sure that the sound and the lighting were right. Make sure I had a table or a podium. Also if needed, download my PowerPoint presentation onto their computer system. Then, because you know my material so well, you could help me rehearse, take notes during the presentation and debrief me afterwards. I will pay all your travel and hotel expenses, plus a daily rate," she offered.

"Julie, that sounds great. Just give me the dates, email me a ticket and I will be there," I said.

This worked out even better than expected! Drive down to Tulsa, park in long-term parking and fly out to San Diego. Do the job, fly back, pick up the car and drive home. Perfect. The job called on skills from all my background: organizing, show business and corporate. I handled any minutia, so that she could have total concentration on her material. It was a perfect combination. Julie was very happy with that outing. This was my first job in a new area of work that could produce more opportunities.

I was now spending almost half of my time in Oklahoma and able to invite friends to experience the Oklahoma life. However, it was painfully evident to me that my cooking skills needed to improve. If you have guests, you have to feed them, right? So, more research found that the Culinary Institute on West 23rd Street offered a wide variety of cooking classes, including a basic one. Quick, sign up. The first thing I learned was that I had never owned a sharp knife in my life. Next, a little of my fear was allayed. Just jump in and try it. Becoming confident in the kitchen has become a long on-going process. Friends have been giving me recipes, but only simple ones, nothing complicated with a lot of measuring. It turned out my favorite recipes were of the "dump and cook" variety, where you just open cans, pour in the ingredients and heat. Casseroles have also become favorites. So far no guest has gone hungry at my table. Dinnertime is improving.

An incident happened the first time that Nicole and Paul Berné came to visit. A lot of thought and time had gone into the preparation of a nice dinner, featuring a pork loin, with roasted potatoes and steamed vegetables. Halfway through dinner they looked at each other, nodded and pulled out

their "barf bags" from the airplane. "Well, I guess we won't be needing these after all," they almost said simultaneously. They got me. As much as I dish it out, I love it when someone gets me good.

My friends, Nicole Barth and Paul Berné, afger having survived my cooking. (Photo by John Sefakis)

Before the Christmas holidays in 2008, it just so happened that my friends, Angus (Mac) and Kay McLean were moving into a new house in Broken Arrow, right outside Tulsa. At the same time my old college roommate and his wife, Donnie and Glennella Doss were moving into a new house in downtown Tulsa.

"How would you like me to come down and spend some time with you and help you get your new home in shape?" was my offer to both couples. They took me up on it. So I spent a few days at each place emptying boxes, hanging pictures and shopping. During the time with Kay and Mac I mentioned that one of my New York clients had called me the "Energizer Bunny."

"No," said Mac, "You're not the Energizer Bunny. You're the Energizer Bunny on steroids!"

Life is continuing in directions that are surprising and fulfilling. It feels very right to spend part of my time in my apartment in New York City and some time in my rental house in Oklahoma. The environments couldn't be more different. On arriving in each place it takes me about two or three days to adapt. In New York it is the noise and the people. In Oklahoma it is the quiet and the solitude. My true Gemini traits must emerge to allow me to be extremely comfortable in each setting. Where do I want to live full time eventually? Let's just say I plan to keep both places until I can't climb the five flights of stairs in New York. Hopefully, that's a few years down the pike.

What has made my life different and interesting? There are a few unusual dichotomies of mine. First, it is fairly rare to be an artist and to have a practical side. They just don't usually go together. But in my case they were both present and active throughout my life. It became increasingly important for me to touch people as a performer. In my later years I really learned how to create an atmosphere on stage, and then let each audience member have that emotional experience of a laugh, a tear or a memory. Yet there was always this drive to keep my everyday life on an even keel. Maybe this is where the innate organizer in me took over the reins. Thankfully, a workable balance has always been there.

Next, it was always important to have fun in the now, yet be future-oriented for security's sake. That also showed up in my handling of money. I treated myself well, but always saved for the future. It is amazing that my mouth has not gotten me into more trouble, because my sense of humor just makes the most inopportune things pop out. Seventy-five percent of the lines elicit real laughter, and then there's the other twenty-five percent that just has to be endured.

And lastly, it is not the norm for someone to have an itinerant life style and maintain lifelong connections with friends. This stemmed from two forces. My natural inclination has always been to be open and friendly. As it became evident throughout the years that a deep "one-on-one" relationship was not to be for me, it was increasingly important to maintain my valued friendships. As was mentioned earlier my glass was definitely half full! No matter how far my travels took me, keeping in touch with my good friends was always on the front burner.

Where will my interests lead me in this new segment of my life? So far, so good. My first year of retirement has been a fairly exciting adventure. To be more accurate, it would have to be my "first year of retirement from the corporate world." Retired in the true sense? I don't think so. There is just too much in this big old world to do and see. Let's just be brave and see what fortune has in store. I'm game. Are you?

LESSONS LEARNED

- Accept the diversity in your life and use it to the fullest.

- A sense of humor will see you through the worst of times.

- Always be the best friend possible.

(Photo by Connie Kitchens)

"Life is not a rehearsal..."

Quote from Rose Tremaine.